STANLEY THORNES ENGLISH PROGRAMME

INSIGHT

Peter Chilver

Stanley Thornes (Publishers) Ltd

Text © Peter Chilver
Illustrations © Stanley Thornes (Publishers) Ltd

All rights reserved. No part of this publication may be reproduced, stored in a retrieval system or transmitted in any form or by any means, electronic, mechanical, photocopying, recording or otherwise, without the prior written consent of the copyright holders. Applications for such permission should be addressed to the publishers: Stanley Thornes (Publishers) Ltd, Old Station Drive, Leckhampton, CHELTENHAM GL53 0DN, England.

First published in 1986 by:
Stanley Thornes (Publishers) Ltd
Old Station Drive
Leckhampton
CHELTENHAM GL53 0DN
England

British Library Cataloguing in Publication Data

Chilver, Peter
   Insight.—(Stanley Thornes English programme)
   1. English language—Grammar—1950–
   I. Title
   428   PE1112

ISBN 0-85950-569-3

Typeset by Tech-Set, Gateshead, Tyne & Wear.
Printed and bound in Great Britain at Butler & Tanner Ltd, Frome.

Contents

This list gives a **guide to texts** (including extracts) and other materials, and to **principal activities**.
All the Units offer opportunities for group and class discussion.

	Acknowledgements	ix
	Insight: Main objectives	xiii

1 INTRODUCTORY — 1

Short story	*Mabel* by Somerset Maugham
Poetry	*A Poison Tree* by William Blake
	'Butch' Weldy by Edgar Lee Masters
	The Ballad of Postman William L. Moore from Baltimore by Wolf Biermann
Play	*The Gioconda Smile* by Aldous Huxley
Film script	*The Short Night* by David Freeman

ACTIVITIES INCLUDE discussing what makes a good story, answering questions on all the texts, and writing stories.

2 CAPITAL PUNISHMENT — 21

Court cases	Evidence drawn from a British murder trial, and an account of an American murder trial
Students' essays	

ACTIVITIES INCLUDE discussing unfair forms of argument, exploring evidence from a jury's point of view, and planning, writing and assessing essays.

3 OPENERS — 37

Four novels	*The Terminal Man* by Michael Crichton
	Weep not, Child by Ngugi Wa Thiong'o
	Frost in May by Antonia White
	The High Window by Raymond Chandler

ACTIVITIES INCLUDE discussing favourite authors and genres, answering questions on all the texts, story-writing, and using a library to select novels to read.

4 **CHARACTERS** 49

Short stories by students

Newspaper stories from local papers

Various pictures, including drawings, paintings, photos and film stills

ACTIVITIES INCLUDE considering some of the various conventions that can be used in the writing of stories, and considering some of the different forms in which stories can be written.

5 **DECISIONS** 71

Autobiography   *Harpo Speaks!* by Harpo Marx
Polemical writing   *The Betrayal of Youth* by James Hemming
Letter to her daughter by Elizabeth Blackwell
Talk on journalism by Doreen Lewis
Newspaper report from *The Times Educational Supplement*

ACTIVITIES INCLUDE conducting interviews, using a library for research, and writing letters.

6 **NEWSPAPERS** 85

Various newspaper stories from local and national papers

Newspaper feature article from the *Mail on Sunday*

ACTIVITIES INCLUDE looking at and evaluating newspapers, and listening comprehension.

7 **WORDS AND MUSIC** 99

Poetry and lyrics   *Mack the Knife* by Bertolt Brecht
Careless Whisper by George Michael
Break, Break, Break by Alfred, Lord Tennyson
Deaths by Pedro Salinas
Thin Ice by Pink Floyd
A Consolation by William Shakespeare
The Lady of Shalott by Alfred, Lord Tennyson
A Red, Red Rose by Robert Burns
My heart leaps up by William Wordsworth
Lover's Secret by William Blake

ACTIVITIES INCLUDE listening to songs, and writing poems and lyrics.

8 SEX DISCRIMINATION ACT — 113

Act of Parliament Sex Discrimination Act, 1975
Newspaper stories from local and national papers
Pamphlet from the Equal Opportunities Commission
Court cases and tribunal reports
Statistics from the Department of Education and Science

ACTIVITIES INCLUDE evaluating all the texts, interviewing, and research.

9 WAR-TIME — 133

Autobiography	*Chelsea Child* by Rose Gamble
	My Early Life by Winston Churchill
Biography	*Hitler, a Study in Tyranny* by Alan Bullock
	The Face of the Third Reich by Joachim Fest
Social history	*Bombers and Mash* by Raynes Minns
Novel	*Schindler's Ark* by Thomas Keneally
Poetry	*Home* by Karen Gershon
	Song of the Bomber by Ethel Mannin
	Lament by Frances Mayo
	War Widow by Margaret Hamilton Noël-Paton
Diary	*Nella Last's War*

ACTIVITIES INCLUDE looking at questions relating to all the texts, research, interviewing, and writing a report.

10 FIVE POEMS — 159

Transcripts of discussions by students

Poetry	*The Everlasting Mercy* by John Masefield
	The Song of the Shirt by Thomas Hood
	Platform Goodbye by H. B. Mallalieu
	The Companion by Yevgeny Yevtushenko
	The Responsibility by Peter Appleton

Essay by a student

ACTIVITIES INCLUDE reading, listening to, talking and writing about poetry.

11	**THE END OF THE STORY**	**175**
	Short story	*I Spy* by Graham Greene
	Autobiography	*Vedi* by Ved Mehta
	Newspaper story from	*The Guardian*

ACTIVITIES INCLUDE looking at questions evaluating all the texts, and dramatic improvisation.

12	**PERSUASION (1) ADVERTISING**	**193**
	Views about advertising	*Advertising and Competition* by Julius Backman
		The Techniques of Persuasion by J.A.C. Brown
	Newspaper reports from	*The Times Educational Supplement* and *The Guardian*
	Advertisements	

ACTIVITIES INCLUDE listening comprehension, research, and evaluating all the various texts.

13	**PERSUASION (2) ARGUMENT**	**211**
	Play	*Hamp* by John Wilson
	Debate	Parliamentary debate on corporal punishment in schools
	Trial	The Loeb–Leopold Murder Case, with the defence lawyer's speech to the judge

ACTIVITIES INCLUDE formal as well as informal discussion.

14	**MAKING FILMS**	**231**
	Informative writing	*An Introduction to Film-Making* by Grace Matchett
	Various film stills	

ACTIVITIES INCLUDE talking, reading and writing about films, and devising stories for films.

15	**DILEMMAS**	**245**
	Biography	*Florence Nightingale* by Cecil Woodham-Smith
		The Destruction of Lord Raglan by Christopher Hibbert
	Polemical writing	*Chaos or Community?* by Martin Luther King
	Poetry	*The Charge of the Light Brigade* by Alfred, Lord Tennyson

ACTIVITIES INCLUDE devising a pamphlet on a controversial issue.

16	**FUTURES**	**259**
	Scientific journalism	Demographic data from *The Sunday Times*
		'Cloned mice' from *Nature Times*
		'Conveyor-belt medicine' from *Time Magazine*
		'What we may learn from animals' from *The Guardian*
		'After the war ...' from *The Guardian*
		'Life in outer space?' from *The Guardian*
		'Is the Earth expanding?' from *The Guardian*
		'The end of the future?' from *The Guardian*
	Polemical writing	*Rethink* by Gordon Rattray Taylor
		Future Fears by Margaret Saple

ACTIVITIES INCLUDE evaluating all the various texts and writing a report.

Acknowledgements

The author and publishers are grateful to the following for permission to reproduce previously published material:

Alan Ross Ltd for the poem 'Platform Goodbye' by H. B. Mallalieu, taken from *The Poetry of War* 1939–45 (p. 167)
Alfred A. Knopf Inc. for the extract from *The Terminal Man* by Michael Crichton (p. 38)
A. P. Watt Ltd, the Executors of the Estate of W. Somerset Maugham, and William Heinemann Ltd for the extract from *The Complete Short Stories* by Somerset Maugham (p. 2)
Associated Newspapers Group plc for the article 'Do we really need these animal tests?' from the *Mail on Sunday* (p. 94)
British Broadcasting Corporation for the extract from *Chelsea Child* by Rose Gamble (p. 135)
Chatto and Windus for the poem 'The Responsibility' by Peter Appleton, taken from *Rhyme and Reason* (p. 169)
Constable for the extract from *Florence Nightingale* by Cecil Woodham-Smith (p. 246)
David Higham Associates for the extract from *The Destruction of Lord Raglan* by Christopher Hibbert (p. 251)
David Whitehouse for the article 'Life in outer space?' which appeared in *The Guardian* (p. 270)
Dr Peter J. Smith for the article 'Is the Earth expanding?' (p. 271)
Elaine Markson Literary Agency Inc. for the extract from *Clarence Darrow* by Arthur and Lila Weinburg (p. 225)
Ellen C. Masters as Executors of the estate of Edgar Lee Masters for the epitaph ' "Butch" Weldy', taken from *Spoon River Anthology* published by Collier-Macmillan (p. 6)
English Operating Board for the poem 'Deaths' by Pedro Salinas, reproduced in *Over to You* (p. 103, no. 4)
Equal Opportunities Commission for extracts from their leaflets (pp. 121, 126)
Hamish Hamilton and College Trustees Ltd for the extract from *The High Window* by Raymond Chandler (p. 44)
Heinemann Educational Books for the extract from *Weep Not Child* by Ngugi wa Thiong'o (p. 40)
Hodder and Stoughton Educational for the extract from *Advertising and Competition* by Julius Backman (p. 194)
Hodder and Stoughton Ltd for the extract from *Schindler's Ark* by Thomas Keneally (p. 146)
Jean Faulks as Executor of the estate of Ethel Mannin for the poem 'Song of the Bomber', reproduced in *Chaos of the Night* (p. 150)

Karen Gershon for the poem 'Home', reproduced in *Selected Poems* published by Gollancz (p. 150)

Laurence Pollinger Limited for the extracts *I Spy* by Graham Greene, taken from *Collected Stories* (p. 177), and *Chaos or Community?* by Martin Luther King (p. 254)

London Express News and Feature Services for the articles 'Red Card for the first lady of soccer' (p. 117), 'Pupils shunning their chance to be equal' (p. 128), and an article from *The Standard* (p. 126)

MARLU Literary Agency for the extract from *The Short Night* by David Freeman, taken from *The Last Days of Alfred Hitchcock* (p. 13)

Marion Boyars Publishers Ltd for the extract from *Betrayal of Youth* by James Hemmings (p. 74)

Michael Joseph for the extract from *Between Ourselves: Letters between Mother and Daughter* edited by Karen Payne (p. 76)

Morrison Leaky Music for the words of the song 'Careless Whisper' by George Michael (p. 101)

Mrs Hamilton Noël-Paton for the poem 'War Widow' (p. 151)

Nature Magazine for the article 'Embryology: Cloned mice' (p. 263)

Newnes Books (a division of the Hamlyn Publishing Group Limited) for the extracts from *Hitler, A Study in Tyranny* by Alan Bullock (p. 140) and *My Early Life* by Winston Churchill (p. 143)

Norman Myers for the article 'After the war' which appeared in *The Guardian* (p. 267)

Penguin Books for the extracts from *Techniques of Persuasion* by J. A. C. Brown (p. 198) and 'The Companion' by Yevgeny Yevtushenko, reproduced in *Selected Poems* (p. 168)

Penny Chorlton for the article 'Girls to get cash for school sex bias' which appeared in *The Guardian* (p. 120)

Pink Floyd Music Publishers Limited for the song 'Thin Ice' by Pink Floyd (p. 103, no. 5)

Pluto Press Ltd for the poem 'The Ballad or Postman William L. Moore from Baltimore', taken from *Poems and Ballads of Wolf Biermann* (p. 7)

Professor Paul Davies for the article 'The end of the future?' which appeared in *The Guardian* (p. 272)

Radio Times and Harold Jackson for the article 'Who killed the Lindbergh baby? (p. 29) and 'The Crime that rocked the world' (p. 29)

Robson Books Ltd for the extract from *Harpo Speaks!* by Harpo Marx (p. 72)

Rosemary Collins for the article 'Advertisers enlist fear as selling aid' which appeared in *The Guardian* (p. 210)

Samuel French Ltd for extracts from *The Gioconda Smile* by Aldous Huxley (p. 8) and *Hamp* by John Wilson (p. 213)

Seumas Milne for the article 'Falklands victims the army tried to forget' which appeared in *The Guardian* (p. 183)

Sidgwick and Jackson for the extract from 'The Everlasting Mercy' by John Masefield (p. 163)
The Guardian for the articles 'Girls face fight for equality in schools' (p. 128) and 'Twin assault by BMA on beer and cigarettes' (p. 208)
The Observer for the article which appeared on 18 November 1984 (p. 127)
Time Magazine for the extract 'Patients undergo surgery on the assembly line' (p. 264)
Times Newspapers Limited for the articles 'Court blow to wine bar feminists' (p. 119) and 'Equality case prompts new timetable' (p. 127); and articles from *The Times Educational Supplement*, 'Engineering loses its macho image' by Adriana Laudney (p. 81), 'Film reinforces male bias on heavy crafts' (p. 129), 'Mathematics bias for boys' (p. 129), 'Girls fall for advertising puffs' (p. 205), 'Aiming at children' (p. 207)
Universal Edition (London) Ltd for the words taken from *The Threepenny Opera* by Weill and Brecht (p. 101)
Virago Press for the extracts from *Frost in May* by Antonia White (p. 43) and *Bombers and Mash* by Raynes Minns (p. 137)
Weidenfeld (Publishers) Limited for the extract from *The Face of the Third Reich* by Joachim Fest (p. 148)

We also wish to thank the following for providing photographs and giving permission for reproduction:

Artificial Eye Film Company Ltd (pp. 100, 231)
Associated British Films (p. 232)
Baird Harris Limited (p. 196)
Barnaby's (pp. 24, 43, 74, 77, 82, 97, 125, 159, 173, 253)
BBC Hulton Picture Library (pp. 20, 37(×6), 61, 62, 71, 72, 102, 107, 141, 157, 191, 215, 245, 249, 267)
Bert Hardy (p. 110)
Bray Leino (p. 201)
British Film Institute (p. 231, bottom)
Campbell/Kensey *The Sunday Times* (p. 259)
Colman RSCG & Partners Ltd (p. 210)
Columbia Pictures Industries Inc. (p. 237)
Contemporary Films Ltd (p. 239)
DACS (p. 99)
Eric Hosking (p. 266)
Harrison Agency (p. 206)
House of Lords (p. 59)
Imperial War Museum (pp. 152, 153)
Jean Mohr (p. 175)
John Hillelson Agency Limited (p. 104)
Mary Evans Picture Library (p. 21)

Metropolitan Police Careers Information Centre (p. 204)
MGM/VA (pp. 17, 28, 85, 242)
National Film Archive (pp. 17, 18, 28, 64, 65, 66, 85, 226, 232, 237, 241, 273)
National Gallery (pp. 49, 51, 54)
National Portrait Gallery (p. 57)
Network Photographers (pp. 113, 131)
New Zealand Meat Producers Board (p. 209)
Photosource (pp. 37 (× 3), 97, 118, 139, 149, 167, 183, 203, 255, 257)
Picturepoint (pp. 41, 114, 123, 189, 211, 219, 268)
Popperfoto (p. 133)
Rank Film Distributors Ltd (p. 18)
Reebok (p. 193)
The British Library (p. 106)
The Guardian (p. 184)
The Press Association Ltd (pp. 120, 185)
The Tate Gallery (p. 99)
Thorn EMI Screen Entertainment (p. 66)
Time Inc. (p. 264)
Twentieth Century Fox Film Company Ltd (p. 226)
United International Pictures (pp. 64, 65, 241)
Universal Pictures, a Division of Universal City Studios, Inc., courtesy of MCA Publishing Rights, a Division of MCA Inc. (p. 273)

Every effort has been made to contact copyright holders. We apologise for any oversights.

INSIGHT: MAIN OBJECTIVES

1. To offer materials for the more academic groups or classes preparing for the GCSE exams in *English*.
2. To stimulate work across the whole range of language activities: talking, listening, reading and writing.
3. To include work in literature, alongside language, but on the understanding that teachers will also introduce their classes to a range of literary texts whether for the *English* or the *English literature* examinations.
4. To meet the need for a range of activities as required for examinations that are either entirely or partly based on coursework.

TALKING AND LISTENING

5. Every Unit offers opportunities for class and group discussion. Some units (8, 12 and 16) are designed for students to explore mostly on their own, in small groups, with a minimum of teacher-intervention.
6. Opportunities are given (and also models), for students to engage in talk of quite different kinds, including debate, formal and structured discussion, solving problems together, and anecdotal chat.
7. Use is also made of various kinds of role-play and improvisation.
8. A number of passages are included for listening comprehension. Generally, these are linguistically complex, and it is intended that the discussion of such texts, after listening to them, should extend the students' confidence and competence in reading texts that they find difficult, so that, through listening and discussing, they develop as readers.

READING

9. There is a wide variety in the kinds of texts offered. They extend from fiction, poetry and drama, to news reports, memoirs, philosophical and scientific writing, biography, autobiography, letters and speeches.
10. Extensive use is made of literature written by students.
11. Students are constantly invited to question the texts they are reading, so that they become involved in using texts generally to find something out for themselves, and to pursue the answers to their own questions.
12. The process of reading is a matter of moving backwards and forwards from the whole to the part. Students need to be constantly encouraged to do this. So almost all the Units give the students practice not only in exploring a single passage but also in relating different passages on a common theme to each other – finding their common threads.

13. The materials for reading are designed not only to stimulate good talking and listening, but also to offer the students a range of models of different registers which they can explore in their own writing.

WRITING

14. The writer's sense of an audience is a major influence on his or her writing. Hence the Units offer constant opportunities for students to write for and with each other.
15. Note-making also is a central part of writing, and the Units give regular encouragement to build on plans, notes and outlines. In particular, there is a constant emphasis on the structuring of written work.
16. Exercises are offered in punctuation, and these will be of use to some classes at some times. Obviously, everything depends on the teacher's perceptions of the needs of the class.

COURSEWORK

17. The Units offer opportunities for a wide range of different kinds of writing, including *creative writing* (poems, stories and plays, Units 1, 4, 7, 10, 11 and 14), *critical writing about literature* (Units 3, 10 and 14), *argumentative and persuasive writing* (Units 2, 5, 6, 8, 9, 12, 13, 15 and 16), *personal writing* (especially Units 5 and 9), *directed writing* in which the writer responds to a number of different texts (especially Units 8, 12 and 16) and *descriptive writing* (especially Units 4, 7, 10, 11 and 14).
18. There are many opportunities for writers to explore different ways of writing about experience, and also to use quite different kinds of stimulus (including pictures and music) in developing their own experience.

USING DICTIONARIES AND LIBRARIES

19. Regular encouragement is given to students to use dictionaries and libraries.

CONCEPTUAL DEVELOPMENT

20. A number of concepts recur throughout the text. These include concepts such as genre, structure, theme, irony, dramatic irony, imagery, figures of speech, and symbolism. It is not intended that these should be seen by students as either simple or rigid concepts. Students need to experiment with their use, to question them, and to begin to make them their own.

1 INTRODUCTORY

'Without a stick of luggage, he leapt on board.'

Stories come in many forms – novels, poems, films, newspaper stories, or plays. Here are some examples.

#

I was at Pagan, in Burma, and from there I took the steamer to Mandalay, but a couple of days before I got there, when the boat tied up for the night at a riverside village, I made up my mind to go ashore. The skipper told me that there was there a pleasant little club in which I had only to make myself at home; they were quite used to having strangers drop off like that from the steamer, and the secretary was a very decent chap; I might even get a game of bridge. I had nothing in the world to do, so I got into one of the bullock-carts that were waiting at the landing-stage and was driven to the club. There was a man sitting on the veranda and as I walked up he nodded to me and asked whether I would have a whisky and soda or a gin and bitters. The possibility that I would have nothing at all did not even occur to him. I chose the longer drink and sat down. He was a tall, thin, bronzed man, with a big moustache, and he wore khaki shorts and a khaki shirt. I never knew his name, but when we had been chatting a little while another man came in who told me he was the secretary, and he addressed my friend as George.

'Have you heard from your wife yet?' he asked him.

The other's eyes brightened.

'Yes, I had letters by this mail. She's having no end of a time.'

'Did she tell you not to fret?'

George gave a little chuckle, but was I mistaken in thinking that there was in it the shadow of a sob?

'In point of fact she did. But that's easier said than done. Of course I know she wants a holiday, and I'm glad she should have it, but it's devilish hard on a chap.' He turned to me. 'You see, this is the first time I've ever been separated from my missus, and I'm like a lost dog without her.'

'How long have you been married?'

'Five minutes.'

The secretary of the club laughed.

'Don't be a fool, George. You've been married eight years.'

After we had talked for a little, George, looking at his watch, said he must go and change his clothes for dinner and left us. The secretary watched him disappear into the night with a smile of not unkindly irony.

'We all ask him as much as we can now that he's alone,' he told me. 'He mopes so terribly since his wife went home.'

'It must be very pleasant for her to know that her husband is as devoted to her as all that.'

'Mabel is a remarkable woman.'

He called the boy and ordered more drinks. In this hospitable place they did not ask you if you would have anything; they took it for granted. Then he settled himself in his long chair and lit a cheroot. He told me the story of George and Mabel.

They became engaged when he was home on leave, and when he returned to Burma it was arranged that she should join him in six months. But one difficulty cropped up after another; Mabel's father died, the war came, George was sent to a district unsuitable for a woman; so that in the end it was seven years before she was able to start. He made all the arrangements for the marriage, which was to take place on the day of her arrival, and went down to Rangoon to meet her. On the morning on which the ship was due he borrowed a motor-car and drove along to the dock. He paced the quay.

Then, suddenly, without warning, his nerve failed him. He had not seen Mabel for seven years. He had forgotten what she was like. She was a total stranger. He felt a terrible sinking in the pit of his stomach and his knees began to wobble. He couldn't go through with it. He must tell Mabel that he was very sorry, but he couldn't, he really couldn't marry her. But how could a man tell a girl a thing like that when she had been engaged to him for seven years and had come six thousand miles to marry him? He hadn't the nerve for that either. George was seized with the courage of despair. There was a boat at the quay on the very point of starting for Singapore; he wrote a hurried letter to Mabel, and without a stick of luggage, just in the clothes he stood up in, leaped on board.

The letter Mabel received ran somewhat as follows:

Dearest Mabel,

I have been suddenly called away on business and do not know when I shall be back. I think it would be much wiser if you returned to England. My plans are very uncertain. Your loving George.

But when he arrived at Singapore he found a cable waiting for him.

Quite understand. Don't worry. Love. Mabel.

Terror made him quick-witted.

'By Jove, I believe she's following me,' he said.

He telegraphed to the shipping-office at Rangoon and sure enough her name was on the passenger list of the ship that was now on its way to Singapore. There was not a moment to lose. He jumped on the train to Bangkok. But he was uneasy; she would have no difficulty in finding out that he had gone to Bangkok and it was just as simple for her to take the train as it had been for him. Fortunately there was a French tramp sailing next day for Saigon. He took it. At Saigon he would be safe; it would never occur to her that he had gone there; and if it did, surely by now she would have taken the hint. It is five days' journey from Bangkok to Saigon and the boat is dirty, cramped, and uncomfortable. He was glad to arrive and took a rickshaw to the hotel. He signed his name in the visitors' book and a telegram was immediately handed to him. It contained but two words: *Love. Mabel.* They were enough to make him

break into a cold sweat.

'When is the next boat for Hong-Kong?' he asked.

Now his flight grew serious. He sailed to Hong-Kong, but dared not stay there; he went to Manila: Manila was ominous; he went on to Shanghai: Shanghai was nerve-racking; every time he went out of the hotel he expected to run straight into Mabel's arms; no, Shanghai would never do. The only thing was to go to Yokohama. At the Grand Hotel at Yokohama a cable awaited him:

So sorry to have missed you at Manila. Love. Mabel.

He scanned the shipping intelligence with a fevered brow. Where was she now? He doubled back to Shanghai. This time he went straight to the club and asked for a telegram. It was handed to him:

Arriving shortly. Love. Mabel.

No, no, he was not so easy to catch as all that. He had already made his plans. The Yangtse is a long river and the Yangtse was falling. He could just about catch the last steamer that could get up to Chungking and then no one could travel till the following spring except by junk. Such a journey was out of the question for a woman alone. He went to Hankow and from Hankow to Ichang; he changed boats here and from Ichang through the rapids went to Chungking. But he was desperate now, he was not going to take any risks: there was a place called Cheng-tu, the capital of Szechuan, and it was four hundred miles away. It could only be reached by road, and the road was infested with brigands. A man would be safe there.

George collected chair-bearers and coolies and set out. It was with a sigh of relief that he saw at last the crenellated walls of the lonely Chinese city. From those walls at sunset you could see the snowy mountains of Tibet.

He could rest at last: Mabel would never find him there. The consul happened to be a friend of his and he stayed with him. He enjoyed the comfort of a luxurious house, he enjoyed his idleness after that strenuous escape across Asia, and above all he enjoyed his divine security. The weeks passed lazily one after the other.

One morning George and the consul were in the courtyard looking at some curios that a Chinese had brought for their inspection when there was a loud knocking at the great door of the Consulate. The door-man flung it open. A chair borne by four coolies entered, advanced, and was set down; Mabel stepped out. She was neat and cool and fresh. There was nothing in her appearance to suggest that she had just come in after a fortnight on the road. George was petrified. He was as pale as death. She went up to him.

'Hullo, George, I was afraid I'd missed you again.'

'Hullo, Mabel,' he faltered.

He did not know what to say. He looked this way and that: she stood between him and the doorway. She looked at him with a smile in her blue eyes.

'You haven't altered at all,' she said. 'Men can go off so dreadfully in seven years and I was afraid you'd gone fat and bald. I've been so nervous. It would have been terrible if after all these years I simply hadn't been able to bring myself to marry you after all.'

She turned to George's host.

'Are you the consul?' she asked.

'I am.'

'That's all right. I'm ready to marry him as soon as I've had a bath.'

And she did.

from *The Complete Short Stories* **by Somerset Maugham**

For discussion

1. What kind of person is Mabel?
2. What is irony? (See the paragraph beginning, 'After we had talked for a little . . .')
3. Are there any other difficult or unusual words? Talk about them before you look them up in a dictionary.
4. Who is the narrator?

Three Poems

A Poison Tree

I was angry with my friend:
I told my wrath, my wrath did end.
I was angry with my foe:
I told it not, my wrath did grow.

And I water'd it in fears,
Night and morning with my tears;
And I sunnèd it with smiles,
And with soft deceitful wiles.

And it grew both day and night,
Till it bore an apple bright;
And my foe beheld it shine,
And he knew that it was mine,

And into my garden stole
When the night had veil'd the pole:
In the morning glad I see
My foe outstretch'd beneath the tree.

William Blake

'Butch' Weldy

After I got religion and steadied down
They gave me a job in the canning works,
And every morning I had to fill
The tank in the yard with gasoline,
That fed the blow-fires in the sheds
To heat the soldering irons.
And I mounted a rickety ladder to do it,
Carrying buckets full of the stuff.
One morning, as I stood there pouring,
The air grew still and seemed to heave,
And I shot up as the tank exploded,
And down I came with both legs broken,
And my eyes burned crisp as a couple of eggs.
For someone left a blow-fire going,
And something sucked the flame in the tank.
The Circuit Judge said whoever did it
Was a fellow-servant of mine, and so
Old Rhodes' son didn't have to pay me.
And I sat on the witness stand as blind
As Jack the Fiddler, saying over and over,
'I didn't know him at all.'

Edgar Lee Masters

The Ballad of Postman William L. Moore from Baltimore

who marched on his own into the Southern States in 1963. He protested against the persecution of the negroes. He was shot after a week. Three bullets struck his forehead.

SUNDAY
Sunday meant rest for William L. Moore
after a hard week's work.
He was only a postman and pretty poor,
he came from Baltimore.

MONDAY
Monday, one day in Baltimore,
he said to Mrs Moore:
I don't want to be a postman no more,
I'm going down south on a tour.
  BLACK AND WHITE, UNITE! UNITE!
  on a placard he wrote.
  White and black – hold repression back!
  And he set off on his own.

TUESDAY
Tuesday, one day on the railway train,
people asked William L. Moore
what was the sign he was carrying,
and wished him luck for his tour.
  BLACK AND WHITE, UNITE! UNITE!
  stood on his placard . . .

WEDNESDAY
Wednesday, one day in Alabama,
walking down the main street,
still a long way from Birmingham,
he'd already got aching feet.
  BLACK AND WHITE, UNITE! UNITE!

THURSDAY
Thursday, the day the sheriff stopped him,
said, 'What the hell – you're white!
What business of yours is the niggers, man?
If it's trouble you want – all right!'
  BLACK AND WHITE, UNITE! UNITE!

FRIDAY
Friday, a dog started following him,
became his only friend.
By evening stones were hitting them both,
but they went on to the end.
  BLACK AND WHITE, UNITE! UNITE!

SAT'DAY
Sat'day, that day it was terribly hot,
a white woman came up to the two,
gave him a drink and secretly whispered:
'I think the same as you.'
  BLACK AND WHITE, UNITE! UNITE!

LAST DAY
Sunday, a blue and summer's day,
he lay in the grass so green –
three red carnations blooming blood-red
on his forehead could be seen.
  BLACK AND WHITE, UNITE! UNITE!
  stood on his placard.
  White and black – hold repression back!
  And he died on his own.
  And he won't be alone.

Wolf Biermann

For discussion

1. All three poems tell a story. Look again at each one and talk about the story that it tells.
2. Discuss any difficult or unusual words or phrases in any of the poems.
3. What do you think the poison tree might symbolise or represent?
4. William L. Moore wanted black and white to unite. How do we know what the poet's own attitude to this is?

 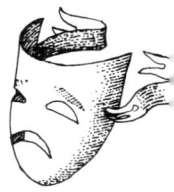

The Gioconda Smile

In Aldous Huxley's play *The Gioconda Smile*, **Henry Hutton** is sentenced to death for the murder, by poisoning, of his invalid wife Emily.

Shortly after the death of his wife, and before he is charged with murder, he marries again. This second marriage, to a much younger woman, is a surprise to all his friends, and especially to **Janet Spence** who has for many years been a friend of Hutton and Emily.

In this scene, after Hutton's conviction, **Janet** is suffering from insomnia and is visited by **Dr Libbard**.

Libbard	I was driving past the house. Thought I'd just drop in to see how things were going.
Janet	Father seems quite well. He's just gone out for his walk.
Libbard	And you? (*He looks at her closely*) Hm. Not much of a credit to your physician, I'm afraid.
Janet	(*after a pause*) If I don't sleep tonight I shall go mad.
Libbard	You've still got some of that stuff I gave you, haven't you?
Janet	It doesn't seem to work any more. I get the most awful dreams and wake up again. Couldn't you give me something that would simply *make* me sleep?
Libbard	I *could*. But I'd much rather not.
Janet	You don't know what it's like, Dr Libbard. Night after night. I can't stand it any longer.
Libbard	(*taking off his coat*) Any fool can stop the symptoms of insomnia. The difficulty is to find the cause – to find it, and then to remove it.
	(*There is a pause*)
Janet	Well, it's going to be removed – next Friday.
Libbard	Next Friday? Oh, I see. Do you hate him as much as all that?
Janet	After all, it was proved, wasn't it? They proved that he killed Emily. How do you expect me not to hate him?
Libbard	Yet you used to be such good friends.
Janet	Never. I always felt there was something wrong somewhere.
Libbard	(*sitting in the armchair*) And yet Emily thought that, if she died, you and he ought to get married.
Janet	(*rising*) Married? But, that's monstrous. How dare you?
Libbard	I'm only repeating what she said. More than once as I remember.
Janet	Talking about me as though I were one of those women of his, as though I were the kind of slut that will tumble into bed with any man that comes along. It's disgusting. It's – it's obscene.
Libbard	I don't know what's so obscene about marriage.

Janet	I won't have it.
Libbard	Getting excited doesn't help you to sleep, does it? (*He feels her pulse*)
	(**Janet** *recovers her self-control and answers in a normal voice*)
Janet	I'm sorry, Dr Libbard.
Libbard	Don't apologize to me. Apologize to yourself. After all, you're the one who has insomnia. And I'll tell you of another who hasn't been sleeping properly; that's the one he actually did marry.
Janet	(*after a pause*) Do you ever think of the child?
Libbard	Hutton's child?
Janet	It's no joke to be the child of a criminal.
Libbard	It's no joke to be anybody's child; it's no joke to be born. And, anyhow, I'm still not convinced that Hutton is a criminal.
Janet	(*picking up a pencil and doodling*) You mean, you don't think he was guilty? After all that came out at the trial?
Libbard	I've just been reading a very interesting book. It's an analysis of well-known cases of people who were condemned for crimes they never committed.
Janet	But they *proved* it.
Libbard	They proved it in these other cases too. Sometimes it was nothing but the circumstantial evidence. It all pointed to one conclusion. And yet, that conclusion was wrong. But, it's rare when that happens. Most often it's a combination of misleading circumstantial evidence and deliberate false witness.
Janet	(*throwing down the pencil and turning*) Do you mean that somebody was telling lies?
Libbard	I don't know. I just can't believe that Hutton was responsible.
Janet	Then – then who was?
Libbard	What about Emily herself?
Janet	Emily? No, Emily wouldn't have committed suicide. She wasn't that sort of person.
Libbard	Yes, I must say, I was a bit surprised when you said that at the trial. She often talked to me about being tired of life – wanting to put an end to it all.
Janet	I never heard her talk that way. Never.
Libbard	Nor did Nurse Braddock, if I remember rightly.
Janet	I don't know what she said. And I don't care.
Libbard	Hutton cared all right. It carried a lot of weight with the jury. (*He rises and crosses to Janet*) Somebody who'd been with Emily, day and night, for the best part of two years. And she says she never heard so much as a whisper of suicide. And suicide was the main line of defence.
Janet	I'm not interested in lines of defence. I'm interested in the truth. I'm interested in justice. (*Her voice rises as she speaks, till it almost goes out of control*) If you're accusing me of telling lies, just because I hated that

	beast . . .(*She suddenly checks herself*) Why do you let me go on like this? Why don't you stop me?
Libbard	People don't like being stopped as a rule.
Janet	I don't really mean it. (*She crosses to the fireplace*) It's just that I get worked up and then it seems to go on by itself. Do you know that awful feeling? (*She moves to the armchair*) As though you were a violin, and somebody were screwing up the strings – tighter and tighter. Oh, God! I wish it were all over. (*She sits*)
Libbard	All over? You seem to think this business is like something in the movies, or in a novel – you seem to think it has an *ending*. At eight o'clock next Friday morning, to be precise. But that won't be the finish.
Janet	What do you mean?
Libbard	Surely, it's obvious. In real life there aren't any endings. Only transitions, only a succession of new beginnings. Hutton's going to be hanged. But don't imagine you're going to be free of him. In one way or another this thing is going on. All you can do is to decide whether it shall go on in the worst possible way, or in some other way.
Janet	What other way?
Libbard	Ask yourself. All *I* know is that the way that's being followed now is the worst way. You can't sleep. And Hutton's going to be hanged for something he never did.
Janet	But it was proved.
Libbard	Not to my satisfaction.
Janet	It's nonsense to say it was suicide. Nurse Braddock never heard her say anything, I never heard her say anything. How could it have been?
Libbard	Very well, let's assume you're right.
Janet	I know I'm right.
Libbard	You know it wasn't Emily and I know it wasn't Hutton. Well, then, it must have come through some other agency.
Janet	I don't know what you're driving at.
Libbard	I'm driving at some way to make you sleep. You can't sleep because somebody is sitting inside your head screwing up the strings. All right, get rid of that somebody. Open the door and show him out. Then the strings will slacken again.
Janet	All these mixed metaphors – strings and doors and throwing people out. Why so poetical all of a sudden?
Libbard	(*after a pause*) Of course you know the basic reason why poor Emily was so dreadfully unhappy?
Janet	What was that?
Libbard	It was because she wouldn't accept the facts as she found them. She was an invalid and she'd lost her looks. But she wanted people to treat her as though she were young and pretty. Hence all the misery.
	(*There is a pause*)

Janet	What has that got to do with me?
Libbard	Nothing. I'm just pointing out that people can come to terms with even the most terrible facts. But they've got to accept them. They've got to adapt themselves to reality. (*He sits on the end of the writing-table*)
Janet	Those are just words, that's all.
Libbard	No, they're more than that. I've known plenty of people who came to terms with death – even with pain, which is a good deal worse.
Janet	(*after a pause*) Do you suppose Henry has come to terms with – with what's happening to him?
Libbard	I know he hasn't.
Janet	Up till now he's always been able to buy his way out of any trouble he got into. Not this time.
Libbard	You're quite right. And that's why it's so hard for him. And yet, it's always in our power to come to terms with the thing. And the quicker we come to terms, the better.
Janet	The better for whom?
Libbard	(*rising*) For everybody concerned. And, especially ourselves, Janet.
Janet	Well, we've had a very interesting talk, Dr Libbard. Now, what about those sleeping tablets? Were you going to give me something a little stronger than you did last time?
	(*Libbard looks at her for a moment, then shakes his head and sighs*)
Libbard	Well, if that's what you really want, I suppose you'd better have it. (*He moves to the writing-table, takes a prescription pad from his pocket, sits, and fills in a form*) (*He looks up*) Janet, do you remember that young Dr Farjeon you met at my house last year?
Janet	Yes.
Libbard	I've known him ever since he was a boy. A very nice fellow, kind, sensible, conscientious.
Janet	No, thanks. I don't want to go to a psychiatrist.
Libbard	But you want to get well, don't you?
Janet	I'm not ill – not that way, anyhow. (*With sudden violence*) You're plotting to get me locked up. That's what it is.
Libbard	Now, Janet, don't talk nonsense. Nobody's plotting anything.
Janet	You think I'm mad. But it's true. You're trying to send me to a doctor for mad people. I tell you, there's nothing wrong with me. I just can't sleep, that's all.
Libbard	He can make you sleep, if you want him to.
Janet	(*horrified*) Do you mean he'll hypnotize me?
Libbard	Well, what's so alarming about that?
Janet	Send me to sleep and then make me say all sorts of things I don't want to say – and I shan't know I've said them. No, no, I won't. (*She crosses to the writing-table*) I know what you're up to, you and your hypnotist. Trying to get things out of me. Trying to drive me out of my mind so that you can have an excuse to lock me up.

Libbard	Listen, Janet. Be reasonable. (*He takes her hands*)
Janet	(*quickly withdrawing her hands*) Don't touch me. I'm not a fool. I can see what you're trying to do.
Libbard	Janet . . . (*He lays a hand on her arm*)
	(**Janet** *strikes savagely at his wrist*)
Janet	I'll kill you. (*She pauses*) Do you understand? (*She breaks to the fireplace*)
	(*The front door bell rings. There is a pause, then* **Libbard** *shrugs his shoulders, turns, sits at the writing-table and resumes writing*)

from *The Gioconda Smile* by **Aldous Huxley**

For discussion

1   Does Dr Libbard think Hutton is guilty?

2   What similarity does Hibbard think there may be between Emily and Janet?

3   What do you learn about Janet from this excerpt? What kind of person is she?

4   What do you think will happen next? How do you think the play will end?

5   Can you think of any other stories (whether plays, films or novels) with a similar theme to this one?

The Short Night

By way of contrast, here is an excerpt from a film. This is the opening scene of a film that Alfred Hitchcock was planning at the time of his death.

(**N.B.** V.O. means voice over)

1   EXT. LONDON – ARTILLERY ROAD – 6:45 P.M.

    A drizzly London evening in the fall.

    Wormwood Scrubs Prison and Hammersmith Hospital sit side by side. Artillery Road, hardly more than a service lane, runs between them.

    A Humber Hawk sits on the prison side facing Du Cane Road, the main drag that runs past the front of both prison and hospital.

    CAMERA is outside the car looking at Brennan, who sits in the front holding a bouquet of chrysanthemums. He's in his early thirties, a little paunchy and very Irish. He's listening to a voice we can't quite make out. It could be the car radio, but Brennan's ear is cocked slightly toward the mums*.

    CAMERA pans off the flowers, toward the prison wall, over the cobblestones and up the rough red bricks toward the top. As CAMERA pans, the voice starts to become clearer.

    As CAMERA goes over the top of the wall and starts down the other side, we realize we're going into the prison, toward the source of the voice.

                  MAN'S VOICE
               (*becoming audible; urgent*)
    ...I'm here...I'm here...hurry on now...can you hear? I said I'm here...

2   EXT. PRISON YARD – NIGHT

    Gavin Brand stands huddled against the wall speaking into a walkie-talkie. He's 39, tall and lean, dressed in prison garb, an intense, aristocratic, imperious man who at the moment is taking a very great risk.

                      BRAND
    Do you read me?...I'm here, damn it, I'm here. Now move!

**mums*: chrysanthemums

3   **ARTILLERY ROAD**

Brennan, still in the car, speaks into the flowers.

> BRENNAN
> (*soothingly*)
> I'm here. You'll be fine ... you'll be fine ... stay calm.

He starts to get out of the car, when his eyes widen in surprise. He stops talking and looks ahead.

4   **HIS POINT OF VIEW – A CAR**

It parks on the other side of the road, near the hospital. A Young Couple sit in front. The headlights go off and the couple embrace.

5   **RESUME SCENE**

> BRENNAN
> (*into the mums*)

Damn ...

> BRAND (V.O.)
> What is it? What's the matter?

> BRENNAN
> It's a bloody lovers' lane.

6   **PRISON SIDE OF THE WALL**

Brand is huddled against the rough bricks.

> BRAND
> What? What are you saying? Just hurry up, man.

> BRENNAN (V.O.)
> Won't take but a second.

7   **ARTILLERY ROAD**

Brennan flashes his headlights into the lovers' car.

The couple, who are in a feverish clinch, look up to see who's bothering them.

Brennan grins at them, lasciviously.

The lovers pull apart, embarassed. The young woman averts her eyes as her boyfriend starts his engine. He pulls forward past Brennan, giving him a dirty look.

Mums in hand, Brennan gets out of his car and hurries around to open the boot.

8   **PRISON SIDE OF WALL**

                    BRAND
                 (*more urgent*)
For Christ sake, man, they'll be back from the cinema. What are you doing?

9   **ARTILLERY ROAD**

Brennan has the boot open, about to remove a rope ladder.

                  BRAND (V.O.)
God damn it, what are you doing there? It's all going to be over ... It's too late ...

Headlights illuminate the boot as Brennan is removing the ladder. He drops it quickly and turns to see an old Morris approaching.

He closes the boot and reaches into the mums, turning off the walkie-talkie, silencing Brand's voice.

The Morris stops adjacent to Brennan. An Elderly Couple are in the car. The woman leans across her husband and speaks to Brennan.

                  ELDERLY WOMAN
Excuse me, young man, we're looking for the hospital.

                   ELDERLY MAN
Hammersmith Hospital. It's on Du Cane –

                     BRENNAN
Yes ... Yes. This is it. Straight on and turn to the left. Visitors' entrance is to the left.

                   ELDERLY MAN
                  (*to his wife*)
What did he say?

                  ELDERLY WOMAN
                     (*loudly*)
He said it's to the left for the visitors' entrance.

10 **OTHER SIDE OF WALL**

                     BRAND
What's wrong? What is it? Answer me damn you, answer. What is it?

11 **ARTILLERY ROAD**

                   ELDERLY MAN
Where should we park?

                  ELDERLY WOMAN
My husband wants to know ...

BRENNAN

On the street. Park on the street. You just go up and turn to the left. Hurry or you'll miss visiting hours. They're very strict.

ELDERLY WOMAN
(*re Brennan's flowers*)

Mums?

BRENNAN

Yes. Hurry along now.

ELDERLY WOMAN
(*holds up a bouquet*)

Me too. For our daughter-in-law. Her liver's shot to hell.

BRENNAN

Lovely. Hurry along.

ELDERLY WOMAN

Thank you . . .

extract from script for *The Short Night* **by David Freeman**

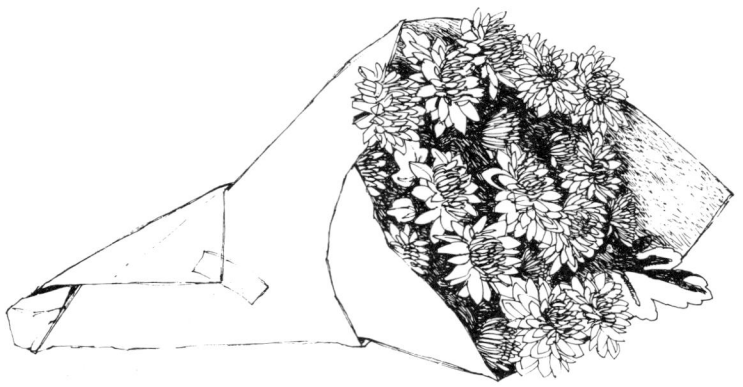

For discussion

1. Very briefly, what is the story so far?
2. Which do you think is more important in the film script: the dialogue, or the descriptions of what is shown by the camera?
3. What do you think will happen next?
4. Which kind (or genre) of film do you think the completed film would have belonged to if it had actually been made?
   Can you think of any other similar films?
5. What is the director's role in the making of a film?

Films Directed by Alfred Hitchcock

North by Northwest (1959)

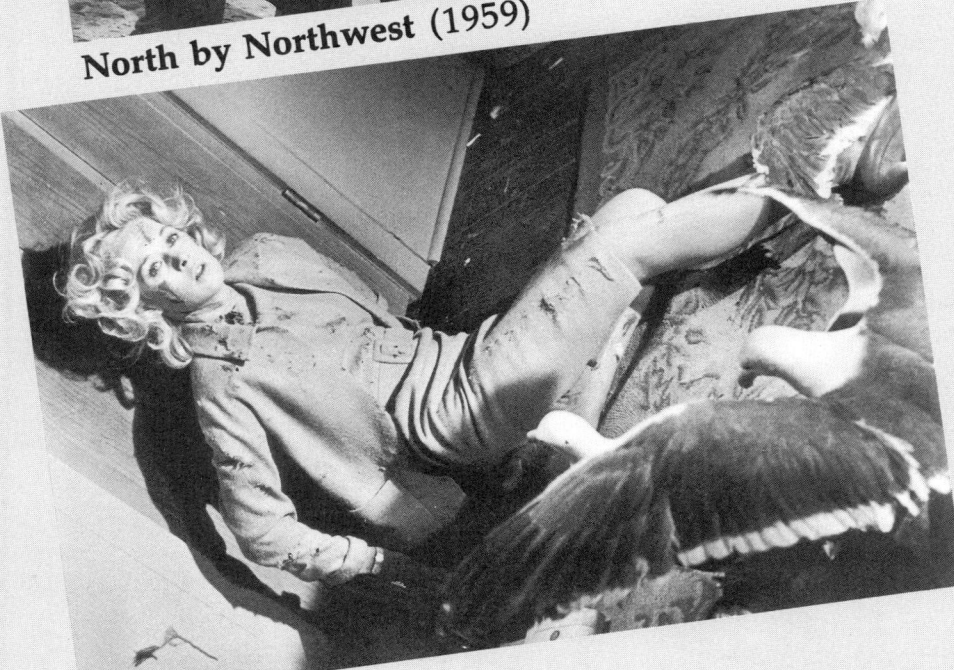

The Birds (1963)

The Lady Vanishes (1938)

The Thirty-Nine Steps (1935)

Questions on all the texts in this Unit

To answer these questions you will need to re-read all four texts in this Unit. You should work individually.

1. What period of time separates the engagement of George and Mabel and their marriage?
2. Where do they get married?
3. When the story-teller asks George how long he has been married (p. 2) George replies, 'Five minutes.' What does he mean by saying this?
4. George goes to a great deal of trouble to avoid marrying Mabel. What is ironic about this?
5. All three poems tell a story. What do the three stories have in common?
6. Explain what the poet means by 'I told my wrath'
7. In the third poem, explain what 'repression' means.
8. Early in the extract from *The Gioconda Smile*, Dr Libbard says, 'Any fool can stop the symptoms of insomnia. The difficulty is to find the cause'. Explain the difference between a symptom and a cause.
9. What does Dr Libbard seem to think is the cause of Janet's insomnia?
10. What is the first thing that Libbard says or does that really annoys Janet?
11. Explain in your own words the point made by the Doctor about the difference between real life and the movies.
12. What is the one thing that is said or done by Janet in this extract that most clearly suggests she could herself be a murderer?
13. The extract from the film is about an attempted break-out from prison. What different things happen to build up the tension for the audience (and also for the main characters)?
14. Suggest something else that might happen (following this extract) to build up the tension still more.

Find and copy out single words from the texts that mean the following.

15. Porch on the outside of a building (*Mabel*, first paragraph)
16. Offensive to standards of decency, or disgusting (*The Gioconda Smile*)
17. Doctor specialising in mental illness (*The Gioconda Smile*)
18. Able to be heard (*film extract*)
19. Domineering (*film extract*)
20. Moves along a horizontal plane (*film extract*)

Favourite Stories

For discussion

Working in small groups, discuss what you think makes a good story. Talk about it in three stages:

1 Think of an example of the best film, novel, play and narrative poem that you know.
2 What do your four choices (for question 1) have in common?
3 In what ways do your choices differ from each other's?

Report back to the rest of the class, compare your ideas, and see whether there is any one kind of story that is particularly popular. Also see which form of story-telling is the most popular: films, novels, plays or poetry.

Suggestions for Writing

Write a story of your own on any theme that appeals to you.

Perhaps write it as a play, or as a film script. Or perhaps write it in two different ways – part of it could be a short story, and part of it could be a poem. It is not essential to write the whole story. One chapter or one scene will do. Nor does it have to be the first chapter or scene.

Later, you may wish to return to the story and write more of it.

2 CAPITAL PUNISHMENT

Contemporary illustration of the execution of Crippen, 1910

Capital punishment

The word *capital* is taken from the Latin *caput*, meaning *the head*. *Capital punishment* is any kind of punishment designed to kill.

Until the second half of the nineteenth century, capital punishment was used in Britain for many offences, not just for murder. For example, a thief could be executed for stealing food, or for stealing goods such as a lace handkerchief. By the end of the century, however, capital punishment was only in use for two main kinds of offence – murder and treason.

In 1965, Parliament abolished capital punishment for *murder*. The punishment for murder is now life imprisonment. This means that the accused can spend anything up to 30 years in prison, although on average it is ten years.

Capital punishment can still be used for cases of *treason*. However, a traitor is nowadays more likely to be charged with an offence under the *Official Secrets Act*, which does not carry the death penalty.

People who are found guilty of more than one offence can receive sentences for each offence. So, for example, a person found guilty of murdering two people could receive two 'life' sentences, to run consecutively, one after the other.

Reintroducing capital punishment for murder

For and against

In the last twenty years there have been a number of attempts to reintroduce capital punishment for murder. Each attempt has been defeated in Parliament.

Here are some of the arguments that have been used. Discuss them together in small groups. Put the items in each list into an appropriate order of importance, beginning with the most important. Just write 1B or 1A and so on.

For reintroduction

A Capital punishment is a deterrent. It makes people afraid to commit murder and will therefore reduce the number of victims.

B It is not possible to reform murderers, so it is better to execute them.

C Capital punishment is the natural punishment for murder; an eye for an eye, a tooth for a tooth.

D Prisons are expensive to run. It is better to execute murderers and avoid the cost of keeping them.

Against reintroduction

W It is never too late for someone to reform. Whilst in prison, a murderer may change his or her ways; we must always give people another chance.

X Capital punishment is inhuman. For society to execute a murderer is just as wrong as for the murderer to kill his or her victim. Two wrongs do not make a right.

Y Mistakes cannot be corrected. If an innocent person is executed, nothing can be done to bring him or her back. Innocent people have been hanged.

Z Capital punishment does not stop murder. The total number of murders committed has not increased significantly since the abolition of capital punishment.

For class discussion

1 Which argument seems to be the most important one for the reintroduction of capital punishment for murder?

2 Which argument seems to be the most important one against its reintroduction?

3 How many students in the class think capital punishment should be reintroduced for murder? How many think it should not?

4 Are there any other arguments which you would use, for or against?

R. v. Jones

The facts of this case are adapted from a real case that came before the British courts some years ago, before capital punishment was abolished. Jones was charged with murder.

Note that most criminal prosecutions are brought in the name of the Queen – hence R. (for *Regina*, or Queen) v. (for *versus*) Jones.

Basic facts of the case

On the evening of April 3rd, a gunman held up a man and a woman in a parked car in a country lane. He spent a long time talking to them; they were in the front of the car; he was in the back. He did not allow them to turn round to look at him. By this time it was dark.

The gunman then told the man to drive the car round the countryside, which he did, and then told him to stop the car in another country lane. The gunman then shot both the man and the woman. The man died, but the woman survived, paralysed from the waist down.

The gunman escaped, presumably thinking that both the man and the woman were either dead or dying. The gunman drove off in the dead man's car.

The murder took place in Sussex. The car was found abandoned the following day, in Ilford, Essex.

Some two months after the crime, *Michael Jones* was charged with the murder of *Henry Smith*. The chief witness for the prosecution was *Alice Brown*, the woman in the car.

Now look at and discuss the evidence as if you are the jury at the actual case. Look at each witness's evidence in turn, discuss it, consider its strengths and weaknesses, and then move on to the next witness.

In effect, you will be in the same position as the jurors were at the actual trial – collecting all the facts and having to decide whom to believe, without having the chance yourselves to question the witnesses. When you have looked at all the evidence and come to your own verdict, you will have the chance to compare your verdict with that of the jury in the actual case.

Take one witness's story at a time. Discuss it in small groups and then compare your opinions with the rest of the class.

Then move on to the next witness.

(**N.B.** You stand much more chance of being fair if you do *not* look through other witnesses' statements until you have finished the discussions on each one in turn.)

Evidence for the Prosecution

1 **Alice Brown**
   a) She did not see the murderer other than very briefly when she turned to look at him in the car at a moment when the lights from another car illuminated his face.
   b) She said in court that she could clearly recognise *Jones* as the murderer. His height, his colouring, and particularly his voice gave him away. He had a Cockney accent and always pronounced *th* as *f* (he said 'fink' instead of 'think'). *Jones* did in fact speak in this way.

   N.B. Her earlier description of the murderer was of someone quite different from Jones. She had also picked out somebody else at an earlier identification parade. This 'somebody else' was cleared by the police.

2 **Mr Waterman**
   He had seen the dead man's car in Croydon, Surrey, being driven at great speed by the accused in the early morning after the crime. The car had overtaken his own in a dangerous manner, and so when *Mr Waterman* caught up with it at a roundabout, he lowered his window and shouted abuse at the driver. He had only seen the driver for those few seconds. He positively recognised *Jones* as the driver

   N.B. *Mr Waterman* had a passenger, a *Mr Fairley*, who was sitting nearer to the other car, and who identified somebody else at another identity parade.

3 **Mr Strickland**
   He saw the dead man's car driving recklessly down Eastern Avenue, Ilford, near to the road where, the morning after the crime, it was found abandoned. He said he could positively recognise *Jones* as the driver of the car. At the time, *Strickland* had been standing outside his own car (*Strickland* saw the car about one hour after *Waterman* saw it.)

N.B. *Strickland's* story was to some extent contradicted by a friend, *Mr Lewis*, who said that *Strickland* had not seen the car while standing in the street but had seen it when it passed by *Strickland's* car while they were travelling to work. (*Strickland* had given *Lewis* a lift to work.)

4 **Mr Martin**

Mr Martin was a friend of *Jones*. He told the Court that *Jones* had recently suggested to him that a good place to hide a gun would be the back seat of a London bus. The murder weapon was later found behind the back seat on the upper deck of a London bus. However, there were no fingerprints.

5 **Mr Sloane**

Mr Sloane was the manager of a hotel in Maida Vale, London, where *Jones* stayed shortly before the time of the murder. *Sloane* told the court that on one occasion he told *Jones* to catch a number 36 bus to get to Queensway from Maida Vale. It was on a number 36A bus that the murder weapon was found by the police.

6 **Mr Davies**

While *Jones* was in prison awaiting trial, he met a prisoner, called *Davies*, who told the court that he and *Jones* talked about the murder, and that Jones confessed he was guilty.

7 **Mrs Muller**

Jones visited *Mrs Muller's* flat in Paddington (London) a couple of days after the murder. They had known each other for some time. She said his face was covered in cuts and his clothes were torn. He told her that he had been in some 'Robin Hood adventures'.

For class discussion

1 **How many of you would be prepared to give a verdict of guilty on the evidence so far?**

2 **Move on to consider the defence evidence in the same way.**

Evidence for the Defence

1 **Michael Jones,** *the accused (aged 20 years)*

   a) He denied that he had ever seen either *Brown* or *Smith* and denied that he had ever been anywhere near the scene of the crime.

   b) He had a criminal record, mainly for theft; he had often been in prison; but had never committed any crime of violence of any kind.

   c) He denied ever having talked with anyone about hiding a gun anywhere; he denied ever having talked to *Davies* in prison.

d) He claimed at first to have been in Liverpool at the time of the murder. He later changed this story to claim that he had travelled further north and stayed at a lodging-house in Edinburgh on the night of the murder. The landlady of the lodging-house gave evidence supporting this claim.

e) He agreed that he had stayed at the hotel in Maida Vale, London, but said he left the hotel to travel north early on the day of the crime.

N.B. The Prosecution accepted that if *Jones* had been in Liverpool or in Edinburgh at any time on the night of the murder then it would have been physically impossible for him to have committed the crime. The prosecution's argument was that he was NOT in Liverpool OR in Edinburgh on the night in question.

2 **Mrs Williams**

She confirmed that *Jones* had stayed in her lodging-house in Edinburgh 350 or so miles from the scene of the crime – on the night of the crime. She confirmed this from her guest-book. She had never previously seen or known him.

No other witnesses who had seen him in Edinburgh were produced in court. (*Mrs Williams* was of good character.)

The instructions to the jury

1 To find the prisoner guilty of murder, you must believe *beyond any reasonable doubt* in the prisoner's guilt.

2 Murder means the intentional killing of another person (or behaving in such a way that any reasonable person would believe you intended to kill even if you did not).

3 Jury verdicts are either unanimous or by a large majority. If more than two out of twelve jurors fail to agree with the rest, then there must be a retrial.

4 Juries can return to court and ask for advice from the judge, but they cannot ask any questions of the witnesses.

N.B. The jury's deliberations are strictly secret and jurors are not allowed to reveal details of them later.

For discussion

1 What is the main weakness in the prosecution evidence?
2 What is the main weakness in the defence evidence?
3 What verdict would you give?

Suggestions for writing

Write a short report explaining in your own words:

a) the basic facts.
b) your views on the evidence for the prosecution. Comment on how you would feel about each of the witnesses and on the prosecution evidence as a whole.
c) your views, similarly, on the defence witnesses.
d) your own verdict and your main reason for it.

from *Witness for the Prosecution* **directed by Billy Wilder**

Who killed the Lindbergh Baby?

Charles Lindbergh was a famous American aviator. He was the first person to fly alone across the Atlantic. In 1932 his baby son was kidnapped from the family home in New Jersey, in the United States. Shortly after, ransom money was demanded for the baby. The Lindberghs paid the money but the baby was then found murdered. In 1936 a German immigrant living in the United States was arrested and executed for the baby's murder. Ever since, there have been serious doubts about the fairness of his trial.

This article was written for the *Radio Times* as an introduction to a television documentary on the case.

The crime that rocked the world

1. 'Work and save, work and save. That was all he did. We wanted so much to get our own little house and to have more children.' The cares of the past 50 years are deeply etched on Anna Hauptmann's features but, at 83, she can still glow with the memories of those modest dreams of her early married years.

2. They came to a shattering end on 19 September 1934. Her son was asleep in his pram as she chatted to a neighbour in the Bronx district of New York. Then, from the yard, they heard noises from her flat and she ran upstairs. In the bedroom she found her belongings scattered over the floor, her husband Richard sitting on the bed looking dazed and two strange men looming over him. It was the last moment of their life together.

3. Within hours the frugal, meticulous, loving carpenter she had married nine years before was accused in screaming headlines around the world of being the unfeeling monster who had kidnapped Charles Lindbergh's baby son, taken 50,000 dollars in ransom and killed the child. For two and a half years the New Jersey police had made no progress in the case. At last the culprit had slipped up; he had paid a petrol station with a note handed over as part of the ransom.

4. Mrs Hauptmann says that, in the nightmare of the arrest and the trial, she knew her husband was innocent. 'When they came to take him I thought it was because he had gone hunting with some friends. He was not in America legally and so he was not allowed a licence. I begged him not to go, and when I saw the men I thought, "Ach, mein Gott, the trouble he is bringing on us with his hunting. I knew he shouldn't go." Then, when I found what it was about, I just thought, "He is innocent, so he will come home soon."'

5. Contemporary newspapers and newsreels show the circus atmosphere that surrounded the trial. The crowds that gathered outside the court screamed 'Kill Hauptmann' and the reports were even more prejudicial than the customary American style. 'They kept saying he was a German

machine-gunner,' his widow remembers, 'but he just did his duty in the war, like the American boys.' In spite of the hysteria, she says she was treated kindly. 'After the arrest, everyone was as nice as they could be. People would send me money – ten or twenty dollars – and tell me to keep it for myself. People in the street would call, "Good luck".'

6   It is not clear if the key piece of evidence in the case still exists – the water-stained cardboard box in which 14,000 dollars of the ransom money was found in the Hauptmann flat. The ransom money handed over by the Lindberghs consisted of 'gold' notes (yellow on one side instead of the standard green) which were subsequently withdrawn from circulation. When Richard paid for petrol with one of them, they had already been phased out and the attendant, commenting that 'you don't see many of these now', made a note of Richard's car number on it – presumably in case it was rejected by the bank. The bank found it to have the serial number of Lindbergh money and the arrest followed.

7   Richard's explanation was that the box had been left for safe-keeping by a former business partner, Isidor Fisch, during a visit to Germany. Fisch had died during the trip and it was only when his family started enquiring about the cash that Richard discovered he had it. So unaware had he been of the box that he had put it where the winter rain had come through to soak the money. He had dried it out and, since Fisch still owed him 7,500 dollars, had taken that and kept the rest for the relatives.

8   It sounded thin at the time but there are indications that, as happens in real life, this improbable explanation was accurate. Mrs Hauptmann, who retains an astounding capacity to recall minute details of her life in those years, sadly remembers all the people bilked by Fisch. 'He was not a very honest man.' It seems a remarkably mild judgement on someone who ruined her life.

9   She has steadfastly refused to rail against her fate and rejected well-meaning advice to change her name or her son's (though she does not appear in the telephone directory and will not meet strangers at her home). In her twilight years, she has some hope that her husband may finally be exonerated of what she calls 'the worst crime, taking a child from his mother'. Through most of the conversation she stays surprisingly detached about her 50-year struggle.

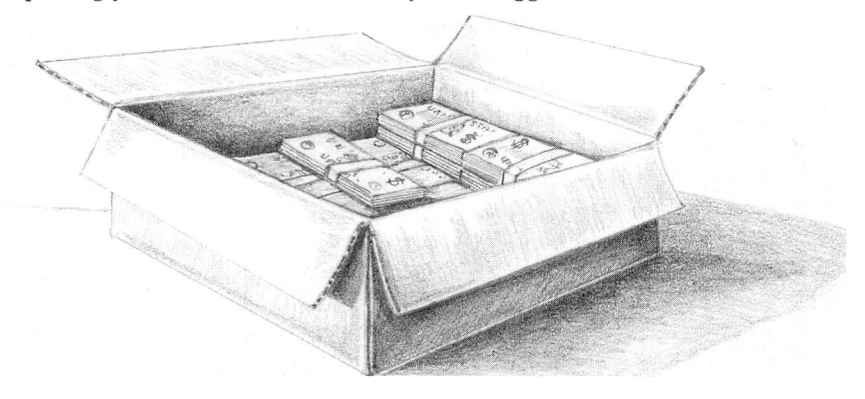

For discussion

1. Make a note of any questions you may now have about the case, and discuss them with the class. For example, do you accept Hauptmann's explanation of the cash and the box?
2. Whose side is the writer of this article on?
3. Discuss any difficult or unusual words. For example, what does 'contemporary' mean (paragraph 5)?.
   Try to work out what the words probably mean from the way they are used. Then check their meaning in a dictionary.

Capital Letters

It has already been pointed out that *capital* is a word derived from the Latin *caput*, meaning *the head*. Thus a capital letter is essentially the head or the chief letter in any word or words. It has a number of different uses. Look again at the Hauptmann article and make a list of the different purposes for which the writer has used capitals. Then compare your lists with each other.

Rewrite the following letter with correct use of capital letters.

> Dear editor i was both impressed and disappointed by the documentary on the lindbergh case by ludovic kennedy last monday. The bbc had taken a lot of care in devising the programme and all the interviews with anna hauptmann in new york were very moving. the article in the radio times was spoiled though by its bias. everything in it was on the side of richard hauptmann. this was also true of the programme itself, the case of the lindbergh baby.

Paragraphs

A well-written paragraph makes one *key point*. The key point of the first paragraph could be summed up as:
   Mrs Hauptmann remembers.
The second paragraph could be summed up as:
   end of a marriage.
Working together in pairs, devise a phrase or a short sentence to sum up each of the remaining paragraphs.

Students' Essays

These are extracts from students' essays on capital punishment. The question was:

Should the death penalty be brought back for those who are found guilty of murder?

1   I find it very difficult to make up my mind on this subject. On the one hand, I disapprove of people killing other people. On the other hand I disapprove of taking anyone's life, even a murderer's.

    I can understand a number of good reasons for executing murderers. In the first place, it is a real punishment. It shows everyone that the killer has done a terrible thing, and that vengeance has been taken. If for example, somebody I loved was murdered, then I would feel angry and bitter if their murderer was simply put into prison for a time and then eventually released. The death penalty makes us all feel that a really serious punishment has been given for something that is serious and unforgiveable.

    I am not sure, though, that all murderers should be executed. Perhaps it is right that you should be put to death for killing a policeman, because the police are having to deal with criminals all the time, and so they should get the greatest possible protection. But I do not think that people should be executed for murders that take place in the heat of the moment, as when people suddenly kill someone, in temper, in their own family.

    Perhaps too, any one who commits murder while committing a robbery or burglary or any act of terrorism, should be sentenced to death. The death sentence acts as a way of stopping such people from going all the way in their criminal actions. It acts as a deterrent.

    The main reason why I am against capital punishment in most cases is that it is very easy for the law to make mistakes. I remember hearing of the case of Timothy Evans who was hanged for a murder that he did not commit. Some years later the real murderer was discovered. Very recently there have been two cases of men being released from prison long after it was discovered that they had *not* committed the murders for which they were imprisoned. In the days of capital punishment they would already have been dead.

Michael Grove

2   Although I am against the reintroduction of capital punishment, I feel that the law should be changed dramatically. I feel that if a person is convicted of murder then he or she should be sent to prison for life and not just for ten to fifteen years. Life sentence should be actual imprisonment for life, or until new evidence is found that proves the person innocent. I feel that a guaranteed life sentence would be a much greater deterrent to would-be murderers than a quick, painless death, and would be just as much revenge for the public.

    So I feel strongly that capital punishment should stay abolished and that Parliament should vote to change the sentence given to convicted murderers. This would make our society a safer place.

Darren Goodwin

For discussion

1. What is the main point made by Michael Grove in his essay? What do you feel about it?
2. What is the main point made by Darren Goodwin? How do you feel about it?
3. Michael Grove has written his essay from a brief plan in which he listed the points he wanted to make. Working together in pairs, write down briefly the main point made in each of his paragraphs.
4. In order to link different points together, both these writers use expressions such as *on the other hand, however, but, perhaps* and *though*. Check both essays to see how often the writers use these expressions, and why.

Capital punishment – a review

Briefly revise the work you have done so far in this Unit, looking again at:

> the introductory information (p. 22);
> arguments for and against (pp. 22–3);
> *R. v. Jones* (pp. 24–6);
> *Who killed the Lindbergh Baby?* (pp. 29–30);
> extracts from students' essays (pp. 32–3).

For discussion

1. What do you now consider to be the two or three main points *in favour* of reintroducing the death penalty for murder?
2. What do you now consider to be the two or three main points *against* its reintroduction?
3. Would you now vote *for* or *against* its reintroduction?

Discuss these points in pairs or small groups. During your discussion mention the various items you have looked at in this Unit.
Make a short note of your discussions, and then report back to the rest of the class.

Fair Comments?

Here are four short extracts from other students' essays. In each case, the students have attempted to justify their opinions and to be fair to those who disagree with them.

> I am in favour of reintroducing capital punishment for murder. I think there is no other way of making clear that we disapprove of murderers and will do everything possible to stop murders taking place. Not only that, but I think a lot of people will feel better just to know that capital punishment has been brought back – they will sleep better in their beds at night. This is important. At the moment, many people feel scared to go out at night or to open the door at night when somebody knocks. Just knowing that murderers are hanged will make such people feel better and safer. So it will make our society a better place to live.
>
> **1**

> I am against the reintroduction of capital punishment. There have always been murders and there always will be murders, and no amount of punishment will make any difference. After all, in the days when children were hanged for stealing lace handkerchiefs or loaves of bread, they still went around stealing. In other words, severe punishments do not stop crime. So there is not a good argument for hanging murderers.
>
> **2**

> I am against the reintroduction of capital punishment because it is always possible to hang an innocent person. Timothy Evans was hanged in 1950, and much later it was discovered that he was innocent. What did the government do? They gave him a pardon and that was that. I know that this kind of thing does not happen often, but even if it only happens sometimes, that seems to me a fair argument for not reintroducing capital punishment.
>
> **3**

> Everyone knows that there have been a lot more murders since capital punishment was abolished. Nowadays it is not safe to open the door at night or to walk down the street after nightfall. Once upon a time, Britain was a safe place. It isn't any more. So I say, bring back hanging!
>
> **4**

For discussion

1. One of the commonest ways of 'cheating' or being unfair in an argument is to *refer to facts and figures but to give no actual evidence of them* (or of where they come from). Do any of the writers of the extracts do this?
2. Another common form of 'cheating' is to *generalise without really giving evidence to justify your opinion*. For example, someone might say, 'We all know that young people nowadays are lazy and deceitful'. Is this done by any of these writers?
3. Another form of 'cheating' is to *pretend to speak or write on behalf of all or most of the people*. For example, 'Good people everywhere are heartily sick of the way children behave nowadays in schools. Everyone wants something to be done'. Do any of these writers use this tactic?
4. Working together in small groups, invent an example of each of the forms of 'cheating' described above for a discussion of examination results in your school. Compare your examples with the rest of the class.
5. Which of the four extracts from the students' essays do you think is the fairest? Why?

Writing an Essay

1. **Should the death penalty be brought back for those who are found guilty of murder?**

Write an essay on this question.
Begin by planning your essay and discussing your plan.
A possible plan could be:

Paragraph 1	Define capital punishment. Explain how it was used in the past.
Paragraph 2	Give main reason for, and also give main reason against.
Paragraph 3	Give second reason for, and also against.
Paragraph 4	Give third reason for, and also against.
Paragraph 5	Give examples of actual cases, such as Jones, Hauptmann and Evans.
Paragraph 6	Give your own opinion and explain it.

In your essay, try to be as fair as possible to both sides of the argument.

Remember the importance of such phrases as *however, on the other hand,* and *but*.

2. You may prefer to choose another issue which is of interest and concern to you, perhaps working in pairs or small groups. In this case you might:

    use the library for initial research.

    prepare a brief questionnaire in order to sound out other people's opinions.

    work out your principal arguments and the evidence you will need to support them.

    consider the principal arguments for those who disagree with you. Work out your response to your critics.

    report back to the class. Discuss your research and consider the attitudes of other members of the class.

    work out a plan for your essay.

3. Later, assess your essays. Read each other's essays and talk about them. Consider especially:

    how far the writer has made use of evidence of different kinds.

    how clearly the writer has thought out his or her opinions or attitudes.

    whether the writer has clearly used a good plan, so that the essay has a definite shape or structure.

    whether the writer is fair to different points of view.

    whether the writer comes to a reasonable conclusion.

3 OPENERS

The opening chapter is perhaps the most important part of any novel. It sets up the story, entices the reader to read on, and raises all sorts of expectations in the reader's mind.

Here is a small collection of openings. Read them and chat about them.

1   They came down to the emergency ward at noon and sat on the bench just behind the swinging doors that led in from the ambulance parking slot. Ellis was nervous, preoccupied, distant. Morris was relaxed, eating a candy bar and crumpling the wrapper into the pocket of his white jacket.

From where they sat, they could look at the sunlight outside, falling across the big sign that said EMERGENCY WARD and the smaller sign that said NO PARKING AMBULANCES ONLY. In the distance they heard sirens.

"Is that him?" Morris asked.

Ellis checked his watch. "I doubt it. It's too early."

They sat on the bench and listened to the sirens come closer. Ellis removed his glasses and wiped them with his tie. One of the emergency ward nurses, a girl Morris did not know by name, came over and said brightly, "Is this the welcoming committee?"

Ellis squinted at her. Morris said, "We'll be taking him straight through. Do you have his chart down here?"

The nurse said, "Yes, I think so, Doctor," and walked off looking irritated.

Ellis sighed. He replaced his glasses and frowned at the nurse.

Morris said, "She didn't mean anything."

"I suppose the whole damned hospital knows," Ellis said.

"It's a pretty big secret to keep."

The sirens were very close now; through the windows they saw an ambulance back into the slot. Two orderlies opened the door and pulled out the stretcher. A frail elderly woman lay on the stretcher, gasping for breath, making wet gurgling sounds. Severe pulmonary edema, Morris thought as he watched her taken into one of the treatment rooms.

"I hope he's in good shape," Ellis said.

"Who?"

"Benson."

"Why shouldn't he be?"

"They might have roughed him up." Ellis stared morosely out the windows. He really is in a bad mood, Morris thought. He knew that meant Ellis was excited; he had scrubbed in on enough cases with Ellis to recognise the pattern. Irascibility under pressure while he waited – and then total, almost lazy calm when the operation began. "Where the hell is he?" Ellis said, looking at his watch again.

To change the subject, Morris said, "Are we all set for three-thirty?" At 3:30 that afternoon, Benson would be presented to the hospital staff at a special Neurosurgical Round.

"As far as I know," Ellis said. "Ross is making the presentation. I just hope Benson's in good shape."

Over the loudspeaker, a soft voice said, "Dr. Ellis, Dr. John Ellis, two-two-three-four. Dr. Ellis, two-two-three-four."

Ellis got up to answer the page. "Hell," he said.

Morris knew what he meant. Two-two-three-four was the extension for the animal laboratories. The call probably meant something had gone wrong with the monkeys. Ellis had been doing three monkeys a week for the past month, just to keep himself and his staff ready.

He watched as Ellis crossed the room and answered from a wall phone. Ellis walked with a slight limp, the result of a childhood injury that had cut the lateral peroneal nerve in his right leg. Morris always wondered if the injury had had something to do with Ellis's later decision to become a neurosurgeon. Certainly Ellis had the attitude of a man determined to correct defects, to fix things up. That was what he always said to his patients: "We can fix you up." And he seemed to have more than his share of defects himself – the limp, the premature near-baldness, the weak eyes, and the heavy thick glasses. It produced a vulnerability about him that made his irascibility more tolerable.

Or perhaps the irascibility was the result of all those years as a surgeon. Morris wasn't sure; he hadn't been a surgeon long enough. He stared out the window at the sunlight and the parking lot. Afternoon visiting hours were beginning; relatives were driving into the parking lot, getting out of their cars, glancing up at the high buildings of the hospital. The apprehension was clear in their faces; the hospital was a place people feared.

For class discussion

1. Are there any difficult or unusual words in the extract? Talk about them. Later, check their meaning in a dictionary.
2. So far, what is the story about?
3. What kind or genre of story is it? How do you know?
4. Do you know any other stories, whether from films, plays, or novels, that are similar in any way?
5. What is likely to happen next?

For group discussion

Read the other extracts and discuss them in small groups. Use the five questions above as the basis for your discussion of each extract.

2   Nyokabi called him. She was a small, black woman, with a bold but grave face. One could tell by her small eyes full of life and warmth that she had once been beautiful. But time and bad conditions do not favour beauty. All the same, Nyokabi had retained her full smile – a smile that lit up her dark face.

'Would you like to go to school?'

'O, mother!' Njoroge gasped. He half feared that the woman might withdraw her words. There was a little silence till she said,

'We are poor. You know that.'

'Yes, mother.' His heart pounded against his ribs slightly. His voice was shaky.

'So you won't be getting a mid-day meal like other children.'

'I understand.'

'You won't bring shame to me by one day refusing to attend school?'

O mother, I'll never bring shame to you. Just let me get there, just let me. The vision of his childhood again opened before him. For a time he contemplated the vision. He lived in it alone. It was just there, for himself, a bright future ... Aloud he said, 'I like school.'

He said this quietly. His mother understood him.

'All right. You'll begin on Monday. As soon as your father gets his pay we'll go to the shops. I'll buy you a shirt and a pair of shorts.'

O mother, you are an angel of God, you are, you are. Then he wondered. Had she been to a magic worker? Or else how could she have divined his child's unspoken wish, his undivulged dream? *And here I am, with nothing but a piece of calico on my body and soon I shall have a shirt and shorts for the first time.*

'I thank you mother, very much.' He wanted to say more. But Njoroge was not used to expressing strong feelings in words. However his eyes spoke all. Again Nyokabi understood. She was happy.

When Kamau came in the evening, Njoroge took him aside.

'Kamau, I shall go to school.'

'School?'

'Yes.'

'Who said so? Father?'

'No. It was our mother. Has our elder mother told you the same thing?'

'No, brother. You know I am being trained as a carpenter. I cannot drop the apprenticeship. But I am glad you're going to school.'

'I am, oh, so glad. But I wish you too would come.'

'Don't you worry about me. Everything will be all right. Get education. I'll get carpentry. Then we shall, in the future, be able to have a new and better home for the whole family.

'Yes,' Njoroge said thoughtfully. 'That's what I want. And you know, I think Jacobo is as rich as Mr Howlands because he got education. And that's why each takes his children to school because of course they have learnt the value of it.'

'It's true. But some, you know, must get learning and others this and that trade.'

'Well, you see, I was thinking that if both of us could learn and become like John, the big son of Jacobo, it would be a good thing. People say that because he has finished all the learning in Kenya, he will now go far away to . . .'

'England.'

'Or Burma.'

'England and Burma and Bombay and India are all the same places. You have to cross the sea before you can reach there.'

'That's where Mr Howlands comes from?'

'Yes.'

'I wonder why he left England, the home of learning, and came here. He must be foolish.'

'I don't know. You cannot understand a white man.'

3

Nanda was on her way to the Convent of the Five Wounds. She sat very upright on the slippery seat of the one-horse bus, her tightly-gaitered legs dangling in the straw, and her cold hands squeezed into an opossum muff. A fog screened every window, clouding the yellow light that shone on the faces of the three passengers as they jolted slowly along invisible streets.

After several sociable but unheeded coughs, the third occupant could bear the silence no longer and began to speak to Nanda's father. She wore a dusty velvet tam o' shanter and a man's tweed coat, and Nanda could tell from her voice that she was Irish. "Excuse me, sir," she asked, "but could you tell me if we are anywhere near Lippington village yet?"

"I'm afraid I can't tell you," Mr. Grey answered in his rich, pleasant voice, "all I *do* know is that we haven't got to the Convent yet, because the driver is putting us down there. The village is further on up the lane."

"The Convent?" exclaimed the Irishwoman, "would that be the Convent of the Five Wounds now?"

Yes," said Nanda's father. "I'm just taking my little daughter to school there."

The Irishwoman beamed.

"Now isn't that beautiful?" she said, "you're a Catholic, then, sir?" She pronounced it 'Cartholic.'

"I am indeed," Mr. Grey assented.

"Isn't that wonderful now? To think of the three of us in this omnibus in a Protestant country and everyone of us Catholics."

"I'm a convert," Mr. Grey explained. "I was only received into the Church a year ago."

"To think of that!" said the Irishwoman. "The grace of God is a glorious thing. Indeed it is. I wonder if the little lady knows what a grace has been given to her to have a father that's been called to the Faith?"

She leant over and put her face close to Nanda's.

"And so you're going to the holy nuns at the Five Wounds, my dear? Isn't it the lucky young lady you are? The saints must have watched over your cradle. There's no holier religious anywhere in the world than the nuns of the Five Wounds. I've a cousin meself . . . Mary Cassidy . . . that's one of their lay-sisters in Armagh. She'll be taking her final vows in February . . . the Feast of the Purification. Do you know when that is, my dear?"

"The second of February," Nanda risked shyly.

The Irishwoman rolled her eyes in admiration.

"Glory be to God, did you ever hear the like?" she asked Mr. Grey. "Are you telling me that young lady's not born and bred a Catholic?"

Nanda's father looked pleased.

"No. She was received only last year, when she was eight. But she's been having instruction and learning her catechism."

"It's wonderful, so it is," the Irishwoman assured him, "and it's a sign of special grace, I'll be bound. Perhaps she'll be called on to do great things in the service of God, who knows? I wouldn't be surprised if she had a vocation later on."

"Oh, it's early days to think of that," smiled Mr. Grey.

Nanda began to feel a little uncomfortable. She had heard a good deal about vocations and she wasn't at all sure that she wanted one.

"They say God speaks to them very early," said the Irishwoman mysteriously, "and that they hear Him best in the innocence of their hearts. Look at St. Aloysius now. And St. Stanislas Kostka. And St. Theresa herself that would have been a martyr for the love of God when she was but three years old. And wouldn't it be a beautiful thing now if she was to offer her life to God as a thanksgiving for the great blessing of your own conversion, sir?"

Nanda began to like the conversation less and less. She was an only child and she had taken to her new religion with a rather precocious fervour. Already she had absorbed enough of the Catholic point of view to see how very appropriate such a sacrifice would be. But although she had already privately dedicated herself to perpetual virginity, and had seriously considered devoting her life to the lepers at Molokai, she did not entirely relish the idea of cutting off her hair and living in a cell and never seeing her home again. She was relieved when the bus stopped and the driver came round and tapped on the window.

"This must be the Convent," said Mr. Grey. "We get down here. Lippington village is a little way further on."

"God bless you both," said the Irishwoman. "Goodbye, little lady. Say a prayer every morning to thank God and his saints for bringing you to the holy faith. And say a prayer sometimes for poor old Bridget Mulligan, for the prayers of children have great power with the Almighty. I'll say five decades for you this very night that you may grow up a good Catholic and a comfort to your father."

As they passed out of the omnibus, Mr. Grey pressed something into the ragged woman's hand.

"God bless you, sir," she called after them.

4

The house was on Dresden Avenue in the Oak Knoll section of Pasadena, a big solid cool-looking house with burgundy brick walls, a terra-cotta tile roof, and a white stone trim. The front windows were leaded downstairs. Upstairs windows were of the cottage type and had a lot of rococo imitation stonework trimming around them.

From the front wall and its attendant flowering bushes a half-acre or so of fine green lawn drifted in a gentle slope down to the street, passing on the way an enormous deodar around which it flowed like a cool green tide around a rock. The sidewalk and the parkway were both very wide and in the parkway were three white acacias that were worth seeing. There was a heavy scent of summer on the morning and everything that grew was perfectly still in the breathless air they get over there on what they call a nice cool day.

All I knew about the people was that they were a Mrs. Elizabeth Bright Murdock and family and that she wanted to hire a nice clean private detective who wouldn't drop cigar ashes on the floor and never carried more than one gun. And I knew she was the widow of an old coot with whiskers named Jasper Murdock who had made a lot of money helping out the community, and got his photograph in the Pasadena paper every year on his anniversary, with the years of his birth and death underneath, and the legend: *His Life Was His Service.*

I left my car on the street and walked over a few dozen stumble stones set into the green lawn, and rang the bell in the brick portico under a peaked roof. A low red brick wall ran along the front of the house the short distance from the door to the edge of the driveway...

After a while a middle-aged sourpuss in a maid's costume opened the front door about eight inches and gave me the beady eye.

'Philip Marlowe,' I said, 'Calling on Mrs. Murdock. By appointment.'

The middle-aged sourpuss ground her teeth, snapped her eyes shut, snapped them open and said in one of those angular hardrock pioneer-type voices: 'Which one?'

'Huh?'

'Which Mrs. Murdock?' she almost screamed at me.

'Mrs. Elizabeth Bright Murdock,' I said. 'I didn't know there was more than one.'

'Well, there is,' she snapped. 'Got a card?'

She still had the door a scant eight inches open. She poked the end of her nose and a thin muscular hand into the opening. I got my wallet out and got one of the cards with just my name on it and put it in the hand. The hand and nose went in and the door slammed in my face.

I thought that maybe I ought to have gone to the back door.

Time passed, quite a lot of time. I stuck a cigarette in my mouth, but didn't light it. The Good Humour man went by in his little blue and white wagon, playing "Turkey in the Straw" on his music-box. A large black and gold butterfly fish-tailed in and landed on a hydrangea bush almost at my elbow, moved its wings slowly up and down a few times, then took off heavily and staggered away through the motionless hot scented air.

The front door came open again. The sourpuss said: 'This way.'

I went in. The room beyond was large and square and sunken and cool and had the restful atmosphere of a funeral chapel and something the same smell. Tapestry on the blank roughened stucco walls, iron grilles imitating balconies outside high side windows, heavy carved chairs with plush seats and tapestry backs and tarnished gilt tassels hanging down their sides. At the back a stained-glass window about the size of a tennis-court. Curtained french doors underneath it. An old musty, fusty, narrow-minded, clean and bitter room. It didn't look as if anybody ever sat in it or would ever want to. Marble-topped tables with crooked legs, gilt clocks, pieces of small statuary in two colours of marble. A lot of junk that would take a week to dust. A lot of money, and all wasted. Thirty years before, in the wealthy close-mouthed provincial town Pasadena then was, it must have seemed like quite a room.

We left it and went along a hallway and after a while the sourpuss opened a door and motioned me in.

'Mr. Marlowe,' she said through the door in a nasty voice, and went away grinding her teeth.

Following your group discussions, compare your answers with those of the rest of the class.

Further group discussion

1 Continuing the discussion you had in Unit 1, make a list of the four or five best novels you have ever read. The list should reflect the choices of the whole group.
2 Which different genres are represented on your list?
3 What novels have you heard of, but have not yet read, which you think you would like to read?
4 Compare your lists with the rest of the class.

Questions on all the texts in this Unit

To answer these questions you will need to re-read all four extracts. You should work on your own.

1. In the first extract the nurse asks Morris and Ellis, 'Is this the welcoming committee?'. What or whom are they likely to be 'welcoming'?
2. Who or what is Benson?
3. In the second extract, what are the two things that most clearly show that Njoroge's family is very poor?
4. In the second extract, how does the author show the difference between what Njoroge is thinking, and what he actually says?
5. In the third extract, what does Nanda say that excites the Irishwoman's admiration?
6. The Irishwoman wants Nanda to become a nun. What is Nanda's own attitude to this?
7. In the fourth extract, who is telling the story? What is his occupation?
8. In this part of the story, what shows that he is well qualified for his occupation?
9. All four of these extracts lead up to something that is about to happen to the main character or characters. Explain what you think is going to happen next to each of them.
10. Explain what all these things that are going to happen next have in common with each other.

Vocabulary

11. Give another word or short phrase meaning the same as 'vulnerability' (first extract).
12. Give another word or short phrase meaning the same as 'irascibility' (first extract).
13. Find and copy out a word in the second extract meaning *thought about*.
14. Give another word or short phrase meaning the same as 'undivulged' (second extract).
15. Make a list of five other words using the same prefix, **un**. (These do not have to be words taken from these extracts.)
16. What does the writer mean in the third extract by describing the woman's coughs as 'sociable'?
17. What does 'provincial' mean? (fourth extract, third from last sentence)
18. What does 'close-mouthed' mean? (fourth extract, third from last sentence)

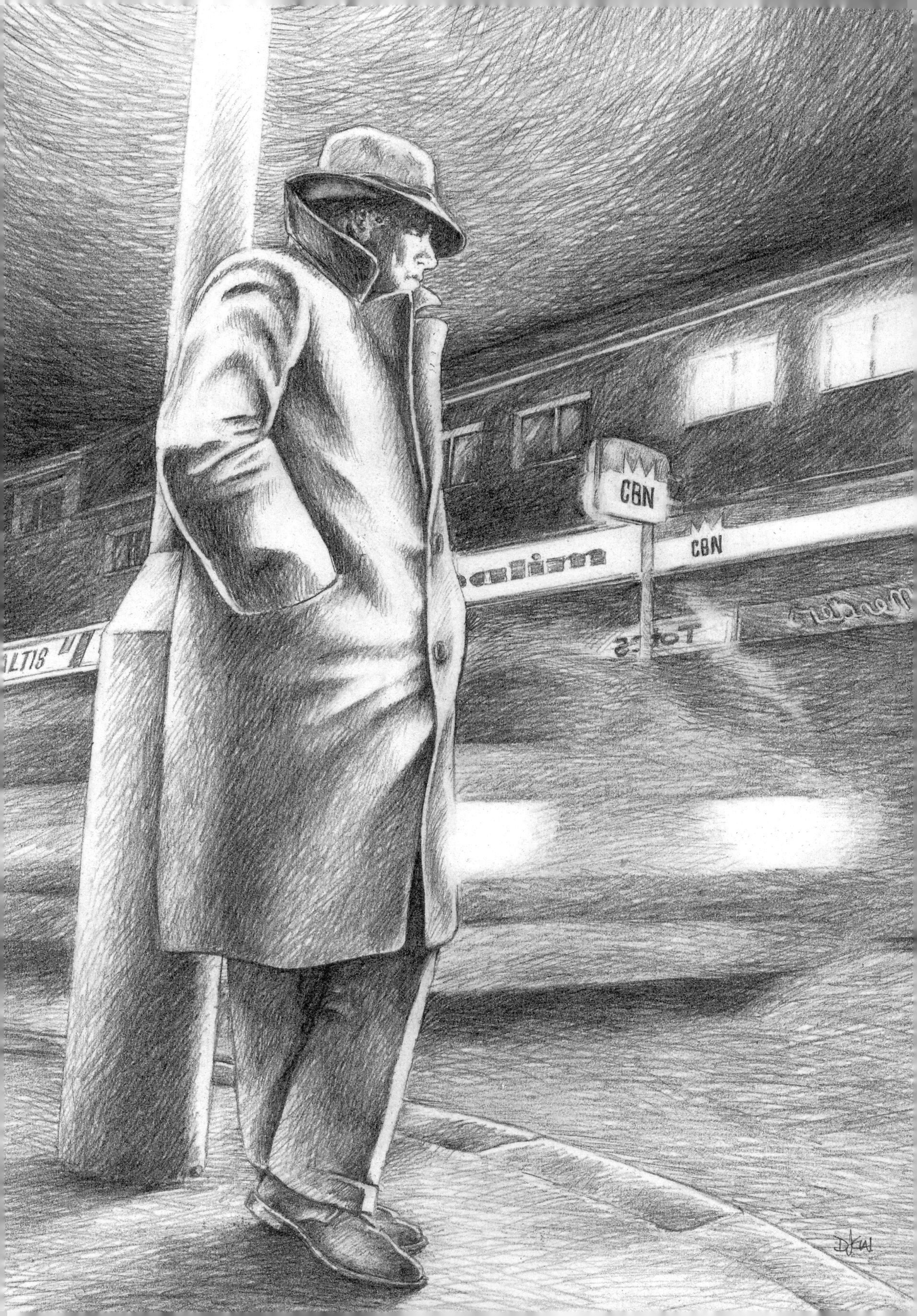
CBN
CBN

Suggestions for reading and writing

1. Choose a novelist of interest to you. Choose two or three of his or her books to read and to talk about.

   Later, write a report on your reading, reporting on such aspects of the books as:

   > the story, in brief;
   >
   > particularly interesting moments in the story;
   >
   > the main character or characters and how they change in the course of the story;
   >
   > similarities between the novels;
   >
   > those aspects of the novels that most attract you.

   Alternatively, you might prefer to look at a particular genre of fiction (including short stories) covering the work of several different writers.

2. As an experiment, write a story (or part of a story) in the style of the writer or writers whose work you have just been reading. You might, for instance, refer back to the story you wrote for Unit 1 (p. 20), and either rewrite it, or write another part of the story.

   N.B. Writing that deliberately sets out to mirror the style of someone else's writing is called *pastiche*.

The pictures on the opening page of this Unit (p. 37) are of:

Top row, left to right H. G. Wells, Charlotte Brontë, Charles Dickens
Middle row, left to right Daphne du Maurier, Edgar Allan Poe, Raymond Chandler
Bottom row, left to right Emily Brontë, Wilkie Collins, Jane Austen.

The openings at the beginning of this Unit are from:

The Terminal Man by Michael Crichton;
Weep Not, Child by Ngugi Wa Thiong'o;
Frost in May by Antonia White;
The High Window by Raymond Chandler.

◀— What genre does the picture on p. 47 seem to be?

4 CHARACTERS

Here is a collection of character studies from short stories written by students.

Annie

Although I clutched Graham's muscular and comforting arm, I could not help feeling afraid. With my other hand I reached out, my heart pounding, wondering what we should do. 'Come on, Graham, please let's get back'. I tugged at his arm. 'Oh, it's all right' he said, 'don't be afraid!'

This would not have happened, however, if we had not been late. For it was already half-past eight when we had left home, and now I wished so much that we had not decided to take the route through the marshes. Janice had been through once and in ten minutes she had arrived at school.

Presently we felt our way through the tunnel. It was damp, oil-smelling and nauseating. The walls were cracked and paint was peeling off; it hurt my palm so badly. The whole atmosphere reminded me of the London Dungeon. The thought of headless corpses and bloody axes reiterated in my mind. I began to feel ill.

Suddenly I heard a piercing squeal; an enormous rat appeared in front of us; we could barely make out its features. He saw us, dashed across a pathway, and hurried off at lightning speed down what seemed a black hole. We both gasped for breath, holding each other's sweating hands.

'Let's get out of here!' Turning around, I saw Graham's face, it had turned as white as a sheet. As for me, I was sure I had fainted.

'Let's go this way. I think I can smell fresh air – hey, are you all right?'

'Just about! Thanks. Yes, let's try this way.' We cautiously moved along a passageway.

I thought about what my mother would say. She had already suffered a shock with my little sister's death; what would happen if she were to be told that I were missing? I dreaded these thoughts. Or even worse, what might happen if we never found our way out? And if no one ever came to look . . . I began to cry. Graham stopped and turned around.

'Oh come on, Annie, we shall find our way out soon. Please, don't cry. Everything will be fine, please don't worry.'

'But what if we don't find our way out?' I reached into my pocket for my handkerchief. I knew I had hurt him. I apologised and we carried on.

Out of the dampness I suddenly heard sounds of what seemed to be a school playground full of children. Hope filled my heart. We gathered pace, and our shuffling feet along the stony ground made echoing noises throughout.

'I think this is it, but don't walk too fast, you might trip.' We loosened our grip a little but still kept very close. There was a confident air around us; I was full of hope; my mind began to relax. We presently passed another junction and continued following the fresh air. I was convinced God had heard our prayers, and I thanked him for answering them. I began to wonder what I was going to tell my mother; some feasible excuse!

The passage curved to the right and brought us to what appeared to be a small room. We felt around for a door or somewhere the air was coming from. It was reassuring to know Graham was still there. I could not think what would have happened if I were alone. Just then, Graham turned around and with a wonderful masculine air, sighed, 'I'm afraid we've taken the wrong path. This is only a ventilating shaft. We'll have to go back.'

'What about the noises I heard? There must be a way out here!'

'It's no use, Annie, I've looked. We've been barking up the wrong tree. Let's waste no time, follow me.'

I had been betrayed. I felt warm, but my heart was empty. I felt a sudden urge to do something; I was near panic, and felt as though my heart had been eaten. I screamed.

'Stop it, Annie! Don't get hysterical!' Graham clutched my shaking hand. I closed my eyes for a second and began to face up to the reality which lay before me. It was soothing to see Graham's normal countenance. I followed, relying solely upon Graham. We walked a little further but then we heard footsteps echoing through the walls. At first I felt relieved but then fear pierced my heart as I thought of other possibilities. A torch shone our way; it hurt my eyes, which had become accustomed to the dim light. Somebody called my name, and so, releasing Graham's hand I ran into my father's arms, crying. I had a lot to explain when we finally arrived home.

Pratish Soni

Stan

Stan sat huddled in a doorway wrapped in a few old newspapers to keep warm. His collection of rubbish that he thought might come in useful, sat in two carrier bags in the opposite corner of the doorway together with his few possessions which he still held on to.

He watched a young couple pass by on the other side of the road carefully not looking in his direction and he wished he could be an accepted person in society again.

It wasn't often that Stan was sober for very long and when he was he always felt this way – sad, miserable, lonely and reminiscent. He wished to himself that he had never started drinking. It had started with a few pints in the pub and an occasional drunken night. Then when he turned to whisky, scotch and gin in order to forget his troubles he had been unable to stop. Now he was unemployed and unable to afford anything more than meths. What he would give, he thought, to be living an ordinary life like so many other people were, and not to be treated as an outcast to be looked down upon.

'No one cares what happens to me,' he said to himself. 'I can't even walk into a cafe to buy a cup of tea. They just tell me to move on and usher me out of the door.' He put his hands in the pocket of his dirty overcoat; the cold October wind was numbing his fingertips. A greasy chip paper tumbled past on the pavement.

'Even the police have stopped bothering with me now,' he told himself. 'They've given up trying to get me into hostels. I just get my soup and the odd proper meal there sometimes, but I couldn't live there – not without my drink.' He wished he had a bottle now, could forget about everything and stop feeling sorry for himself.

He thought how everybody walked by him, as though he didn't exist or they didn't want him to exist, except for the gangs of small boys who sometimes teased and abused him – and felt even more lonely than before. He wished again for a bottle of something.

He was shivering with the cold of the wind and the grey concrete step beneath him and he decided not to stay there any longer. He bundled his papers into one of the carrier bags and shuffled off along the road. Maybe he could find the other meths drinkers on the old bomb-site. Perhaps they would have a fire going and a bottle of meths with which he could drown his sorrows.

David Shrimpton

For discussion

1 What difference is there in the way these two stories are written?
2 Is there any difference in the way the stories begin?
3 Is there any difference in the way they end?

The Companion

At around about six o'clock the screaming stopped; the town folk picked up their deck-chairs and stumped back towards their cars to drive back home. 'Coronation Street' was due to start in a few minutes and this was my cue to slip quietly out of the house. As I looked over towards the beach, I could see a small girl paddling in a rock-pool with her trousers pulled up to her knees. The purple clouds were starting to roll towards her and loom threateningly above her. The girl looked up and quietly scurried away towards the sand dunes.

As I waded through the piles of litter towards the beach I could hear the monotonous squeaking of the ice-cream sign flapping backwards and forwards in the wind. I knew that this was the day.

Before I reached him I knew what I wanted to do. The desire to kill the bird had flared up once more. I ignored the old fisherman snoring in his deck-chair beside his boat, his little ginger cat, and the pretty girls who were going to a disco. I was totally oblivious of anything until I reached the craggy cliffs that stuck out from the bay like a cyst on a bald man's head.

Managing to find a secure foothold, I started my ascent. After a few minutes I caught sight of him sitting in his usual nest, sheltered from the sun. He greeted me with his usual squawk. Instead of this warming my heart, as it usually did, it resonated with a distinctively harsh sound which actually made me wince. I staggered towards the bird and put out a surly hand to it, with the customary piece of cheese balanced on my fingertips. The bird refused it with a turn of his head, and this deeply hurt me. I was ashamed with myself that this should have touched me so much.

I sat down and peered across the sea, fixing my eyes on a piece of wood being tossed up and down like a cork at the bottom of a waterfall. It reminded me of myself and I wondered why I continued to come to see a very ordinary sea bird every night. The hatred swelled up again inside me, but before I could do anything, I heard a flutter of wings. There, away from me, the creature floated majestically over the sea. Our companionship had ended.

Guy Wilkinson

54

Eddie

That Sunday afternoon was the first really warm afternoon we had experienced for some time. It was one of those hazy days when everything is bathed in a rich golden glow. Where I was sitting, on the grass by the pond, I had the shadow of an oak tree falling on me as I watched the children paddling and splashing each other by the water's edge.

There were many couples strolling about, and, looking up, I noticed a pair standing at the top of the bank just across the pond. She had dark hair like mine; she was gazing up at a boy who was talking animatedly about something. He had his arm loosely around her waist and stood, very still, watching her as he spoke. Suddenly she laughed and, as she laughed, he kissed her lightly on the brow.

It seemed as though I was watching a scene from my own life being acted out. Not so long ago I had stood there with someone, just as they did now, laughing and listening. 'I wonder how you will end up!' I thought, remembering what had happened to Eddie and myself.

At first, Eddie and I had been friends. We had practically grown up together and had shared each other's secrets and joys. Then when we were about fourteen, everything changed. Now I could not look at him without a certain amount of love. Soon we were seeing each other regularly, with nobody else between us. Both had given up all other boy- or girl-friends. We got on well until a few days after Christmas when we were at a friend's house, helping to prepare for a New Year's party. Eddie and I were putting up some decorations when he turned to me and asked,

'Do you love me, Vik?'

I didn't quite know what to say.

He added, 'Really love me?'

'I suppose so,' I said, 'I've never really thought about it.'

Later that night he was taking me home when a boy suddenly appeared out of the mist, like a ghost, and bumped into Eddie. It was just an accident and the boy muttered, 'Sorry!' and walked on. But for some reason Eddie was very annoyed. He yelled out in the lonely street, 'Hey, you! Come here!' The boy stopped just under a street lamp, and I could see that he was really very young, probably no more than 12 years old, and very scared. I wondered what he was doing out on his own at that time of night. But I had no time to wonder any longer, for Eddie went up to him and hit him on the shoulder.

'What do you think,' he said to him, hitting him again, 'what do you think you're doing, barging into people? Eh?' I told Eddie to shut up and leave the boy alone but he ignored me. By this time the boy was very frightened indeed and Eddie was still hitting him on the shoulder. It was nothing terrible but it hurt the boy, and now he started to cry. 'Stop it, Eddie!' I called to him. But it was the boy's tears that made him stop, not my calling out to him. The boy just stood there crying and so Eddie said, 'You watch it another time. You hear me? Watch it!'

Still sobbing, the boy stood waiting for another blow as I said to Eddie, 'You asked me not so long ago if I loved you. Well I don't when you behave like this.' Then I turned to the boy and said, 'Go on, go home. Stop crying. He didn't mean it. Go on.' I was gently pushing the boy away from Eddie who looked ready to murder the defenceless creature. Finally he turned and fled, disappearing in an instant into the night.

Then I turned to Eddie. 'One day,' I said, 'that boy will get even with you. And when it happens, may God help you, because I won't.' And with that I turned and left him and made my own way home.

Vikki Parr

For discussion

1. What kind of person is Eddie?
2. What kind of person is Vikki?
3. This is just an extract from the story. What do you think will happen next? How do you think the story will end?
4. What is the difference between the way this story is written and the way *The Companion* is written?

Gloria

Frank opened the oven door and pulled out his Sunday dinner. As usual the instant steak and the baked potatoes could have passed for lumps of coal. As with most things in his life, Frank had not quite got the knack of cooking yet. He added a tin of green blobs which masqueraded under the name of processed peas, and sat down to eat. His eyes glanced around the room of his 'bachelor flat'. He called it that because it made him feel younger. He stopped at the image of his mahogany-effect wall unit, and, inside it, the countless copies of *Readers Digest* and his beloved mono record player.

He left his steak, potatoes and peas, and made his way across the floral-patterned carpet and placed a Mantovani L.P. on the turntable. Had Mantovani been within earshot, he would have squirmed to hear the aural mess made by Frank's ancient stylus of his finest moments. Frank, however, loved it all and sat in front of his gravy-stained plate, humming the wrong tune and tapping his feet in four-four time to a waltz.

He left both his dessert and the washing up as he wanted to leave himself plenty of time for the ten-minute walk to the station – the ten-minute walk to meet Gloria.

Oh, how even the mention of that name filled him with ecstasy. Women had always treated him with scorn, but Gloria was different. She loved him as he loved her.

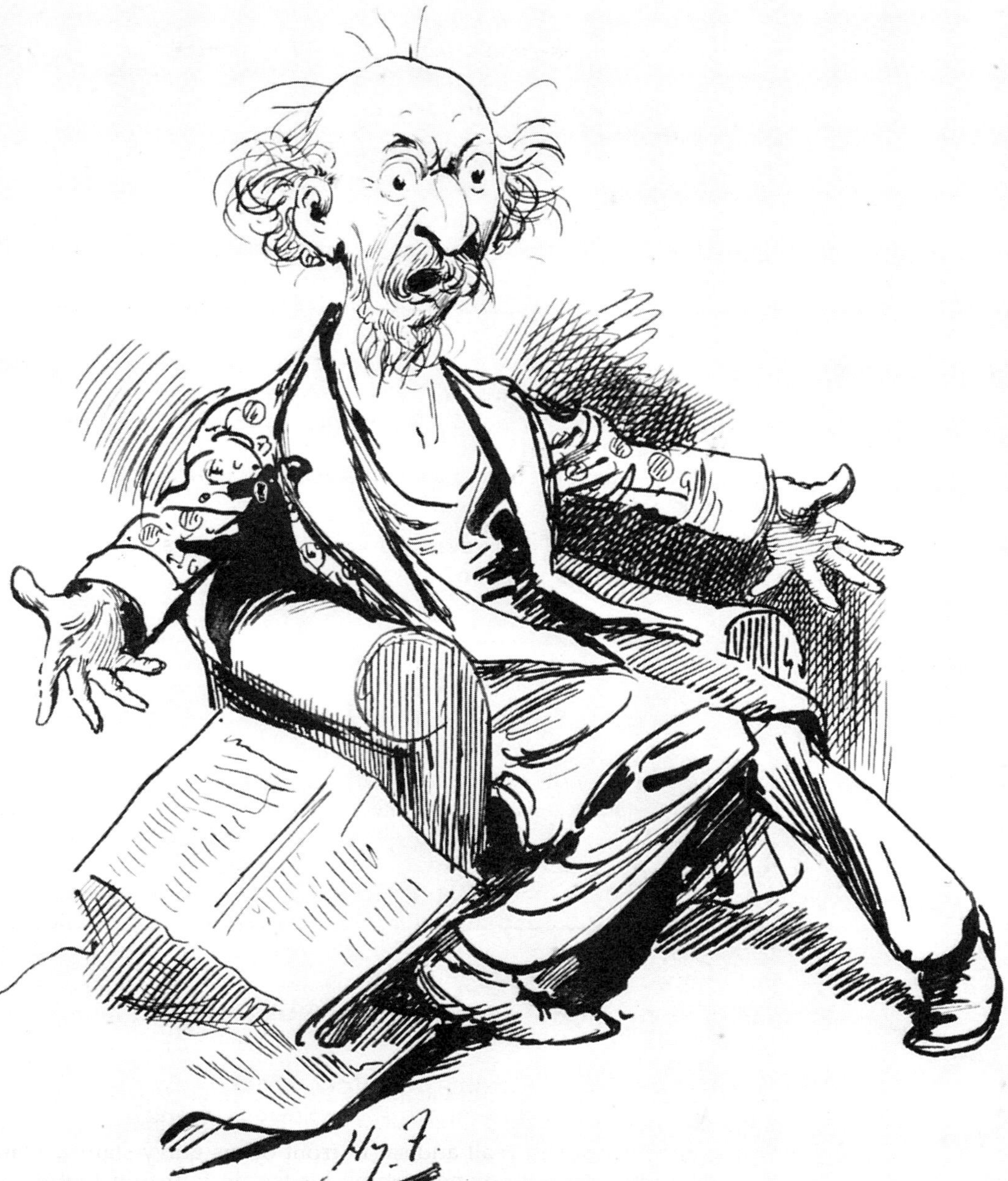
Hy. F

(A few miles away, the woman occupying his thoughts applied her third layer of make-up and second tin of hairspray.)

Frank thought of the nondescript little man he had once been. He had a respectable job – something in the City, he always said. He was not that old, although even with a few years knocked off for vanity's sake, he was obviously in the Sunday afternoon of his life. But all this could not make up for the vacuum which existed in his life until Gloria came and filled it. Oh, how she had changed him. He pictured the scene, in the film of his life-story, when he first met Gloria. He thought how the soundtrack would change from dull and gloomy cello to bright, lively piano. His deliberations as to whether to allow Attenborough or Schlesinger to direct his autobiography were interrupted by a loud click as the record came to an end.

(A few miles away, Gloria pulled on her six-inch stiletto-heeled shoes and imitation-fur coat and set off to catch the bus to the station.)

Frank made the half-mile walk with a brisk, jovial stride, occasionally kicking his way through a pile of fallen, autumn leaves. He was happier than ever before in his life.

(Gloria sat on the number 69 bus, blowing hard on her fingers to dry the still-tacky nail varnish.)

Their date was for two-fifteen...

Graham Vidler

For discussion

1. Is there anything in this story that you either do not understand or wish to ask about?
2. This is just an extract from the story. What do you think may happen next? And how do you think the story will end?
3. Is there anything about the way this story is written that makes it different from the other stories in this Unit?
4. What kind of person is Frank? What do you learn about him from the story so far?
5. What kind of person is Gloria? What do you learn about her from the story so far?

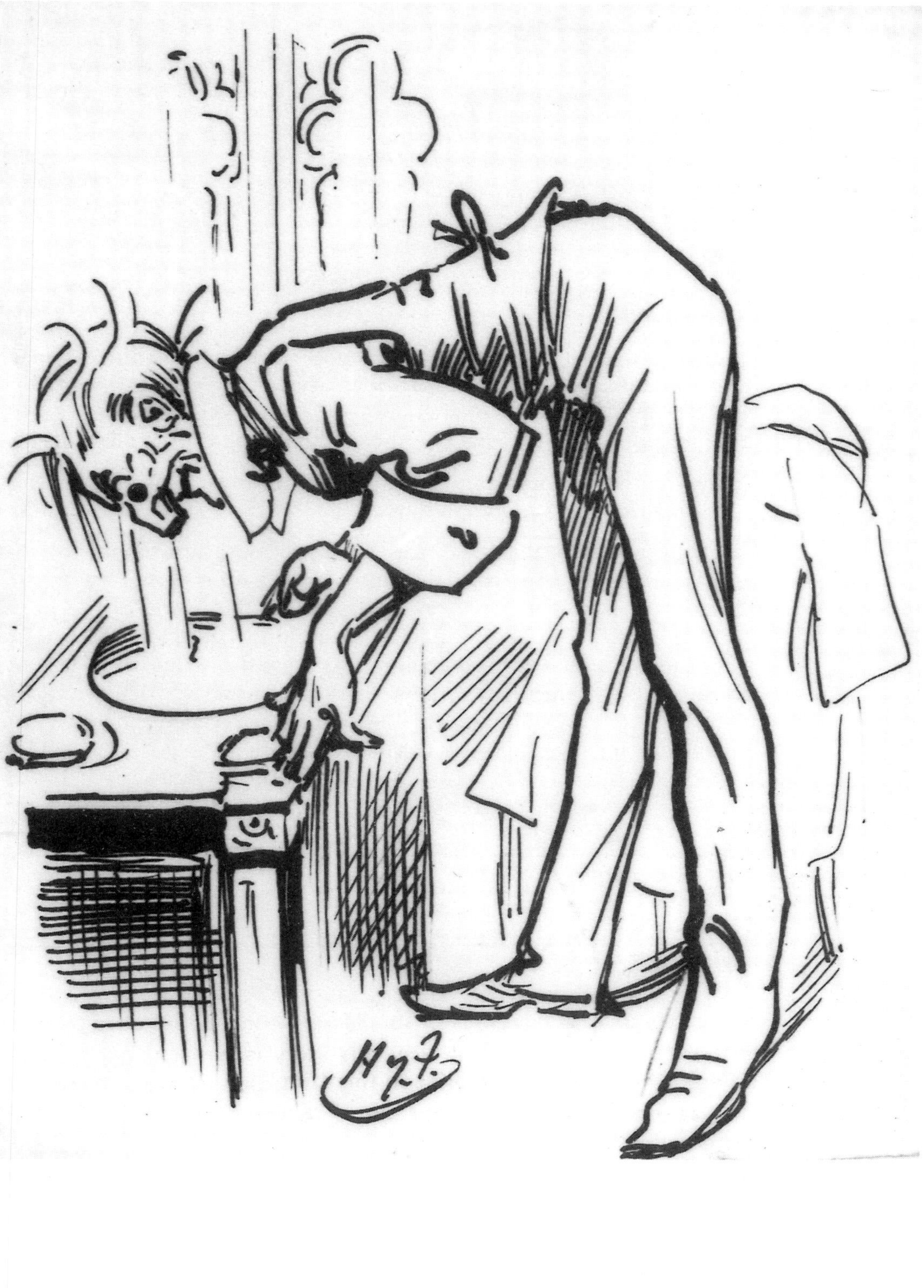
H.F.

The Conventions of Storytelling

Stories can be told in many different ways, using many different conventions. Different conventions include:

1. telling a story in the *first person*. For example:
   I will always remember when...
   In the third person, this would be:
   He (or she) would always remember when...

2. the *flash-back*, in which the story teller shifts the action back to an earlier time.

3. changing the setting. For example, you begin a story in one place and then change the scene to show what is happening meanwhile (at the same time) somewhere else. The film director Alfred Hitchcock used to call this the 'meanwhile, back on the farm' scene.

4. presenting the character's thoughts and feelings as if the writer is *inside the character's head*.

5. showing how the character feels by connecting him or her to what is happening in the world outside. An example would be a very depressed person suddenly noticing the terrible noise of the traffic in the street. Another example, commonly used in films, is a character who is very sad looking through the window as it starts to rain; or a character who gets very good news suddenly noticing that the sun is shining. This is sometimes called *projecting* the characters' feelings onto the world around them.

For group discussion

1. Can you think of any novels or films which have used any of these conventions?
2. Browse through the five stories in this Unit. Do any of them use any of these conventions?
3. Can you think of any other conventions used in telling stories, whether in films or novels?
   Later, discuss your answers with the rest of the class.

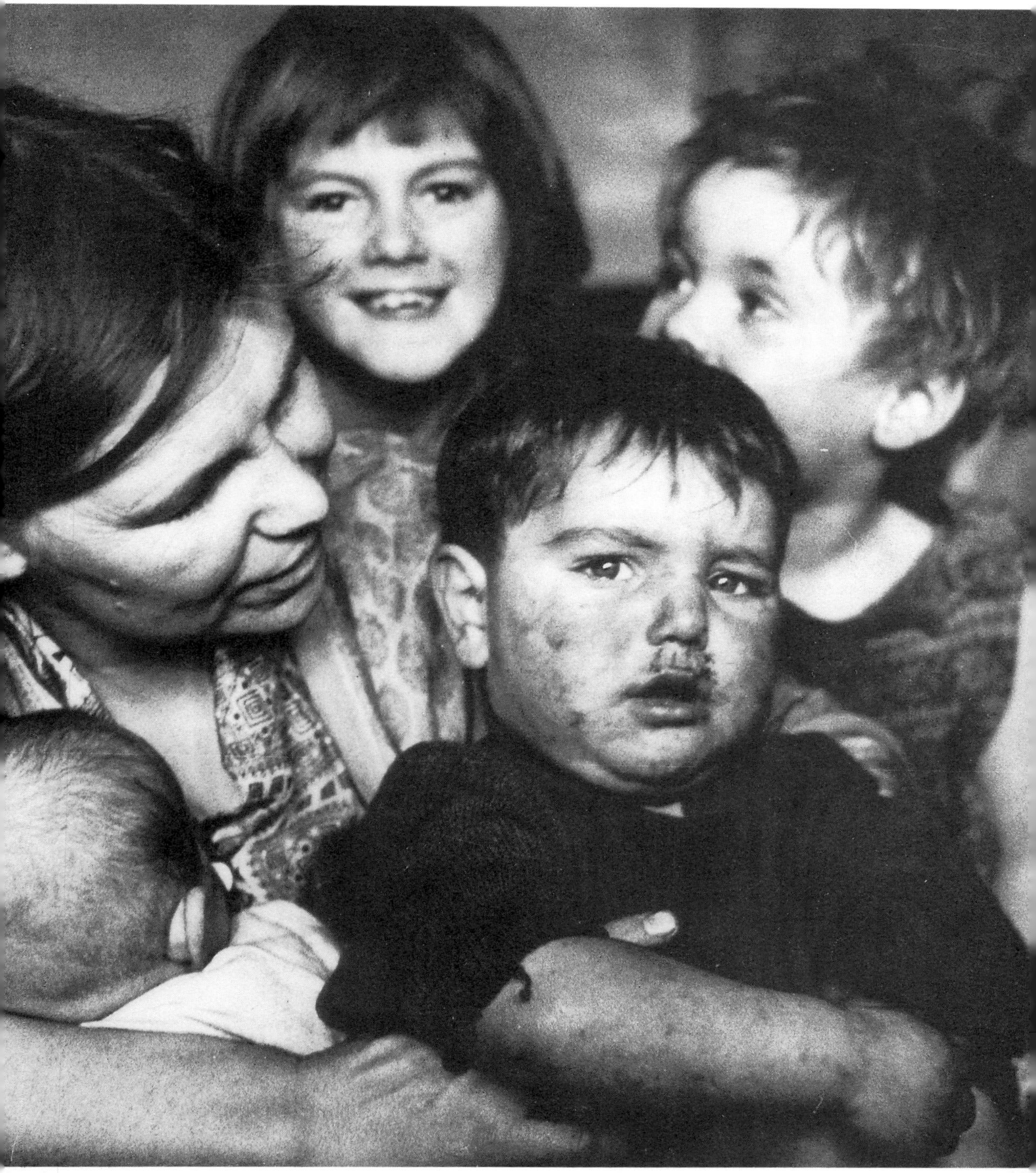

Two News Stories

Rewrite the first paragraph of these two news reports as short stories. In each story, use two different conventions of storytelling.

Sally Saves Don

A drowning boy was plucked to safety from the River Dell last week. Don Lambert got out of his depth while swimming, and nobody noticed him. Then a girl heard his calls for help.

Don's saviour was Sally McClune, a 15-year-old student at Mansfield High School. The lucky boy was 16-year-old Don, a student at the same school.

Thief nearly suffocates

A masked raid on Fanshaw Post Office last Wednesday ended when one of the raiders nearly suffocated in a stocking he used to cover his face.

Postmistress May Hallet said that he started to choke and pulled off the stocking. 'I need air,' he cried, and then both thieves ran out of the Post Office into the pouring rain outside.

'I think that stocking saved us,' said Ms Hallet. 'I don't know how it would have ended otherwise.'

Characters in Pictures

Characters can be portrayed not only in stories but also, of course, in pictures. Look at the various pictures in this Unit, and working together in pairs, make a short list of two or three things you learn about the kinds of people shown. For example, do they seem intelligent, pleasant, happy, calm, brave or vain? Briefly list the adjectives you would use to describe each of them.

The pictures in this Unit are:
>Young man (painting by Botticelli p. 49).
>Young woman (painting by Otto Scholderer p. 51).
>Young general (painting by Joshua Reynolds p. 54).
>Gentleman in armchair (drawing by Harry Furniss p. 57).
>Gentleman at wash basin (drawing by Harry Furniss p. 59).
>Children in Cardiff (photograph by Bert Hardy p. 61).
>Family in Cardiff (photograph by Bert Hardy p. 62).

For class discussion

1. Compare the various adjectives you have used to describe the characters in the different pictures. See if you can agree on any *two* adjectives which most precisely describe each one.

2. Look again at each picture and discuss whether you think the artist (painter, drawer or photographer) has a definite *attitude towards* the character. For example, is there an example of the artist admiring a character? or laughing at one?

3. In talking about the pictures, we have considered the way in which a picture reflects not only the character of the person in the picture, but also the attitude of the artist towards that person.

   This also happens in stories. For example, what is the attitude of the writer towards Stan in David Shrimpton's story, or towards Frank in Graham Vidler's story?

4. In films also, characters are represented from different points of view. There is often a character that other characters think is good, but the film-maker warns the audience that he or she is actually bad. For example, many horror films have a character such as Jack the Ripper, who seems to be an ordinary decent man to those around him, but the film-maker gives all sorts of clues to the audience about his real character.

Can you suggest any examples of other films where:

> the audience know the character is good, but other characters think he or she is bad?
>
> the audience know the character is bad, but other characters think he or she is good?

Audiences are told the film-maker's attitude to a character through various kinds of clues. What kinds of clues are they? And can you suggest examples from films you have seen?

5   What do you feel is the film-maker's attitude to the characters in the following set of stills from films? What kinds of comments is the film-maker suggesting about them?

The film stills in this Unit are:
> Mary Pickford and Buddy Rogers in *My Best Girl* (p. 64).
> Lukas Haas in *Witness* (p. 65).
> Orson Welles in *The Third Man* (p. 66).

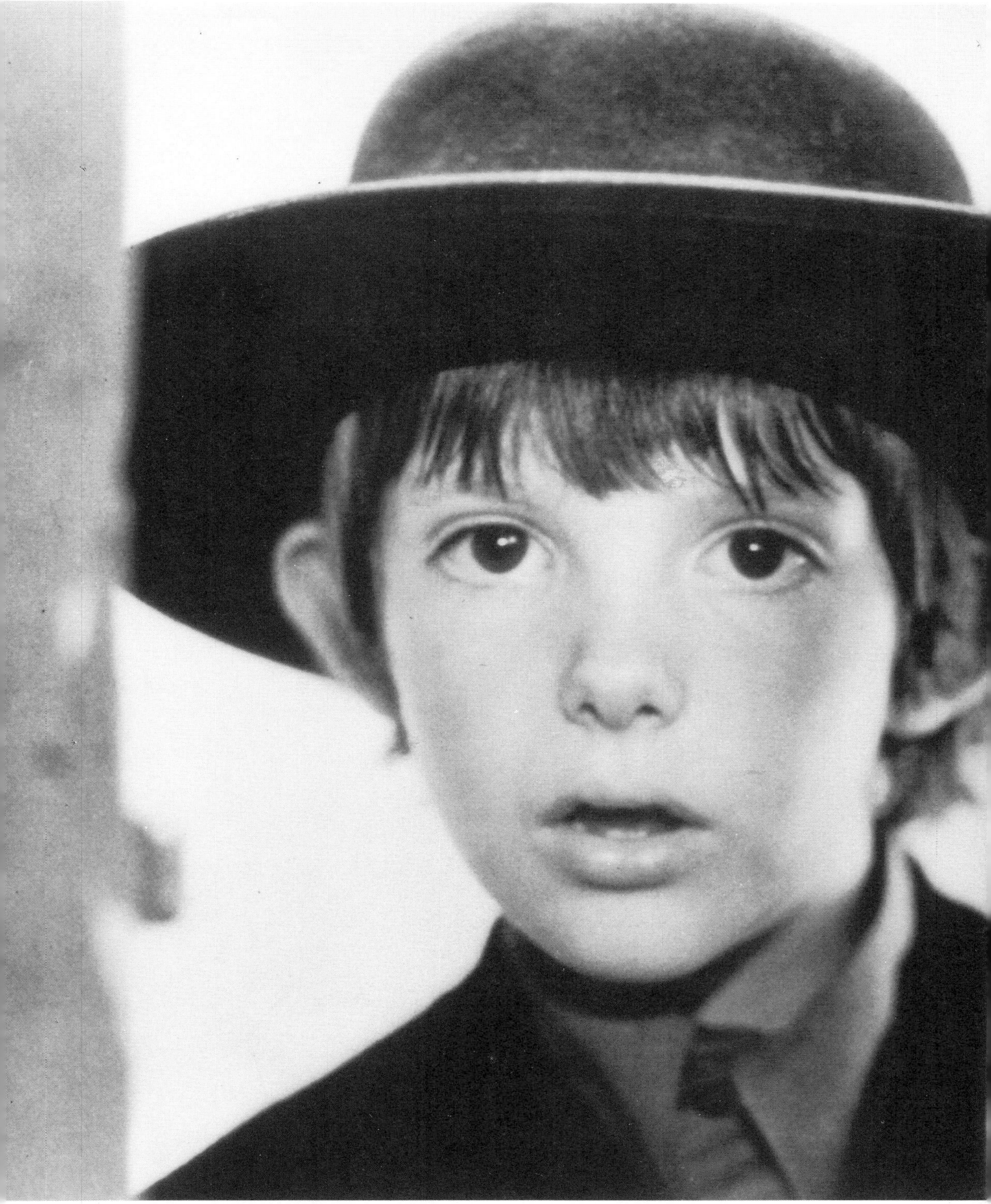

etteln & Hausieren
verboten
BEKANNT
BERÜHMT
BEGEHRT
DIE
alität

Punctuation: the comma

The students who have written the five stories in this Unit have all made fairly extensive use of the comma. After the fullstop, the comma is the most important mark of punctuation.

1. The word itself is from a Latin word (*comma*) meaning a *cut* or a *break* (and the Latin is itself derived from a Greek work *komma*). In other words, a comma 'cuts up' or 'breaks up' a sentence into parts.

2. Strictly speaking, it is not helpful to talk of rules for the use of any mark of punctuation (especially the comma), since everything depends on the writer and on his or her intentions when writing. But speaking very generally, the overall purpose in using a comma is to encourage the reader to pause briefly when reading, and in so doing, to help the reader make clear sense of what he or she is reading.

3. This overall purpose can be broken down into a number of more specific intentions. Look again at the first paragraph of Pratish Soni's story (*Annie*) and discuss the different purposes for which he uses the comma.

4. Pratish also uses a comma for a slightly different purpose in the first sentence of the second paragraph. What is the purpose?

5. Graham Vidler uses the comma for another purpose in the first sentence of the second paragraph of *Gloria*. What is the purpose?

6. It is worth noting that there are times where the comma makes a major difference to the overall meaning of a sentence. What is the difference in meaning, for instance, between:
   a) The dancing couples, who were awarded a special prize, were very proud of their achievement.
   and
   b) The dancing couples who were awarded a special prize were very proud of their achievement.

   Invent a pair of sentences of your own to illustrate a similar use of the comma.

7. In the examples above, the comma indicates which one of two possible meanings the reader should attach to a sentence. There are also occasions when the comma is almost as important, but where its function is to save the reader from having to read back to the beginning of the sentence to find where a break needs to occur. For example:

   If you shoot, your friends will have to phone for the police.

or
> When you move, the gun will go off.

In both of these, the comma makes it easier for the reader to construct the sense of the sentence. There is another example of a similar use of the comma in the fourth sentence of *Gloria*.

8. Briefly revise the different purposes for which the comma is used, and then rewrite the passage below with the addition of commas where necessary.

    When you have finished, make a brief list of the different purposes for which you have used the comma.

    > It had been a miserable time for all three of them for Tom his mother and his brother ever since the letter had arrived from the school. It was a simple enough letter though no letter from the school could ever have been simple enough for his mother. The Headmaster who appeared to be a man of few words declared 'I would like to discuss Kenneth's behaviour with you.' The idea of discussing anything with the Headmaster filled his mother with terror. 'You boys you'll be the death of me' she cried and she clearly meant it. Kenneth though was only miserable because Tom and his mother were.

Questions on the five stories

To answer these questions, you will need to re-read all the stories in this Unit.

1. In the story *Stan*, what is the attitude of Stan towards 'ordinary' people?
2. In *The Companion*, why does the piece of wood (in the last paragraph) remind the story-teller of himself?
3. What is the main thing you learn about the character of Eddie (in the story of that name) in addition to the fact that he falls in love with Vikki?
4. Describe the kinds of things you learn about the character of Frank in the story *Gloria*. Write a paragraph about it, using your own words, but quoting from the story.
5. What are the two main things you learn about Annie's character in the first story?

6. **Conventions of storytelling**
   a) Which if any of the stories are told in the first person?
   b) Which if any of the stories use a flashback?
   c) Which if any of the stories use the convention of 'meanwhile back on the farm'?
   d) In which of these stories is there the least action?

7. **The writer's attitude to his or her characters**
   a) Which of the writers is slightly or gently laughing at his or her characters? Give an example.
   b) What is David Shrimpton's attitude to Stan?
   c) What is Pratish Soni's attitude to Annie?

8. **Vocabulary**
   a) What is the meaning of 'oblivion' in the first paragraph of *Annie*?
   b) Find a word in the third paragraph of *Stan* that means *looking back and remembering*.
   c) What does the word 'resonated' mean in the last paragraph but one of *The Companion*?
   d) What does 'animatedly' mean in the second paragraph of *Eddie*?
   e) Find a word in the first paragraph of *Gloria* that means *disguised itself*.

9. **Similes and metaphors**
   Find and copy out an example of a *simile* in The Companion, and explain why the writer uses it.
   In the paragraph beginning, 'Frank thought of' (in *Gloria*) find an example of a *metaphor* and explain what it means.

Suggestions for writing

1. Write about a character, real or imagined, and create a story in which he or she looks back at an important experience.
2. Write the next part of *Gloria* or of *Eddie*.
3. Write a story about yourself, but write it from the point of view of another character in the story.
4. Write a story about one of the characters in one of the pictures in this Unit.

Before you write anything go through the following role-play section.

For role-play

Discuss with the class the particular character you intend to write about. Take the part of that character in a class interview.

The whole class should join in the interview, asking a wide range of questions concerning the following points about the character:

- attitudes
- past experiences and history
- schooling and family
- likes and dislikes
- relationship with other characters
- ambitions
- hobbies

N.B. In your writing focus on different ways in which you can build up the reader's own mental picture of the character. For example, explore the setting, the style of speech, the attitudes, manners, clothes, appearance – all those things that in life tend to influence us in forming our opinions of the people around us.

5 DECISIONS

This Unit looks at some of the various factors that influence people in their choice of career.

Harpo Marx

Harpo was the silent member of the Marx Brothers, a comedy team who appeared in stage shows and films in America throughout the 1930s and 40s. Their films still have an enormous following on television and video. In this extract from his autobiography Harpo describes one of the first influences that led him as a small boy in New York towards the life of an entertainer.

> The man who first inspired me to become an actor was a guy called Gookie. Gookie had nothing to do with the theatre. He rolled cigars in the window of a cigar store on Lexington Avenue.
> This was the store with card games and bookmaking in the back room, the nearest thing to a social club in our neighbourhood. It was Frenchie's home away from home and, along with the poolroom, Chico's too. Since gambling was never the obsession with me that it was with Chico, I didn't spend much time in the back room. Where I had the most fun was on the street, in front of the store.
> Gookie worked at a low table, facing the Avenue through the window. He was a lumpy little man with a complexion like the leaves he used for cigar wrappers, as if he'd turned that colour from overexposure to tobacco. He always wore a dirty, striped shirt without a collar, and leather cuffs and elastic armbands. Whether he was at his table in the window or running errands for the cardplayers, Gookie was forever grunting and muttering to himself. He never smiled.
> Gookie was funny enough to look at when he wasn't working, but when he got up to full speed rolling cigars he was something to see. It was a marvel how fast his stubby fingers could move. And when he got going good he was completely lost in his work, so absorbed that he had no idea what a comic face he was making. His tongue lolled out in a fat roll, his cheeks puffed out, and his eyes popped out and crossed themselves.

I used to stand there and practise imitating Gookie's look for fifteen, twenty minutes at a time, using the window glass as a mirror. He was too hypnotized by his own work to notice me. Then one day I decided I had him down perfect – tongue, cheeks, eyes, the whole bit.

I rapped on the window. When he looked up I yelled, "Gookie! Gookie!" and made the face. It must have been pretty good because he got sore as hell and began shaking his fist and cursing at me. I threw him the face again. I stuck my thumbs in my ears and waggled my fingers, and this really got him. Gookie barrelled out of the store and chased me down the Avenue. It wasn't hard to outrun such a pudgy little guy. But I'll give Gookie credit. He never gave up on trying to catch me whenever I did the face through the window.

It got to be a regular show. Sometimes the guy behind the cigar-store counter would tip off the cardplayers that I was giving Gookie the works out front. When they watched the performance from the back-room door and he heard them laughing, Gookie would get madder than ever.

For the first time, at the age of twelve, I had a reputation. Even Chico began to respect me. Chico liked to show me off when somebody new turned up in the poolroom. He would tell the stranger, "Shake hands with my brother here. He's the smartest kid in the neighbourhood." When the guy put out his hand I'd show him a Gookie. It always broke up the poolroom.

I didn't know it, but I was becoming an actor. A character was being born in front of the cigar-store window, the character who was eventually to take me a long way from the streets of the East Side.

Over the years, in every comedy act or movie I ever worked in, I've "thrown in a Gookie" at least once. It wasn't always planned, especially in our early vaudeville days. If we felt the audience slipping away, fidgeting and scraping their feet through our jokes, Groucho or Chico would whisper in panic, "Sssssssssst! Throw me a Gookie!" The fact that it seldom failed to get a laugh is quite a tribute to the original possessor of the face.

from *Harpo Speaks!* **by Harpo Marx**

For discussion

1. In effect, what talent did Harpo reveal when he started to impersonate Gookie?
2. What does the extract tell the reader about the kind of childhood Harpo had?
3. In general terms, what does Harpo suggest that comedy is based on?
4. Is there any vocabulary in this extract that is specifically American?

Listening Comprehension

The Betrayal of Youth...

One of the functions of education is to help young people think about and make decisions about their future. Here is an extract from a study by an educationalist in which he attacks the majority of schools for the unimaginative way in which, as he sees it, they go about their task.

An inept deficiency in education is the lack of any serious attempt on the part of our schools to convey a sense of the exciting realities now opening up before us. Most students have been taught nothing about astronomy during their last two years at school. The fascinating story of evolution is usually put across as an aspect of biology, not as the dynamics of nature's splendour, and a continuing factor in human life. Or again many children leave school without any awareness of the human being's symbiotic relationship with the planet, or even that we are all totally dependent on the sun and the soil for our food. One teacher commented: 'We aren't giving them any sort of vision. Expediency can never be inspiring.' Thus, the wonders of existence are commonly ignored.

By such glaring omissions, we deprive young people of a modern perspective, and then complain that they are cynical, apathetic and materialistic. One of the best antidotes to cynicism, apathy and materialism today is an imaginative grasp of the nature and responsibilities of human existence within the context of evolution on this planet. We see this demonstrated in one form in the spread of ecological morality in the world; the struggle between those who care for the planet and those who only care about exploiting it. A minority of schools are doing something towards developing ecological understanding but the majority seem to be blind to its social and moral importance.

Not only ecological values, but human values also emerge naturally from an education which deals properly with the human condition. Basic moral values – telling truth to one another, being honest, caring, compassion and concern, a dedication to justice and fair play, responsibility – are really just the names that humanity has created to identify what are the essential values of human relationships. Happy personal relationships and effective social organization are impossible unless such values can be assumed to be operative. Moral values are, in fact, as pragmatic as the values of nutrition. Either you respect them and thrive, as a person or society, or you ignore them and grow sick. A school that is honest about the human situation, that conveys the challenge and excitement of existence, that surrounds children with a community in which the human values are constantly in evidence, and that helps children to make contact with great lives and great human achievements, will be doing for the modern child what religious absolutism did for earlier generations – making it clear what moral values are and why they matter. Today the young will not receive moral values as precepts; they need, rather, to learn them through encounter with life, and through the moral content of the subjects they learn.

The young are longing for commitment, hence their tendency to identify with all kinds of cults and hero figures. Yet they cannot become committed within a vacuum. The schools are failing the younger generation because in outlook as well as curriculum they are harking back to traditional ways and ideas that have lost their impact. One feature of this is an outmoded authoritarianism in the presentation of values. It used to be thought that, in perspective and values, the adults knew while the young were expected to listen. Now we know that nobody knows with that much certainty. And the society around us is hardly convincing evidence to the young of the older generation's particular wisdom. Many of the young people around the world are in revolt against the materialistic values of the catch-as-catch-can society. They are looking for something more fulfilling. Young and old, we are in the search together – for ourselves, for relationships, for understanding. In this search, as in everything else, the appropriate bond between teachers and students today is the bond of shared humanity as they move forward in partnership towards the future.

from *The Betrayal of Youth* by **James Hemming**

For discussion

1 Discuss any words used in the passage that you do not understand.
2 How does Hemming feel the schools could do a better job?
3 Hemming talks of the need for schools to 'convey a sense of the exciting realities'. Where does Harpo Marx seem to have found such a sense?

Listen to the passage a second time, making notes while you listen, with a view to discussing:

4 What are the four or five main points made by the writer? And how do you think a school might reply to these points?

N.B. You should keep these notes for use later when you are answering questions on all the texts in this Unit.

The First Woman Doctor

Elizabeth Blackwell (1821–1910) was the first woman to obtain a degree in modern medicine. She applied for a place at a college in New York and the authorities, thinking that the woman's name was a joke, accepted her. Later, when she started to practise as a doctor, she met a great deal of opposition and ridicule. Colleagues as well as members of the public found the idea of a woman practising medicine, 'shocking' and 'immoral'.

When she was 33 years old, she decided she would never marry. Instead she would adopt a homeless child, Kitty Barry, a seven-year-old waif. Kitty grew up to become her assistant and travelling companion.

Here is a part of a letter Elizabeth wrote to Kitty (who was then 40), explaining why she had decided to become a doctor. By this time Elizabeth had retired from medical work.

20 January 1887

My Dear Child,
    I will now really try to comply with your earnest and repeated request that I will note down for you some of the facts of my past life. I should hardly care to do so if I were not prompted by my affection for you . . .
The idea was first forced upon my attention by a valued lady friend of the family (Miss Donaldson) who was a sufferer from a most painful disease requiring surgical intervention . . . She asked me whether, as I had health, leisure and cultivated intelligence, it was not a positive duty to devote them to the service of suffering women.
    The thought of studying medicine was to me so utterly repugnant that I instantly put it aside and tried to forget it. I had always despised the body, as the greatest hindrance to all that I most valued. I disliked everything that related to our physical organisation, even studies in natural history were antipathetic to me. I cannot at all trace the source whence I derived this contempt for the body, but I well remember trying as a child to subdue my body. When going to school in New York I had tried to go without food for days, and had tried to sleep on the bare floor . . . This spirit of asceticism and deep-rooted opposition to the conditions of human existence was rudely shocked by Miss Donaldson's prayers that I should become a physician.
    I therefore wrote to six well-known physicians in different parts of the U.S. for counsel as to whether it would be a good thing for a lady to become a physician and, if so, what course she should pursue. The replies received were identical in substance. All agreed that a thoroughly qualified woman physician would be a great boon to society; but all equally agreed that it was impossible for a woman to become an equally educated physician, and that it would be foolish and even improper to attempt such a course. These answers made a great

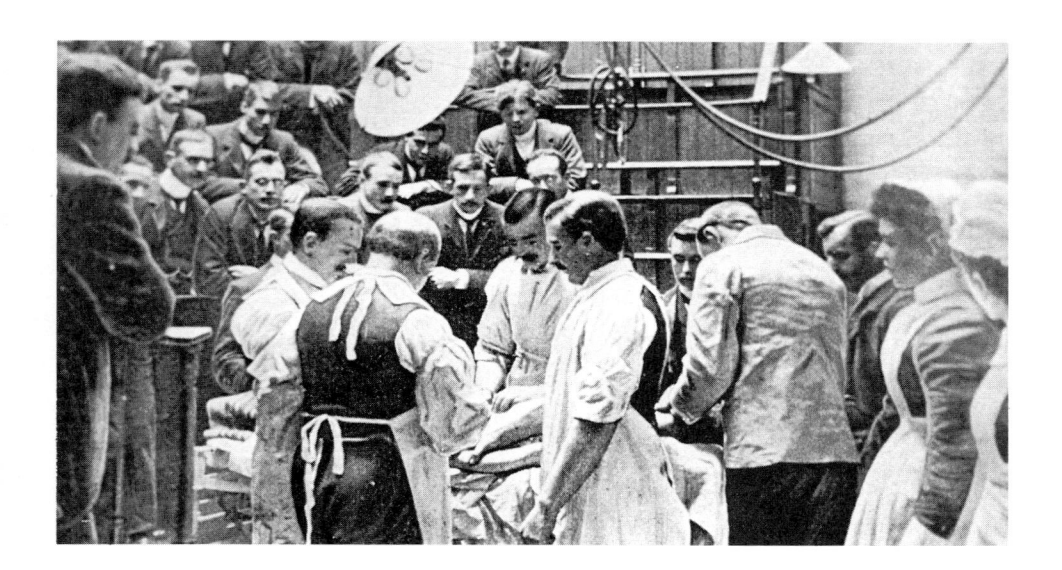

impression upon me. I accepted the first part and rejected the second part of the counsel. I reasoned that if a thing was a great good, in itself, there must be some way of doing it – and I would do it! I was young, strong, accustomed to study, and I needed an absorbing occupation.

This felt need of engrossing occupation and effort requires a statement of one of the chief reasons which finally decided my work. Up to this date I had scarcely ever been free from some strong attraction which my sober judgement condemned but which nevertheless made me uncomfortable, often very unhappy, and yet which I seemed powerless to eliminate from my daily life. I hold my own personal or other attractions in very low esteem, or rather it never occurred to me to consider them; and I was extremely shy. At that very time when the medical career was suggested to me I was experiencing an unusually strong struggle between attraction towards a highly educated man with whom I had been very intimately thrown and the distinct perception that his views were too narrow and rigid, to allow of any close and ennobling companionship.

I grew indignant with myself at a struggle that weakened me, and resolved to take a step that I hoped might cut the knot I could not untie and so recover full mental freedom: I finally made up my mind to devote myself to medical study, with the belief that I should thus place an insuperable barrier between myself and those disturbing influences, which I could not wisely yield to, but could not otherwise stifle. I long retained a bunch of flowers which had passed between us, done up in a packet which I sentimentally but in all sincerity labelled 'young love's last dream'.

I look back now with real pity at the inexperience of that enthusiastic young girl who thus hoped to stifle the master passion of human existence. But it was then a very truthful effort, and after some weeks of fierce mental contest, I drew a deep breath of relief and prepared for the fresh departure in life.

I have always enjoyed one great blessing in my life, *viz* the fullest sympathy of my own family. The mother and nine brothers and sisters who were left to struggle through life on my father's death were a very united family. So when I determined to study medicine, although none of us realised what the study might involve, it was with the entire approbation of all the dear brothers and sisters that I prepared for my studies. We were all very poor in worldly goods. My first step therefore was to accept a position as music teacher offered to me at Asheville amongst the mountains of North Carolina, in a school kept by a clergyman who was also a physician and where I hoped to commence a course of medical reading as well as gain money . . .

The excellent head of the Asheville school, the Rev. John Dickson, proved an intelligent and sympathetic counsellor; he gave me the use of his library, and under his direction a course of medical reading was commenced. Considerable time was needed before the natural distaste to medical subjects could be overcome. It was an irrational prejudice and I resolved to conquer it; and in the end I became thoroughly ashamed of my repugnance to the physical side of human nature and entered at last with thorough interest into my new studies: but the struggle was not an easy one.

One day a fellow teacher laughingly brought me a 'subject for dissection'. It was a cockchafer that had been smothered in a pile of pocket handkerchiefs and it was jokingly offered to me to try my skill upon. I accepted the task and absurd as the fact may seem, it proved a difficult one. I seized the insect with a hairpin, placed it in a shell, and then opened my pearl-handled pen-knife to make an incision – but I could not make it. I stood over that shell for an hour before I summoned up resolution enough to cut into the insect and discover only a little dry yellowish dust! Clearly however a greater victory was then gained than I was aware of at the time: for in the serious and necessary studies of a later date, I never experienced again a similar repugnance.

from *Between Ourselves: Letters between Mothers and Daughters,*
edited by Karen Payne

For discussion

1   What was it in Elizabeth herself that drew her to the idea of becoming a doctor?
2   What was it in herself that repelled her from the idea?
3   What does Elizabeth mean by 'the spirit of asceticism'?
4   In what ways might such a spirit be valuable to anyone pursuing a difficult career?
5   To what cause does she attribute her need for 'an engrossing occupation'?
6   When and why does the writer use (a) the colon and (b) the semi-colon?

Telling the News...

This is an extract from a journalist's talk to students about what a journalist does and how he or she learns to do it.

Who are journalists?

Perhaps the best way of explaining what a journalist does is to spell out the different places where you will find journalists. Of course, newspapers are written and edited by them. They go out and find the news, they find out all they can about it, and they come back to their offices and write it all down. But that is only one of the places where they work. Radio and television are equally important. The scripts for every news programme, whether it is the day's news or a sophisticated documentary, are written by journalists. All the evidence they use is the end-product of their patient (or impatient) attempts to find out what has happened, to whom it has happened, and where and why and how and when.

Most journalists become specialists. For example, they may specialise in crime, or politics, or sport, or finance. Some of them no longer find out the news, but become commentators, giving the public a broad but informed view of what is happening, linking up the past and the present or what is happening here with what is happening there. Some of these commentators achieve great distinction; their views are widely read and influential; they become authorities.

Some of these rather specialised journalists also have the good fortune to travel extensively. For example, they may become overseas correspondents, based in one particular place or area. Or they may travel all over the world in pursuit of a particular story or of a particular figure, such as a leading politician. Or they may be sent to cover a war.

Sometimes a journalist's special interests leads to work with a specialised magazine devoted solely to that particular activity. Just out of interest, the next time you are in a reference library, have a look at the list of magazine titles on their shelves.

What sort of person is a journalist?

Well, you need to have a good command of language. Not only do you have to be able to write well, but you also have to be a good talker, for otherwise, how can you possibly get other people talking and so collect the news in the first place? You do not have to be academic. In fact, you could be a brilliant writer of essays (or of short stories, for that matter) but be no good at all as a journalist. The writing required of a journalist is of a different kind entirely. It also needs to go with a certain amount of toughness and coolness. You cannot collect the news if you are particularly shy or sensitive. You would give up too quickly. After all, most of the time most of the people you have to talk to DO NOT WANT TO TALK TO YOU. This was the first discovery I made when I first began work as a reporter on a local newspaper – the people who know what you want to know, do NOT want to tell you. And they work hard at NOT TELLING YOU!

I soon learned a second rule too. The people who DO want to talk to you are not often worth spending time with. For example, if a local politician wants to chat with you, it will generally be because he or she wants some free publicity. This will not usually make for interesting news.

You also need to be persistent, and willing to work long and difficult hours. You can't discover the news in office hours. You find it when it happens and when it's available. You also need to be tough enough to accept criticism – and you get plenty. It comes not only from your readers and from the people you write about, but also from your editor and your colleagues. Heaven help the reporter who finds nothing to report, or who slips up on the 'facts'.

What are the rewards?

I'm not going to talk about money, because so much depends on how far you go up the ladder. Generally, you earn more on a national than on a local paper. You earn more on radio and television. And so on. I'm going to talk about the enjoyment. There's something marvellously exhilarating about knowing that you have written the news. You have told it. Until you put it all together, nobody knew what was happening. There's that extraordinary sensation of being in the middle of events, and while trying to be fair and honest in reporting what you see, also creating from it stories that the world will find worth reading or worth listening to. When you come to think of it, journalists play an important part in the lives of all of us . . .

Doreen Lewis

For discussion

1. What in particular does Lewis find enjoyable about a journalist's work?
2. In what ways might sensitivity be a hindrance to a journalist?
3. Can you suggest any example of insensitivity in the various news programmes you have seen on television or heard on the radio?
4. What would *you* find enjoyable about being a journalist?

Engineering loses its macho image

by Adriana Caudrey

The Women Into Science and Engineering campaign has managed to bring women engineers out of the wilderness by emphasizing that their profession no longer involves heavy and dirty work, it was claimed last week.

This achievement was recognized by several speakers at a London conference of the Women's Engineering Society, which was attended by 200 women engineers, scientists and educationists. But there were warnings that the progress must not be allowed to peter out if women are to increase their showing in traditionally male preserves.

The WES is therefore urging the Equal Opportunities Commission and the Engineering Council to keep up the momentum of WISE well beyond the end of the year.

It is also calling on the DES to:
☐ encourage more girls to study maths and science to 16 years and over;
☐ change the science curriculum to make it more attuned to girl's perceptions;
☐ foster stronger links between schools and industry; and
☐ help overcome sex differentiation in primary schools.

It is also pressing the Confederation of British Industry and the Engineering Employers' Federation to:
☐ show a commitment to employing women in technical, supervisory and management postions; and
☐ advance their careers in accordance with their abilities.

The Government is being urged to provide funding for women who have taken career breaks, to enable them to go on retraining courses.

Currently, only 1 per cent of Britain's professional engineers are women. Both in schools and industry there are barriers which discourage women from entering science and technology, the conference heard.

Although there is no longer blatant sex discrimination, sex bias is rife. Scientists and engineers are still portrayed as male stereotypes. School texts and employers' recruitment literature tend to use masculine examples and case studies.

Once they have entered the male preserve of the engineering industry women frequently face prejudice, sexual harassment, and fewer promotion prospects than their male counterparts, several speakers said.

The pressures attached to being the "token woman" sometimes force young female engineers to quit their jobs — and their employers assume this is for "family reasons".

Professor Daphne Jackson president of the WES and the first female physics professor in Britain, said that information technology firms were pushing for a 56 per cent increase in the number of science and technology graduates over the next five years.

Professor Jackson said that already the trend was for more girls to graduate in science subjects. In 1956 only 0.3 per cent of engineering graduates were women, whereas in 1982 it was 7 per cent. The proportion of women physics graduates doubled in those years from 6 to 12 per cent. Similarly, the percentage of A level passes in maths gained by girls went up from 11.3 per cent in 1956, to 25.8 per cent in 1982, and in physics from 11.9 to 19.2 per cent.

In urging more women to go into information technology. Professor Jackson said: "I see too many egotistical and immature young males attracted to the 'I' of information technology, who can communicate only with their computers, and too few literate and numerate young people who can contribute to the 'I'."

Dr Jan Harding, of the Centre for Science and Maths Education, at Chelsea College, said that masculine influence dominated school science.

Her research indicates that it is the more mature girls who choose science subjects, and the less mature boys. She argues this is because girls choose science in order to "make a contribution to the world", whereas the boys see it as a "reliable, unemotional subject." While 25 per cent of girls interviewed said they hoped their job would enable them to help others, only 4 per cent of boys made that their priority.

Dr Marilyn Davidson, research fellow at the Department of Management Science, University of Manchester Institute of Science of Technology, carried out an "equal opportunities audit" at BP — and as a result of recommendations BP changed recruitment literature, filling it with case studies of female engineers, and they created a special brochure to encourage women into the company.

from THE TIMES EDUCATIONAL SUPPLEMENT 2nd November 1984

For discussion

1. What does Professor Jackson mean by 'immature'?
   And what does Dr Harding mean by it?

2. The WES is urging the Department of Education and Science to "encourage more girls to study maths and science to 16 and over". How could the Department do this?

3. What seem to be the two main factors that have resulted in relatively few women becoming engineers?

4. According to this article, what seem to be the most important qualities needed by an engineer?

Group work

Work on the following questions in pairs or small groups, but keep your own individual records of the answers.

To answer these question you will need to refer back to all the texts in this Unit.

Vocabulary

1. What is the meaning of 'obsession' as it is used in the extract from *Harpo Speaks!* (paragraph 2)?
2. According to James Hemming, adults complain that young people are 'cynical, apathetic and materialistic'. Explain what each of these words means.
3. What does Elizabeth Blackwell mean when she writes about an 'engrossing occupation' (paragraph 4)?
4. In what sense does Doreen Lewis use the word 'academic' (first paragraph of the second section)? In what other way can the word be used?
5. What does Adriana Caudrey mean when she writes about 'traditionally male preserves' (paragraph 2)?

Punctuation

6. In Elizabeth Blackwell's letters there are several places where a *string of full stops* is used. Explain why they have been used.
7. In the same letter, explain the use of the *semi-colon* in the first sentence of the penultimate paragraph (the last paragraph but one).
8. In the same letter explain the use of the *colon* in the final sentence of the last paragraph.
9. A *rhetorical question* is one that requires no answer. The listeners or readers know precisely the answer they are expected to provide. For example, a politician might say to his audience: 'Shall we allow this country to be ruined by the evil ambitions of our opponents?' Find an example of a *question mark* following a rhetorical question in Doreen Lewis's article. Copy out the sentence.
10. Adriana Caudrey uses a *colon* for two quite different purposes. Explain what they are.

> **Interpretation**

11. What is the connection between the passage by James Hemming and the article from *The Times Educational Supplement?*
12. What does Doreen Lewis's talk tell you about her as a person?
13. Does Doreen Lewis seem to have had any of the qualities that (a) Harpo Marx, or (b) Elizabeth Blackwell had?
14. What qualities did (i) Harpo Marx and (ii) Elizabeth Blackwell have that would have made them (a) successful and (b) unsuccessful journalists?
15. Blackwell, Marx and Lewis all seem to have succeeded in overcoming various kinds of resistance in pursuing their careers. What different kinds of resistance did they learn to overcome?

> **Planning a career**

Working in pairs or small groups

1. Make a short list of the various careers that interest you personally.
2. Prepare a set of questions that will help you to find out more about these careers. For example, you may want to know more about the following:
     - entry qualifications
     - training and entry
     - conditions of work
     - prospects
     - qualities most needed
3. Use any available libraries to track down the answers to your questions.
4. If at all possible, find ways of meeting a number of people connected with your career choices and talking with them.
5. Find out the name and address of any organisation or institution that will send you further details about these careers. Write to them.
6. Prepare a short report for discussion with the rest of the class.

6 NEWSPAPERS

Cary Grant and Rosalind Russell
in *His Girl Friday* **(USA, 1940)**

What is a News Report?

Many different kinds of writing (as well as pictures) go to make up a newspaper. They include news reports, letters, editorials, feature articles, reviews and advertisements. News reports are generally written in a very distinctive way so that they are instantly recognisable for what they are.

Here is a short collection of extracts from different kinds of stories. Working together in pairs or small groups, read each of them through and work out what they are. If they are *not* reports from newspapers, what are they?

1

It was about three o'clock on a Friday afternoon when Annette decided to leave school... I am learning nothing here, she thought. From now on I shall educate myself. I shall enter the School of Life. She packed her books up neatly and rose. She crossed the room, bowing gravely to the tutor, who had interrupted her reading and was looking at Annette with disapproval.

2

Dad	Left your job, then?
Terry	Yes.
Dad	What for this time?
Terry	I don't think it was bringing out the best in me.
Mum	It was a good job... as good as you're likely to get.
Terry	I didn't *like* it.
Dad	Who says you're supposed to like it?

3

Tadpoles have a familiar smell

THE FAMILY life of a tadpole is, on the face of it, pretty limited. The parents are long gone by the time their offspring, several thousand strong, struggle out of the gelatinous mass of eggs deposited in the pond by the female. But, contrary to all appearances, tadpoles are not without their familial ties. Bruce Waldman of Cornell University has discovered that tadpoles of the American toad (*Bufo americanus*) can recognise brothers and sisters. Moreover, the siblings prefer to stick together.

4

24th June
19 20   220°C. $5\frac{1}{6}$k.
20 50   Tacked to port tack, 330°C. Unreefed main, handed No. 2 jib, and bagged it. Bagged No. 3 jib. Set genoa. Reset Miranda. Changed genoa sheet and leads.
21 45   Sun shining. Light air. Took opportunity of filling 12 bottles of paraffin from 2-gallon can. Not approaching New York fast on this course, however. But delightful change of weather.
22 20   345°C. $3\frac{1}{3}$k.

5

RICHARD BURNETT, 16, sees the same faces in the queue at the Social Security office every week. Tired, expressionless old men, too long out of work to worry any more.

Richard from Twickenham Close, Ings Road Estate, Hull, Yorks, says: "They don't seem to care any more that they're unemployed."

6

MISSING CAT

HAVE YOU SEEN THIS CAT?

FEMALE TABBY - SMALL BUILD - BEIGE AND DARK BROWN MACKEREL SPOTTED AND STRIPED MARKINGS. WEARING A BLUE COLLAR WITH A TRIANGULAR SHAPED MAGNET MARKED "ITT CAT DOOR" ON IT.

SHE IS VERY FRIENDLY AND IS NAMED ALICE. SHE HAS BEEN MISSING SINCE SUNDAY 3RD JULY. LAST SEEN IN THE WESTCOMBE PARK STATION AREA LAST FRIDAY AND IN THE WESTCOMBE HILL AREA LAST MONDAY 11TH.

COULD YOU CHECK YOUR GARAGE. GARDEN SHED, WATER BUTT, ETC.

INFORMATION PLEASE TO:

7

December love

The first time they went out was in December,
The twenty-second. As he walked her home
The pavements were alive with frosty glitter,
And long clouds lay milk-white beneath the moon.

8

To plan the education of Crown Prince Rudolf presented a great problem. Much thought went into it, especially because the three people closest to Rudolf – his mother, father and grandmother – all had entirely different views.

The Emperor was keen to maintain the family traditions.

9

To whom it may concern

Evelyn Oluwi was a student at this school from 1978 to 1985. During this time she worked hard to achieve good results in her public examinations. She took the ...

10

By IAN HEPBURN

A ROW broke out last night after two sixth-formers were ticked off for holding hands in school.

Headmaster William Orchard said: "There are appropriate times for all things. I don't think holding hands is appropriate in school."

For discussion

1. Which of these is an extract from a newspaper report?
2. If any of these are not news stories, what are they?
3. How do you know?

Now compare your answers with the rest of the class.

How are News Reports Written?

What rules does a reporter seem to follow in writing a story? Before you decide finally, look at the news stories below.
They are reproduced here without headings.

1. Devise a suitable heading for each.
2. Check whether they seem to follow the rules you suggested.

Dunston Riverside primary school in Gateshead has won first prize of £1,000 in a national scheme designed to promote better communications between the young and the elderly.
  Under the scheme, organized by Help the Aged and financed by the Legal and General, about 100 schools ran projects in which children worked side by side with old-age pensioners in the classroom. At Dunston Riverside about 70 children were involved in craft-work projects with up to a dozen old-age pensioners.

PENSIONER Mrs Ivy Harris was fatally injured last week when she was involved in an accident with a car in London Road, Wilsey.
  The accident happened on Thursday at the junction of London Road and Station Parade, Wilsey, while Mrs Harris is believed to have been crossing the road.

From Paul Johnson in Belfast

Rioting continued yesterday in West Belfast for the fourth day running. Vehicles were hijacked, burning road blocks set up, and security force patrols attacked with petrol bombs.

The incidents came as Mr Thomas Reilly, aged 23, of Turf Lodge, shot dead earlier this week, was buried. He was a road manager, and the pop world sent wreaths.

More than 1,000 mourners attended a requiem mass conducted by local priests and the Bishop of Down and Connor, the Most Revd Cahal Daly. During the ceremony a priest described Mr Reilly's death as "tragic and unwarranted."

Disturbances in Belfast and Londonderry left two police officers and two civilians injured. Eight people were arrested. Police said that a dozen vehicles were hijacked in Belfast, and another 16 burned out. Shots were fired at Fort Whiterock army base.

An RUC spokesman has claimed that "Godfathers of violence" were deliberately organising the rioting.

An 18-year-old solidier, Private Ian Thain, has been charged with murdering Mr Reilly.

The Language of News Reports

Asked by a group of students how he wrote his reports, a journalist replied:

1. Keep it simple; keep it short; keep to the facts.
2. No introduction. No waffle. No repetition.
3. Who, what, where, when, why and how: that's all!

The newspapers that sell the most copies (many millions) are the ones that keep to these rules.
They are, in other words, the easiest to read.
A child of twelve could read them!

In their training, journalists learn to pay attention to the following.

1. Length of Words

The more syllables there are in a word, the harder it is to read – in general! Sometimes, to make language easier, one long word may have to be replaced by a group of short words. As examples, replace each of these with a group of short words:

syncopation
improvisation
optimistic
dehydrate
astronomy

Sometimes, of course, one longer word can be replaced by one shorter word. As examples, replace each of these with one shorter word:

exhibit
prohibit
insane
homicide
discourteous

Work together in pairs, using the three short stories on page 88 to make a list of all the words (other than names) that consist of more than two syllables. See if you can replace them with shorter words without destroying the sense of what is written. You may have to replace one long word by more than one short word. Compare your answers with the rest of the class.

2. Length of Sentences

The more words in a sentence, the harder it is likely to be to read. Sometimes it is possible to replace a long sentence with a shorter sentence, without loss of meaning or sense. For example, can this be done with the following sentence?

> The accident caused the deaths of a large number of people who were unlucky enough to be there at the time, and who had done nothing to cause the accident to happen.

Sometimes, a long sentence can only be replaced by a group of two or more short sentences.

Working in pairs, find the longest sentence in the three news reports above. Rewrite it as a group of short sentences.

3. Length of Paragraphs

Generally, news reports are written in short paragraphs.

Working in pairs, find the longest paragraph in this group of reports. See if you can make it shorter without losing the sense or meaning of it and without increasing the total number of syllables. (Take length to mean the total number of words.)

Writing News Reports (1)

Now try putting some of these rules into practice. Here are the facts collected by a reporter before writing his or her story. They are written here more or less as they might appear in the reporter's notebook.

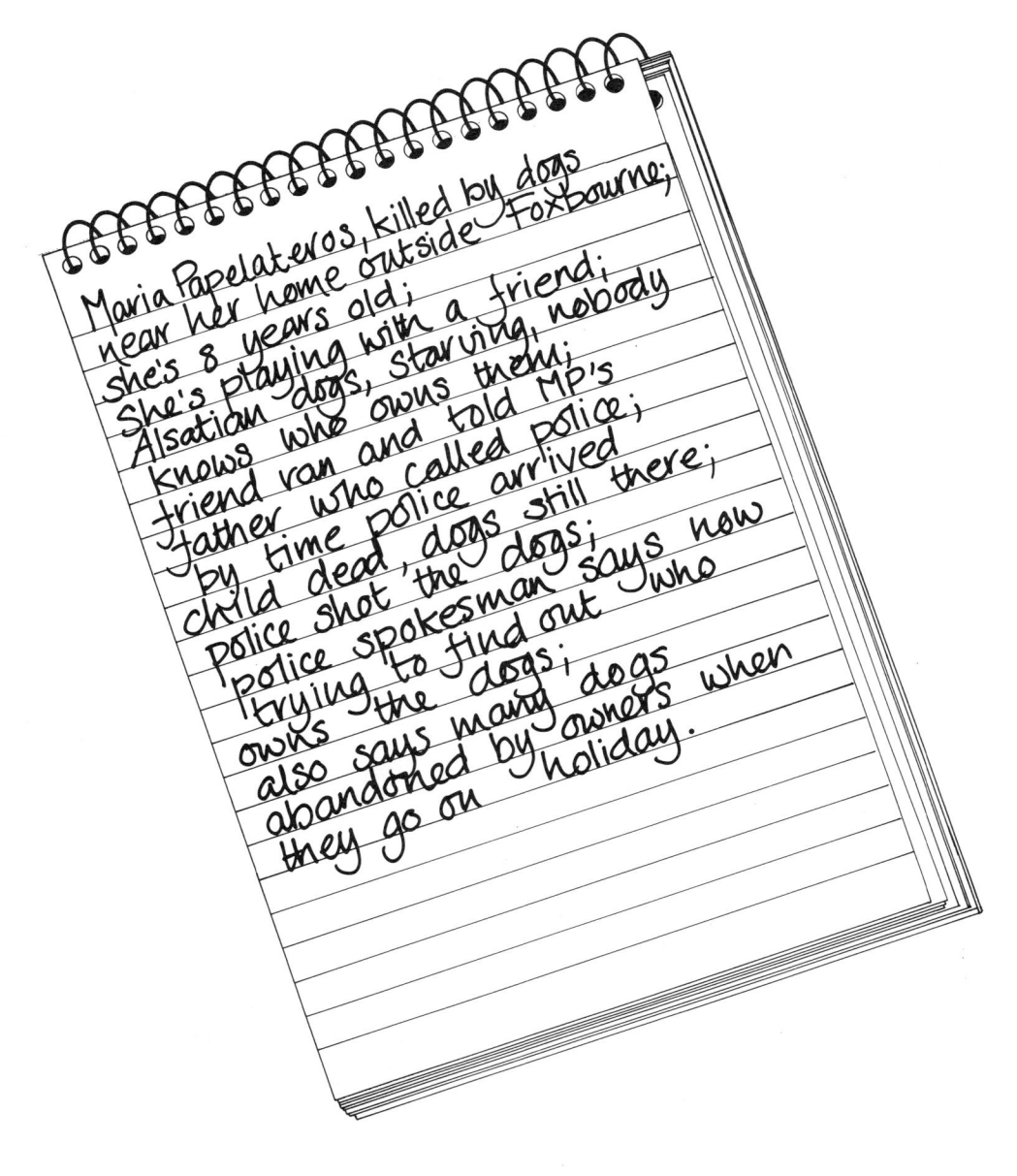

> Maria Papelateros, killed by dogs near her home outside Foxbourne;
> she's 8 years old;
> she's playing with a friend;
> Alsatian dogs, starving, nobody knows who owns them;
> friend ran and told MP's father who called police;
> by time police arrived child dead, dogs still there;
> police shot the dogs;
> police spokesman says now trying to find out who owns the dogs;
> also says many dogs abandoned by owners when they go on holiday.

Write a news story based on these facts.
Compare your different versions.

Writing News Reports (2)

Fair or Unfair?

Imagine that the following incident has happened and that it comes to the notice of a local newspaper reporter.

> A pedestrian is knocked down and killed trying to cross the road near to the newspaper offices. The road is always rather busy and local residents have, on several occasions, asked the local authority and the police to create a safety crossing at the place where the accident occurred.
>
> There are no witnesses to the accident, other than the driver of the car, who claims that the pedestrian (a youngster of 17 years) suddenly ran out into the street without any kind of warning. The driver stopped, and immediately reported the accident. By the time the victim had been taken to hospital she was dead.
>
> Several residents phone up the newspaper to complain that this shows how important it is to have a safety crossing at this point in the road.
>
> The police have decided that the death was an accident for which the motorist cannot be held criminally responsible.

Acting as news reporters, the class should now:

1. interview the driver of the car to get his or her story of what happened;
2. interview two or three local residents regarding their views on the need for a safety crossing;
3. write a report of the incident for the newspaper. Different students should agree to write different kinds of reports:
   - a report that is completely fair and impartial;
   - a report that is sympathetic to the residents who want a safety crossing;
   - a report that is not sympathetic to the residents who want a safety crossing.

Before interviewing, agree on all the basic facts as regards who did what, where, when, and to whom. Give names of people, places and roads, and specific times.

Before writing, discuss ways in which a news report can show bias or prejudice, including the importance of:
   - headings and sub-headings;

- the 'size' of the story and its placing in the newspaper;
- the decision whether or not to report a story at all.

Remember newspapers are affected by the law of libel. They must not say anything against anyone, that they cannot either prove to be true, or that is not a fair comment on a matter of public interest.

Punctuation: the Hyphen

Re-read the three news reports on page 88 and look especially at the use of the hyphen in the first and third reports.
Why is the hyphen used in these reports?
When and why would you use the hyphen in the following sentences?

> He was a well spoken person.
> She had a red hot face.
> He wore a sky blue jacket.
> Out came a jack in the box.

Punctuation: Revision

Read the same three news reports again, and list all the different marks of punctuation.
Briefly indicate why each mark of punctuation is used. Also list and explain the different uses of capital letters.

Listening Comprehension

Do We Really Need These Animal Tests?

a feature article

Listen to the article, discuss it, and then answer the questions below.

Mail on Sunday inquiry
by Angus Macpherson

THE rights of animals, for so long shrugged off as a preoccupation of cranks and the oversentimental, have, for the first time, become an issue that politicians, businessmen and scientists admit they cannot ignore.

Anyone who takes a righteous stance against man's traditional treatment of animals – hunting them, eating them, and experimenting on them – is no longer to be regarded as a fanatic.

There are still paint-spray graffiti demanding 'an end to animal torture'; and the shadowy underground army that calls itself the Animal Liberation Front has promised more raids on animal laboratories.

But far more hopeful is the scene that received little public attention last week in the stately chambers of the Royal Society just off Piccadilly.

There were some 300 experts, many of them scientists from Government laboratories and drug firms actively engaged in animal experiments, who spent three days discussing ways of cutting down the use of laboratory animals. And the underlying assumption was that the total elimination of such experiments was a goal to be worked towards.

Quite apart from humane feelings about animals, the frequent failures of these experiments are now too well known to be shrugged off.

Animal tests failed for example to reveal the hazards to humans of the arthritis drug Opren.

While reporting man's drive to the moon a decade ago, I became convinced that the scientists' research on animals was not only of no help, but a constant source of false alarms.

Chimps died in their space capsules, raising fears of unsuspected hazards. But when men went (the warnings having been ignored) they sailed through the same space journeys quite unaffected.

OFFICIALS of the Research Defence Society, pledged to preserve the right to experiment on animals, point out that the vaccines that have taken almost all the terrors out of polio were first developed 20 years ago in tests on monkeys.

And medical compounds from antibiotics like streptomycin and anti-inflammatory drugs for crippling arthritis were also first tested on animals. 'Not just to see if they were safe,' said an official, 'but in the first place to see if they worked, and were worth going on with.'

And nobody can say for sure exactly how many tragedies have been avoided by experiments on animals.

Yet at this week's discussion one scientist after another complained that up to half of the four million animal experiments in Britain each year were 'virtually useless', done for bureaucratic rather than scientific reasons.

There is nothing unusual about this view, but the sources of this criticism and the wide agreement were unprecedented.

It was a breakthrough for FRAME – the Fund for the Replacement of Animals in Medical Experiments – who had called the meeting. And it led FRAME's president, Nottingham University scientist Michael Balls, to say: 'We are making progress at last – great things are about to happen.'

The overall number of animal experiments after reaching a peak in 1971, does appear to have declined by over one million in the last decade. But some of the most objectionable are on the increase according to the latest Home Office figures; for instance, those performed on man's closest companions, cats and dogs and those putting animals under severe psychological stress.

FRAME is campaigning, for a start, for an end to the now-widely criticised LD-50 test. Required for virtually any new product, from drugs to anti-freeze, it consists of force-feeding the chemicals to a large batch of animals until 50 per cent of them are dead.

At last week's meeting, this body count was condemned as 'old-fashioned and revolting' by Professor Denis Parke, of Sussex University. Yet at least half a million animals a year are killed in Britain in LD-50 tests, the victims mostly being rats, mice, rabbits or dogs.

from THE MAIL ON SUNDAY
7th November 1982 (extract)

Questions on the listening comprehension

1. Tests on animals are often said to be cruel. What other main point is made against them in this article?
2. What is the main point made in this article in defence of such tests?
3. According to this article, have the total number of such tests increased or declined since 1971?
4. There is now a campaign to put an end to the LD-50 test. Explain what this test is.
5. According to this article, which group of people is most likely to bring down the numbers of tests on animals: scientists, animal-lovers, or members of the Animal Liberation Front?

Punctuation

These sentences have been adapted from the article but the punctuation has been left out. Rewrite them with the correct punctuation but do not alter the order of the words.

6. The rights of animals for so long shrugged off as a preoccupation of cranks and the oversentimental have for the first time become an issue that politicians businessmen and scientists admit they cannot ignore.
7. There are still paintspray graffiti demanding an end to animal torture and the shadowy underground army that calls itself the animal liberation front has promised more raids on animal laboratories.
8. Chimps died in their space capsules raising fears of unsuspected hazards.
9. Yet at least half a million animals a year are killed in Britain in LD-50 tests the victims mostly being rats mice rabbits or dogs.

Vocabulary

Explain what these words mean:
10. 'graffiti' ('There are still paintspray graffiti demanding an end to animal torture.')
11. 'psychological' ('These tests put the animals under severe psychological stress'.)
12. 'liberation' ('They are members of the Animal Liberation Front'.)

Prefixes and suffixes

13. The article refers to 'antibiotics'. What does the prefix *anti* mean?
14. In front of which of these words can the prefix *anti* NOT be used?
    climax, freeze, clockwise, thought
15. The article refers to a meeting of the scientists as 'hopeful.' What does the suffix *ful* mean?
16. At the end of which of these words can the suffix *ful* NOT be used?
    meaning, happy, use, cheer, tear
17. The article refers to 'unsuspected' dangers. What does the prefix *un* mean?
18. In front of which of these words can the prefix *un* be used?
    hero, happy, sad, cheerful, affect, affected
19. The article refers to tests that were 'useless'. What does the suffix *less* mean?
20. At the end of which of these words can the suffix *less* be used?
    meaning, use, cheer, event, thought, cheerful

Group work

In small groups or pairs, work on one of the following:

1. Collect as many news reports as you can of a single story. Ideally collect them from all the national newspapers published on the same day. Discuss the differences in the ways they tell the story, and write an account of the differences between them.
   Your account might be in four parts:
   a) the basic facts of the story;
   b) any differences in the facts given in the reports (including differences as regards the omission or deliberate exclusion of facts);
   c) any differences in the newspapers' attitudes to the story (including differences in spacing and presentation);
   d) which of the reports you regard as the fairest and the most informative, and why.

2. Collect a small number of newspapers, perhaps two or three, published on the same day, and compare them. Write a report of your evaluation of the papers, considering such factors as:
   a) any differences in the kind of stories that are reported;
   b) any differences in the ways they are reported;
   c) the different categories of news represented in the papers (for example, crime, fashion, international news, finance, sport, entertainment);
   d) any apparent bias or prejudice in any of the papers.

3. Collect a sequence of news reports on any event that takes place over a period of time, such as the reporting of a major crime, the later quest for the criminal, the eventual capture of a suspect, the trial and the outcome of the trial. Put all the stories together and write a report on the complete 'story', explaining clearly what has happened from beginning to end. Write it in the form of a news report.

7 WORDS AND MUSIC

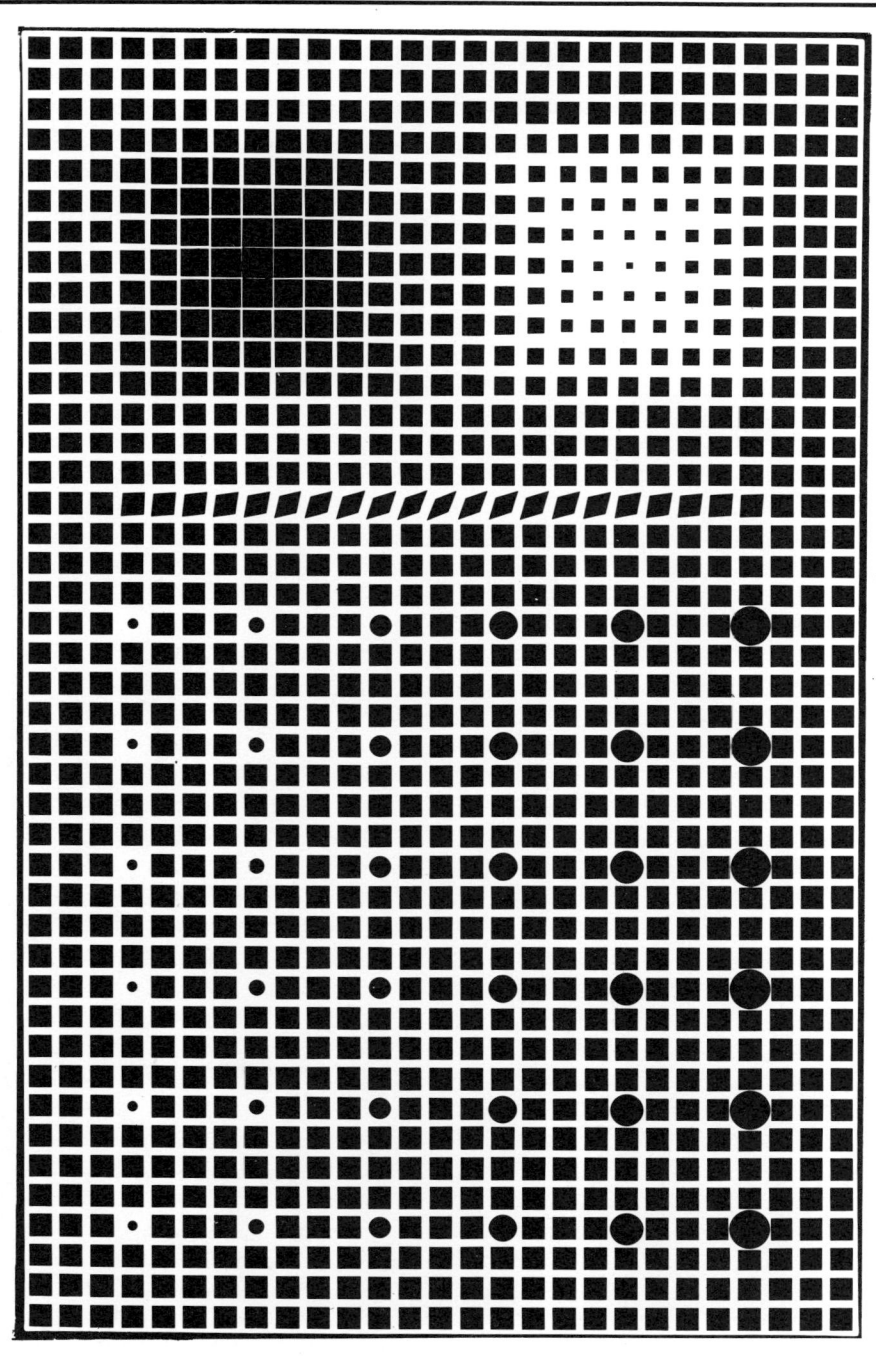

'Supernovae' 1961 **by Victor Vasarely**

Songs and poems have much in common. Many, for example, have a definite rhythm; and lyrics, the words of songs, are often interesting in their own right, without the music.

Before reading the poems and lyrics below, briefly discuss:

1. What else do songs and poems have in common?
2. When musicians write songs, do they generally begin with the music or the lyric?
3. Do you know any songs whose lyrics are especially interesting?

Read this selection of poems and song lyrics. Some of them you will already know.

from *Nostalgia* **directed by Andrei Tarkovsky**

1   Oh, the shark has pretty teeth, dear,
And he shows them pearly white.
Just a jack-knife has Macheath, dear,
And he keeps it out of sight.
When the shark bites with his teeth, dear,
Scarlet billows start to spread.
Fancy gloves, though, wears Macheath, dear,
So there's not a trace of red.

On the side-walk, Sunday morning,
Lies a body oozing life;
Someone's sneaking round the corner.
Is the someone Mack the Knife?
From a tug-boat by the river,
A cement bag's dropping down;
The cement's just for the weight, dear,
Bet you Mackie's back in town.

Louie Miller disappeared, dear,
After drawing out his cash;
And Macheath spends like a sailor.
Did our boy do something rash?
Sukey Tawdry, Jenny Diver,
Polly Peachum, Lucy Brown:
Oh the line forms on the right, dear,
Now that Mackie's back in town.

from *The Threepenny Opera* **by Kurt Weill and Bertolt Brecht**

---

2   I'm never gonna dance again
Guilty feet have got no rhythm
Though it's easy to pretend
I know you're not a fool
I should have known better
Than to cheat a friend
And waste the chance that I'd been given
So I'm never gonna dance again
The way I danced with you

Time can never mend
The careless whispers of a good friend
To the heart and mind
Ignorance is kind
There's no comfort in the truth
Pain is all you find

Tonight the music seems so loud
I wish that we could lose this crowd
Maybe it's better this way
We'd hurt each other with the things we want to say
We could have been so good together
We could have lived this dance forever
But now who's gonna dance with me – please stay

Now that you're gone
Now that you're gone
Was what I did so wrong
That you had to leave me alone

Careless Whisper **by George Michael**

For discussion

Both of these are songs.

1. Does either of them evoke a picture or image in the reader's mind? What words or phrases especially do this?
2. Is there anything in either of them that clearly shows it is a lyric for a song?
3. What moods do the lyrics capture and express?

Liverpool **by Bert Hardy**

Now read and discuss the following song lyrics and poems in the same way.
1. What images do they evoke?
2. Do they in any way look as though they are lyrics for songs?
3. What moods or feelings do they most express?

3   Break, break, break
      On thy cold grey stones, O Sea!
   And I would that my tongue could utter
      The thoughts that arise in me.

   O well for the fisherman's boy,
      That he shouts with his sister at play!
   O well for the sailor lad,
      That he sings in his boat on the bay!

   And the stately ships go on
      To their haven under the hill;
   But O for the touch of a vanished hand,
      And the sound of a voice that is still!

   Break, break, break,
      At the foot of thy crags, O Sea!
   But the tender grace of a day that is dead
      Will never come back to me.

---

4   First I forgot you in your voice
   And if you were beside me now
   And spoke, I would not know you.

   Next, it was your step I forgot
   And if you flee me, flesh or shade,
   Into the wind, I can not tell,
   For certain, if it is you.

   When Winter came your petals fell
   From my memory, one by one:
   Your smile, the colour of your dress,
   Your special look, your size in shoes;
   The cold wind stripped them from you.

   And then your body disappeared:
   Your flesh fell as the rest had fallen.
   Even then you lived, body, soul,
   Bones, voice, agony and laughter –
   In your name – those seven letters
   Were all that remained of you.

   Finally, I forgot your name;
   Suddenly, those seven letters
   Became strangers and met only
   On envelopes bearing other
   People's names, and you were assumed
   Into an alphabet heaven;
   And I had forgotten you.

---

5   Momma loves her baby
   And daddy loves you too
   And the sea may look warm to you babe
   And the sky may look blue
   But Ooooh babe
   Ooooh baby blue
   Ooooh babe

   If you should go skating
   On the thin ice of modern life
   Dragging behind you the silent reproach
   Of a million tear-stained eyes
   Don't be surprised, when a crack in the ice
   Appears under your feet
   You slip out of your depth and out of your mind
   With your fear flowing out behind you
   As you claw the thin ice

6 When in disgrace with fortune and men's eyes
    I all alone beweep my outcast state,
And trouble deaf heaven with my bootless cries,
    And look upon myself, and curse my fate;
Wishing me like to one more rich in hope,
    Featured like him, like him with friends possest,
Desiring this man's art, and that man's scope,
    With what I most enjoy contented least;
Yet in these thoughts myself almost despising,
    Haply I think on Thee – and then my state,
Like to the lark at break of day arising
    From sullen earth, sings hymns at heaven's gate;
For thy sweet love remember'd such wealth brings,
That then I scorn to change my state with kings.

from *Ran* **directed by Akira Kurosawa**

7   On either side the river lie
    Long fields of barley and of rye,
    That clothe the wold and meet the sky;
    And thro' the field the road runs by
        To many-tower'd Camelot;
    And up and down the people go,
    Gazing where the lilies blow
    Round an island there below,
        The island of Shalott.

    Willows whiten, aspens quiver,
    Little breezes dusk and shiver
    Thro' the wave that runs for ever
    By the island in the river
        Flowing down to Camelot.
    Four gray walls, and four gray towers,
    Overlook a space of flowers,
    And the silent isle imbowers
        The Lady of Shalott.

    By the margin, willow-veil'd,
    Slide the heavy barges trail'd
    By slow horses; and unhail'd
    The shallop flitteth silken-sail'd
        Skimming down to Camelot:
    But who hath seen her wave her hand?
    Or at the casement seen her stand?
    Or is she known in all the land,
        The Lady of Shalott?

    Only reapers, reaping early
    In among the bearded barley,
    Hear a song that echoes cheerly
    From the river winding clearly,
        Down to tower'd Camelot:
    And by the moon the reaper weary,
    Piling sheaves in uplands airy,
    Listening, whispers, ''Tis the fairy
        Lady of Shalott.'

---

8   O, my Luve's like a red, red rose,
      That's newly sprung in June;
    O, my Luve's like the melodie
      That's sweetly play'd in tune.

    As fair art thou, my bonnie lass,
      So deep in luve am I;
    And I will luve thee still, my Dear,
      Till a' the seas gang dry.

    Till a' the seas gang dry, my Dear,
      And the rocks melt wi' the sun!
    O I will love thee still, my Dear,
      While the sands o' life shall run.

    And fare thee weel, my only Luve!
      And fare thee weel a while!
    And I will come again, my Luve,
      Tho' it were ten thousand mile!

9   My heart leaps up when I behold
      A rainbow in the sky;
    So was it when my life began,
    So is it now I am a man,
    So be it when I shall grow old,
      Or let me die!
    The Child is father of the Man:
    And I could wish my days to be
Bound each to each by natural piety.

---

10 Never seek to tell thy love,
      Love that never told can be;
    For the gentle wind does move
      Silently, invisibly.

    I told my love, I told my love,
      I told her all my heart;
    Trembling, cold, in ghastly fears,
      Ah! she did depart!

    Soon as she was gone from me
      A traveller came by,
    Silently, invisibly:
      He took her with a sigh.

The 3 h.p. Royal Enfield motorcycle

Key

3   *Break, Break, Break* **by Alfred, Lord Tennyson**
4   *Deaths* **by Pedro Salinas, translated by Martin James**
5   *The Thin Ice* **by Pink Floyd**
6   *A Consolation* **by William Shakespeare**
7   *The Lady of Shalott* **by Alfred, Lord Tennyson**
8   *A Red, Red Rose* **by Robert Burns**
9   *My heart leaps up* **by William Wordsworth**
10 *Lover's Secret* **by William Blake**

Of this group, only number five was written as a song, although numbers six and eight have been set to music since they were first written as poems.

For further discussion

1   **Of those that were not written as songs, which do you think could most clearly be set to music?**
2   **Which of the poems and songs most contrast with each other in mood and rhythm and theme?**

Favourite Songs

In groups

1. Make a short list of your favourite songs – say five or six.

2. Make a list of four or five statements about each one, perhaps including statements about:

    the melody, such as:
    It is sad; or gentle; or romantic.

    the rhythm, such as:
    It is strong; or happy; or syncopated.

    the lyrics (if it is a song)
    Consider whether the lyrics are important.
    What do the lyrics say? (Perhaps quote briefly from the lyrics.)

    the music itself, and how it is made
    For example, is it played by particular instruments? by a group? by an orchestra? is it electronic? does it use any special effects?

    what kind of song it is
    For example, is it romantic? Is it a ballad? Is it a protest song?

3. Then choose one song that is the most popular in your group, and, if possible, play it (on tape or record) to the rest of the class.

As a class

4. Before listening to any of the songs, make a note of the various points made about the song by the group who have chosen it.

5. Compare these with your own response to the music.

6. Later, vote (as a class) for the two songs that you have most enjoyed. Play them again and discuss four or five points you would make about them that most fairly describe how you feel about them. (For example, you could say that a piece of music has a rather sad and gentle melody, but the rhythm is in contrast to this, as it is strong and lively, or that the melody contrasts with the lyric.)

Writing about music

The Music that I Like

This is an essay written by a student. She had been talking with others in her class about the music she likes and why she likes it.

I like music a great deal, and I like many different kinds of music. Music has a lot to do with mood and feeling. I have many different moods, and there seems to be music to match almost all of them. I can think of music that makes me sad, that makes me happy, that makes me want to dance, that makes me want to sit still and silent. I cannot remember a time when I have not enjoyed music of one kind or another, and I hope there never will be.

Kinds of Music

You only have to walk into a record shop to realise that music comes in many different kinds or categories. On one side are the very popular singers and groups of today. On another are the jazz records. On another are the various kinds of classical music. Or perhaps one particular kind of popular music, such as rock or reggae, may fill the entire shop. Many shops also have a section devoted to nostalgia – these are records of music that used to be popular once and that are still liked by a small (or fairly small) section of the public. Quite often they are records made by stars of twenty or more years ago.

Some people are very definite about the kinds of music they like. They say, 'I like jazz but I hate rock!' Or, 'I like classical but I cannot imagine what you see in pop!' But really this is all just plain snobbery. We are all entitled to like whatever kinds of music we like, and there is no way of proving that one kind of music is better than another. The great thing is to be prepared to listen to all kinds. In other words, we should not be small-minded or arrogant.

B So, what are my favourite kinds of music? Fairly near the top of the list I would place the music that I can listen to on my own, when I am feeling relaxed and want to have an hour or so to do nothing but sit and listen and carry on relaxing. Some of the piano music of Chopin and Schubert (especially Schubert's waltzes) comes into this category. So do many of the songs of The Beatles, some of Michael Jackson, some of Elvis Presley, and some of the orchestral music of Elgar, such as his Song of Morning and Song of Night.

I also like music that is probably best listened to when you are with a lot of other people. For example, I have enjoyed seeing musicals in the theatres in London. I saw and enjoyed three American musicals – *West Side Story, 42nd Street* and *Oklahoma*. These were shows with different kinds of music in them, ranging from sad and lonely to lively and excited. Although I like the music, I think I enjoy it most in the theatre, as part of a large audience. I also enjoy the music of *Cats*, the show by Andrew Lloyd Webber. But I have not yet seen it on the stage.

C Another way of thinking about the music I like, is to think about the people who perform it. There is no question that I like certain singers more than others, even when they sing the same songs. I like the voices of David Bowie, of Diana Ross, of Nat King Cole, of Billie Holliday, of Luciano Pavarotti, of Joan Sutherland – I could go on and on. These are musicians who sing very different kinds of music, ranging from jazz to opera, but they all have very special qualities that make their recordings special.

There are also certain individual performers I like, who are not singers but players of certain instruments. For instance, I love to hear the guitar played by Julian Bream. His playing of the Rodrigo guitar concerto is simply wonderful. And I like almost anything played on the flute by James Galway. I also have enjoyed the violin-playing of Isaac Stern (of a violin concerto by Elgar) and the piano-playing of Philippe Entremont (of the Second Piano Concerto of Rachmaninov).

D I've mentioned some of the kinds of music that I like. I must now add that some of my favourite music is not so much a kind of music as a mixture of kinds. In other words, it is very difficult to say exactly what kind of music it is. For example, I enjoyed the film of *Tommy*, a rock opera by The Who; although it is rock music, it is also opera! It has lots of qualities that make it more than rock and more than opera: it is a kind of music all of its own. I think the same can be said of much of the music of the American composer George Gershwin; his *Rhapsody in Blue* is partly jazz, partly classical and partly something else again. In much the same way, Gershwin's opera *Porgy and Bess*, seems to be a mixture of opera, jazz and negro spiritual. Two of the songs from *Porgy and Bess* that I like especially, are 'It Ain't Necessarily So' and 'Summertime'.

I should also mention songs that seem to be a mixture of folk and rock, such as many of the songs of Bob Dylan and of Tom Robinson. These are often songs of protest: they are attacking the way people or governments behave. And I like them very much.

E As you can see, it's very difficult to talk about all the music I like without leaving out lots of different music or without going on for ever. So I will end up by mentioning music of all different kinds, simply because it would be unfair to leave them out: they have given me so much pleasure. The list includes background music to films – some of my favourite films would have been nothing without their musical background. Examples would be the films *Star Wars*, *Gone With the Wind* and *The Magnificent Seven*. I must also mention almost every waltz I have ever heard, especially the waltzes of Johann Strauss. And finally – last but not least – all the music I have ever heard of Scott Joplin, the great master of syncopation.

Claire Ryan

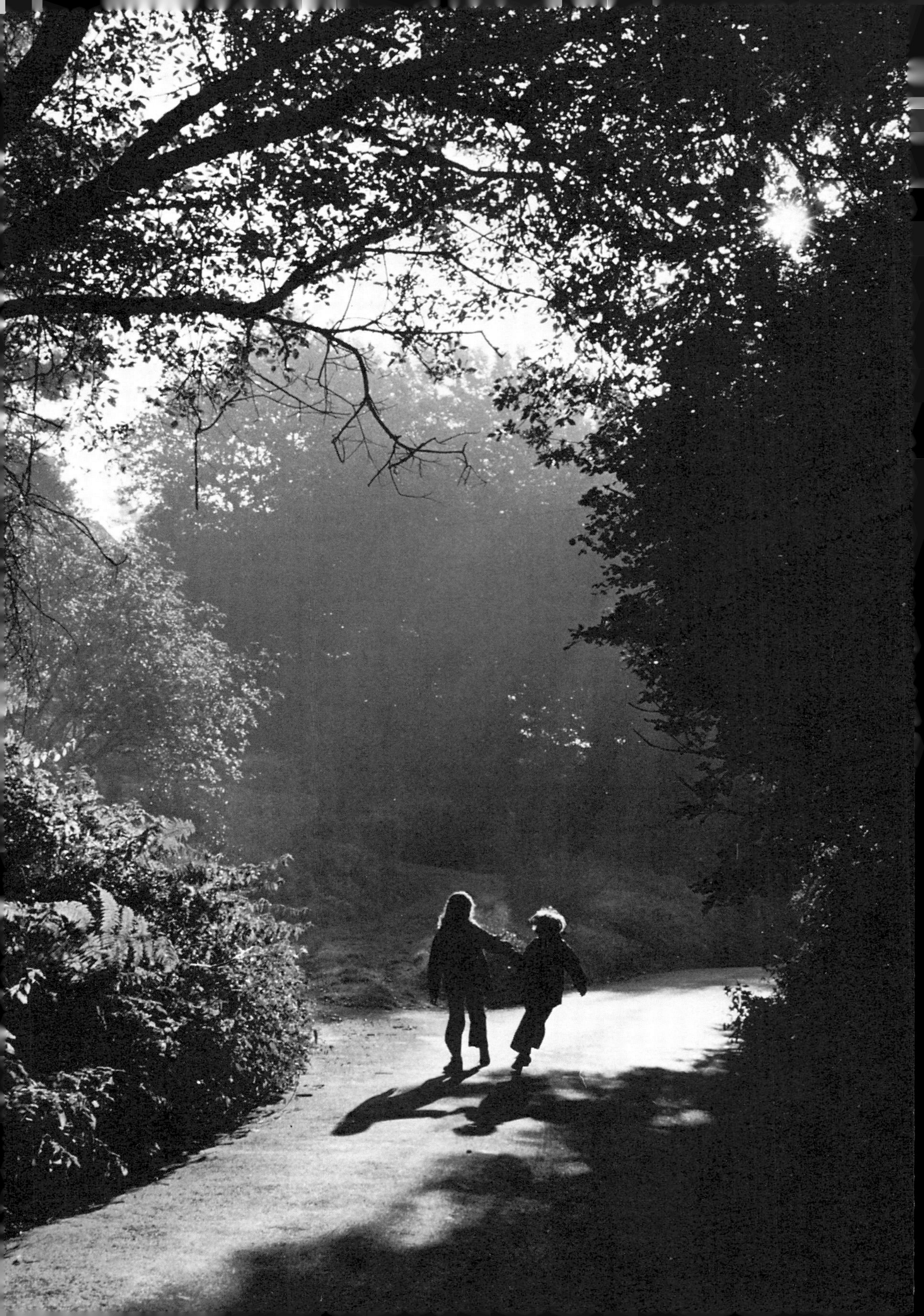

Group work

Dictionaries

Make a list of any words that you find difficult or unusual. Write down briefly what you think they probably mean. Then check them in a dictionary.

Questions

1. Claire Ryan has given sub-headings to the various parts or sections of her essay. The first one is shown here ('Kinds of Music') but the rest of the sub-headings are left out. Re-read the essay and suggest a good sub-heading to replace the letters B, C, D and E.
2. Claire Ryan writes about the different kinds of music that she likes. What *different* kinds do you like?
3. She also writes about favourite performers of music. Make a list of some of your own favourites.
4. She mentions music that seems to be a mixture of kinds and styles. Can you think of any more examples?
5. Do you think your taste in music has changed over the last few years? Can you give some examples? Can you suggest why it has changed?

Punctuation

6. Make a note of each different item of punctuation used in section D, and explain the different purposes for which these different items of punctuation are used.

Compare your answers with the rest of the class.

Words and pictures

Poetry and music can capture and express moods and feelings. So too can many kinds of pictures.

1. Look at and discuss the six pictures in this Unit and suggest half a dozen or so words or phrases to describe the mood or feeling of each one.
2. Two are paintings (or drawings); two are scenes from films; two are photographs. What different moods do they seem to express?
3. Can you suggest a piece of music to accompany any of the pictures?

← *My Grandchildren* **by Bert Hardy**

Writing poems and lyrics

1. Write a poem to go with one of the pictures, or bring along a picture of your own and use that as the basis for a poem.
2. Think of a rhythm and write a lyric to go with it.
3. Think of a melody and write a lyric to go with it.

Read your work to each other and discuss the kinds of moods and rhythms and melodies that each of the lyrics or poems suggests.

8 SEX DISCRIMINATION ACT

The **Sex Discrimination Act** was passed by Parliament in 1975. The materials in this Unit illustrate some of the effects of the Act in the decade following its enactment.

The materials are in four sections:
- some extracts from the Act itself
- decisions of the Courts and Tribunals in interpreting the Act
- employment
- education

Research

Read the materials; talk about them; ask questions about them.
See what further information you can find regarding events since 1975. For example, your library may stock Keesing's Contemporary Archives, and if you look up 'Sex Discrimination Act' in the index you will be able to locate a number of events, court cases and parliamentary discussions that have occurred quite recently.
You may also be able to interview people both inside and outside the school with a view to finding out more about attitudes towards the issue.

Writing

Choose one particular aspect of the issue to write about. It could, for example, be a review of the various court cases you have read about, explaining what was decided and why, and showing what you would have decided (in the light of the Act itself). Or it could be a review of the results of your interviews with people of different ages in your own community.
Write your report for use as a discussion document with another class, and be careful not to assume that your readers know much about either the Act or its effects.

Sex Discrimination Act 1975

1975 CHAPTER 65

An Act to render unlawful certain kinds of sex discrimination and discrimination on the ground of marriage, and establish a Commission with the function of working towards the elimination of such discrimination and promoting equality of opportunity between men and women generally; and for related purposes.

[12th November 1975]

BE IT ENACTED by the Queen's most Excellent Majesty, by and with the advice and consent of the Lords Spiritual and Temporal, and Commons, in this present Parliament assembled, and by the authority of the same, as follows:-

PART I
DISCRIMINATION TO WHICH ACT APPLIES

1.—(1) A person discriminates against a woman in any circumstances relevant for the purposes of any provision of this Act if- *(Sex discrimination against women.)*

(a) on the ground of her sex he treats her less favourably than he treats or would treat a man, or

(b) he applies to her a requirement or condition which he applies or would apply equally to a man but—

(i) which is such that the proportion of women who can comply with it is considerably smaller than the proportion of men who can comply with it, and

(ii) which he cannot show to be justifiable irrespective of the sex of the person to whom it is applied, and

(iii) which is to her detriment because she cannot comply with it.

(2) If a person treats or would treat a man differently according to the man's marital status, his treatment of a woman is for the purposes of subsection (1)(a) to be compared to his treatment of a man having the like marital status.

2.—(1) Section 1, and the provisions of Parts II and III relating to sex discrimination against women, are to be read as applying equally to the treatment of men, and for that purpose shall have effect with such modifications as are requisite. *(Sex discrimination against men.)*

PART II
DISCRIMINATION IN THE EMPLOYMENT FIELD

Discrimination by employers

6.—(1) It is unlawful for a person, in relation to employment by him at an establishment in Great Britain, to discriminate against a woman — *(Discrimination against applicants and employees.)*

(a) in the arrangements he makes for the purpose of determining who should be offered that employment, or

(b) in the terms on which he offers her that employment, or

(c) by refusing or deliberately omitting to offer her that employment

(2) It is unlawful for a person, in the case of a woman employed by him at an establishment in Great Britain, to discriminate against her—
  (a) in the way he affords her access to opportunities for promotion, transfer or training, or to any other benefits, facilities or services, or by refusing or deliberately omitting to afford her access to them, or
  (b) by dismissing her, or subjecting her to any other detriment.

PART III
DISCRIMINATION IN OTHER FIELDS
Education

22. It is unlawful in relation to an educational establishment . . . for a person . . . to discriminate against a woman — [Discrimination by bodies in charge of educational establishments.]
  (a) in the terms on which it offers to admit her to the establishment as a pupil, or
  (b) by refusing or deliberately omitting to accept an application for her admission to the establishment as a pupil, or
  (c) where she is a pupil of the establishment—
    (i) in the way it affords her access to any benefits facilities or services; or by refusing or deliberately omitting to afford her access to them, or
    (ii) by excluding her from the establishment or subjecting her to any other detriment.

PART VI
EQUAL OPPORTUNITIES COMMISSION

53.—(1) There shall be a body of Commissioners named the Equal Opportunities Commission, consisting of at least eight but not more than fifteen individuals each appointed by the Secretary of State on a full-time or part-time basis, which shall have the following duties— [Establishment and duties of Commission.]
  (a) to work towards the elimination of discrimination,
  (b) to promote equality of opportunity between men and women generally, and
  (c) to keep under review the working of this Act and the Equal Pay Act 1970 and, when they are so required by the Secretary of State or otherwise think it necessary, draw up and submit to the Secretary of State proposals for amending them. [1970 c. 41.]

The Courts and Tribunals

RED CARD FOR THE FIRST LADY OF SOCCER

Theresa loses £250 and is outlawed by judges

Express Staff Reporter

SOCCER rebel Theresa Bennett, the tough-tackling schoolgirl who floored the mighty Football Association, was beaten in the replay in court yesterday.

It means that she will never again be allowed to play in a boys' league team.

For the F.A. won its appeal against a county court ruling that it was wrong to ban her from her local youth eleven.

The appeal court decision also cancels the £250 damages awarded to her by the county court.

After the verdict, which will hit the hopes of Soccer girls everywhere, 12-year-old Theresa of Little Carlton, Newark, Notts, said: "I am disappointed, but I didn't ever really expect to play for Arsenal, anyway."

Shame

"I love soccer and I suppose I can still take part in practice games with the boys. I had meant to buy a bike with the damages money but that will go now."

She insisted: "The result was really a draw. One for the F.A., one for me. There will be no return match."

The Equal Opportunities Commission, which financed her case, hit out: "What a shame that the Football Association should bring their big guns to bear on a little girl who is good at football."

The blow fell when Master of the Rolls, Lord Denning, and two appeal judges held that there was nothing in the Sex Discrimination Act which could allow girls under 12 to play football with boys.

"It is plain as can be that football does not come within the Act." said Lord Denning. "If the law says that it does then it is an ass and an idiot. I do not think it does."

Last night Sir Harold Thompson, chairman of the F.A. wished Theresa "all the luck in the world".

"I have been labelled a bully but I'm certainly not that," he said.

The Equal Opportunities Commission promised to back Theresa if she wants to take the battle to the House of Lords. It is the first sex discrimination case involving women in sport.

from THE DAILY EXPRESS
29th July 1978

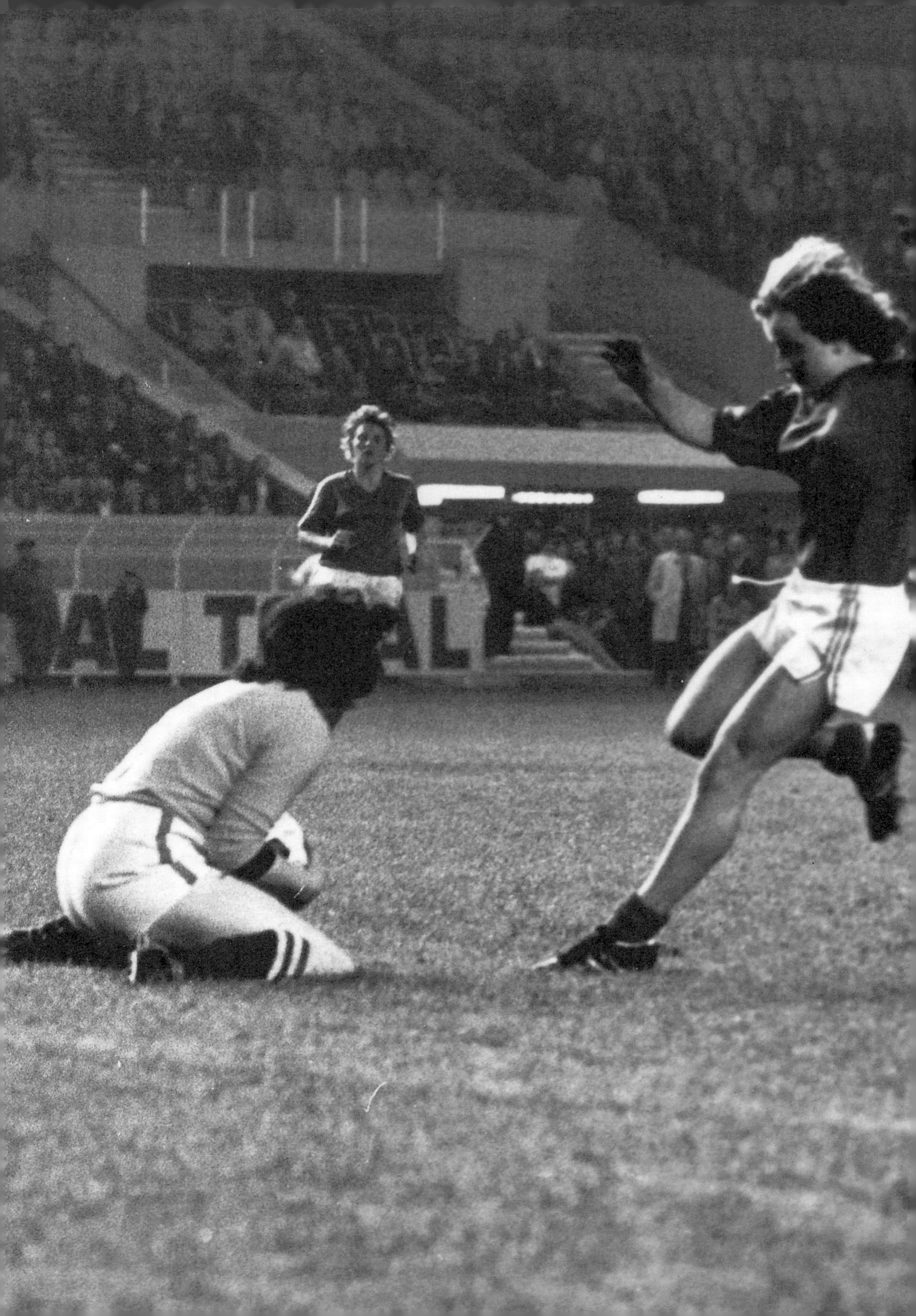

Court blow to wine bar feminists

By David Nicholson-Lord

Women's rights campaigners yesterday lost the first round in their renewed battle with El Vino, the Fleet Street wine bar, which refuses to serve women unless they are seated at a table.

In a reserved judgement a county court judge ruled that the practice, introduced 37 years ago, did not contravene the Sex Discrimination Act because women did not receive "less favourable treatment" at El Vino.

Judge Ranking also told the Mayor's and City of London Court that the women who brought the action, Miss Anna Coote and Mrs Tess Gill, had exaggerated their dismay at the house rule.

Their reaction was "somewhat extreme", he said. Objections to the rule had been minimal and only a handful of people had said it was discriminatory.

The judgement brought a strong reaction from Miss Coote and Mrs Gill, whose action, the fourth against El Vino under the Act, is being financed by the Equal Opportunities Commission. The Commission believes it may serve as a test case in interpreting Section 29 of the Act governing less favourable treatment in the provision of services to women.

Miss Coote said she was "very upset" but added: "I was not surprised, because we thought this might happen in the county court".

Mrs Gill said she was confirmed in her view that "male judges are the worst kind of people to judge this kind of case".

Judge Ranking said it was not Parliament's intention that the Act should be used to intervene in every circumstance, such as the daily management of places like El Vino. The "vast majority" of people would accept the house rule, and the Act, from the reasonable person's point of view, had thus not been breached.

from THE TIMES 16th July 1981

Mrs B. Price versus the Civil Service Commission Employment Appeal Tribunal, 1977

Mrs Price applied for a post as an Executive Officer with the Civil Service but was rejected because she was 35. The Civil Service required that candidates should be between $17\frac{1}{2}$ and 28 years old. Mrs Price (a mother of two children) argued that this discriminated against women, since many women of that age group would be involved in bringing up a family and would be unable, therefore, to gain admission to the Civil Service.

The Tribunal agreed that this unfairly discriminated against women and ordered the age bar to be removed by 1980.

TRIPLE VICTORY — Michelle Debell (left) Michelle Teh and Selmin Sevket who were kept back a year at school because they are girls

Girls to get cash for school sex bias

By Penny Chorlton

THREE 12-year-old girls who suffered sexual discrimination at school are each to receive £351 agreed compensation after winning their case at Bromley County Court, London, yesterday.

They were not allowed to move up from the third to fourth year at St George's Church of England Primary School, Bromley, solely because of their sex, the court was told.

Michelle Debell, Selmin Sevket and Michelle Mei Lin Teh were kept down a year when they were 10 because the headmistress, Miss Pamela Smith, found there were too many pupils in the class with which they should have moved.

Parents were told that the youngest pupils in the year would have to stay down. But the parents of the three girls discovered that no boys had been kept back and reported the matter to the Equal Opportunities Commission.

Eight girls were not moved up to the next class at the school, which had a policy of keeping back the youngest children when classes were oversubscribed.

Bromley education authority and Miss Smith, now retired, admitted sexual discrimination. A further £278 compensation is to be paid to Miss Sevket for private tuition fees.

Mr Geoffrey Stephenson, for Bromley council, told the court: "The decision was taken in perfectly good faith by the teacher concerned believing that this was the best way in educational terms to organise the third and fourth year classes."

Mr Anthony Lester, QC for the Equal Opportunities Commission, said that the girls were not kept down because of their abilities but purely because of their sex. This was clearly illegal under the Sexual Discrimination Act.

The case was the first of its kind, but the EOC says it has received similar complaints from other parts of the country.

After the hearing, Michelle Debell said: "Some people thought we were not bright enough to go into the other class. We were very angry when we found out about the boys."

Her father James, of Nightingale Lane, Bromley, said: "We only hope that the court case will stop this happening to other children."

Michelle Teh said: "I was turned down for the secondary school I chose even though I was the only girl at St George's to pass the entrance exam."

A spokesman for the education authority said that the case was an isolated one and was not the result of official policy.

*from THE GUARDIAN
13th November 1984*

The Debell, Sevket and Teh case

Extracts from a leaflet published by the Equal Opportunities Commission explaining the importance of the *Debell, Sevket and Teh case*.

Background Facts

Michelle Debell, Selmin Sevket and Michelle Teh were pupils at St. George's Church of England Primary School, in the London Borough of Bromley. At this school the children were grouped into classes by age. Class 10 was the top Junior class for fourth-year pupils and was the last class pupils entered before leaving to go into secondary education.

On returning to school after the summer holidays in September 1982, the three girls – who were then fourth-year pupils – expected to enter class 10. At assembly they were told that fourth-year boys with some fourth-year girls would be going into class 10, and that they and five other fourth-year girls would be staying in class 9 with third-year pupils. When the parents of the three girls contacted the school to find out why the girls were not moving to class 10 they were told that there were too many children in the fourth year for class 10: 17 boys and 22 girls. The parents also learned that:

- Class 10 had been organised to contain 17 boys and 14 girls. The eight youngest fourth-year girls had been kept in class 9 rather than the eight youngest pupils, of whom four were girls and four were boys. No boys were made to stay in class 9 with third-year pupils.
- The three girls were not among the eight youngest fourth-year pupils, and fourth-year boys younger than them had been moved to class 10.
- The three girls had not been kept in class 9 because of lack of ability or aptitude or any other failing.
- Contrary to the written policy of the school, the class division had not been made on the basis of age alone, but also made on the basis of balancing the number of girls and boys in classes.

Despite repeated requests by the parents, the Local Education Authority and the school refused to re-allocate the girls from class 9 to class 10.

Complainants' Case

The parents of the three girls complained that their daughters were fourth-year pupils who had been treated less favourably than boys who were fourth-year pupils, contrary to section 1(1)(a) and 22(c) of the Sex Discrimination Act.

In the parents' view, the top Junior class was an important part of their daughters' education. In that class all the pupils were preparing for the move to secondary education and for tests and examinations which would determine either which ability stream they would enter at the next school, or whether they had the ability to enter one of the two selective schools.

The parents were greatly concerned at the situation in terms of both the practical and emotional effects on their daughters. The parents said that the three girls, by being denied access to class 10, composed entirely of fourth-year pupils:

- Had been deprived of continuity of association with their friends and former classmates; access to the higher level academic stimulation they would receive from working in the wholly fourth-year class; the benefit of teaching which was entirely at fourth-year level.
- Had been placed in a class where, owing to the lower average age of the children, the average level of educational attainment would not be as advanced as that of the class of older, solely fourth-year pupils; they would inevitably repeat or hear repeated work they had done the year before; the difference in average age between class 9 and class 10 would inevitably affect the level of presentation of material and sophistication of discussion.

The parents also felt that because the three girls had not been moved to class 10 their performance in examinations taken before transfer to secondary education would be affected.

All the parents considered that their daughters:

- Had suffered a loss of status both in self-esteem and in the estimation of their peers being regarded as pupils who had been 'kept down' through an apparent lack of ability.
- Had experienced a loss of self-confidence and felt that they had not been treated fairly.

Respondents' Case

The Local Education Authority stated that eight fourth-year girls had been allocated to a different, but not lower, class, and pointed out that it is not an uncommon practice in primary schools to form mixed-age groups. The Local Education Authority made the following points:

- This is a $1\frac{1}{4}$–$1\frac{1}{2}$ form entry school where age group numbers have made unavoidable a number of mixed-age classes for some years.
- It was necessary to allocate a number of pupils to class 9 because class 10 would otherwise have contained more than the maximum permitted number of pupils. The teachers were experienced in this kind of class organisation.
- The curriculum was not organised in terms of work to be covered in successive years. Rather, the emphasis, within the school was in terms of progression for the individual pupil. To pursue this effectively, the teachers used a blend of class, group and individual teaching.

- The opportunity exists for all fourth-year children to mix socially. They have the same break time and share the same play areas. Classes 9 and 10 join together for games lessons and for craft options.

With regard to the school's policy on making class divisions based on age alone, the reasons given for departing from that policy were:

- The Headteacher attempts to organise classes from oldest to youngest throughout the school. Age as a sole criterion, however, can cause a great imbalance of girls and boys in particular classes. Therefore, the Headteacher also tries to even up numbers of each sex in each class for socialisation and curriculum opportunity reasons.

- In this case the Headteacher allocated the eight youngest girls to class 9, first because it had a female teacher and she thought this was in the best interests of those pupils; and secondly to ensure a balance between male and female pupils in classes 9 and 10. The allocation was, therefore, based on an individual assessment of pupils according to their educational needs.

Settlement

In settlement of this action the London Borough of Bromley on behalf of itself as first defendant and Miss P.N.L. Smith as second defendant:

- Gave notice on 27th July 1984 that they had paid the sum of £351 into Court in respect of each of the plaintiffs, together with the sum of £278 in respect of Selmin Sevket's claim for the cost of her private exam tuition.
- Admitted in an open letter dated 4th October 1984 that the acts complained of were breaches of the Sex Discrimination Act.
- Agreed to a statement being read in open court.
- Agreed to pay the plaintiff's legal costs.

Potential Implications for Schools

The difficulty in the case described in this leaflet arose from the school's attempt to achieve a balance of the sexes in classes. This resulted in decisions concerning the placing of individuals which were based upon their sex rather than upon some common set of criteria which treated all pupils in the same way.

Such sex-based decisions are likely to result in unlawful sex discrimination. The Commission's legal advice is that attempts to introduce quotas of boys and girls in relation to educational provision is likely to result in unlawful acts. This has possible implications in the following situations:

- Access to co-educational schools or to educational courses within those schools;
- Access to ability bands, streams or sets within co-educational schools;
- Access to benefits, facilities and services either within schools or within an Authority's overall educational provision;
- Access to particular kinds of education, such as selective schooling.

The guiding principle is that pupils should be treated on their individual merits, regardless of their sex.

Mrs Steele versus The Post Office and the Union of Post Office Workers
Employment Appeal Tribunal, 1976

Until September 1975, the Post Office only employed postwomen on a temporary basis even though many postwomen might work for them for a long time. Mrs Steele was employed as a temporary postwoman from 1961 and her job became "permanent" after the change of regulations in September 1975. The following year she applied for a vacancy delivering letters in another area but was turned down on the basis that she had not been a permanent employee for as long as another applicant who was given the job. The successful applicant was a man who had been employed on a permanent basis since 1973.

Mrs Steele complained to the Tribunal on the grounds that the principle of awarding jobs according to length of permanent service within the Post Office, unfairly discriminated against women since no matter how long they had been working for the Post Office, they had only been allowed the status of permanent workers since 1975.

The Tribunal agreed that this was unfair, and ruled that for future occasions, Mrs Steele's permanent status should be backdated to 1969, thus making it fairly certain that she would be the most senior applicant and with the best prospect of getting the job.

Employment

A former air hostess who went up in the world today became the first woman to captain a 747 Jumbo Jet across the Atlantic.
Lynn Rippelmeyer flew in to Gatwick with 470 passengers aboard her People Express jet...

from THE STANDARD *19th July 1984*

Miss Susan Batten, aged 30, passed out yesterday from London Fire Brigade training, as Britain's first full-time firewoman...

from THE TIMES *30th September 1982*

Firefighter Lynn Gunning, who was subjected to gross harassment by several male firefighters while she was the only woman stationed at Soho, London, is negotiating with the Greater London Council for compensation.

from CITY LIMITS *26th July 1985*

MEN are winning the race for top jobs in the women's world of teaching, according to a London schools' survey out today
Now Inner London education chiefs are to launch a drive to encourage more women to apply for senior posts, most of which are held by promotion-hungry men.
Although four out of five ILEA primary teachers are women they take only half the headships.
In secondary schools where half the staff are women well under half hold top positions.
A survey by the authority's statistics branch says that when women do apply for promotion they stand as good a chance as men. But twice as many men apply for posts...

from THE STANDARD *22nd July 1982*

Of 635 MPs, only 19 are women...

from THE TIMES *1st September 1981*

The new Lord Mayor of London is Lady Donaldson. She is the first woman Lord Mayor of London...

from THE TIMES *30th September 1983*

What can I do if I think that, in connection with work, I am being discriminated against because I am a woman?

If, for example, you feel that you have been refused a job or a promotion or have not been offered training or if you have been dismissed, you may have a claim under the Sex Discrimination Act. The Guide to the Act, which you can get from an employment office, Jobcentre or unemployment benefit office, explains these matters more fully and describes the special procedure to enable you to obtain more information from your employer. Form SD 74 is used for this purpose and is obtainable from the same offices. If you do decide to make application to a tribunal you must do so within three months of the discriminatory act complained about. You can seek further advice from the Advisory, Conciliation and Arbitration Service or from the Equal Opportunities Commission.

from 'Equal Pay for Women' published by the Equal Opportunities Commission

Sheila Edmundson, now sailing as Second Mate aboard an Ellerman City Liner on the way to pick up a cargo of sugar from Mauritius, looks set to become the first woman captain in the Merchant Navy...

from THE OBSERVER 15th March 1981

This week the General Synod of the Church of England debates again whether the law should be changed to allow the ordination of women in the Church...

from THE GUARDIAN 12th November 1984

JOYCE BENNETT leads her congregation in hymns and prayer every Sunday. But she will not be able to celebrate Holy Communion or conduct the marriage service for perhaps 10 years. Dr Bennett is the only ordained Anglican woman priest with a regular congregation in Britain. Last week's decision by the General Synod in favour of the principle of the licensing of women priests is unlikely to take effect until the mid-1990s....

from THE OBSERVER 18th November 1984

Education

Equality case prompts new timetable

East Sussex County Council has issued guidelines on the Sex Discrimination Act to all its schools after a councillor discovered that her daughter was being refused metalwork lessons.

In a survey prompted by her complaint, the county found seven out of 39 secondary schools were still offering craft subjects along traditional lines – needlework and cookery to girls, metalwork and woodwork to boys.

The schools have now been told they must change their timetables by next September so that a range of craft subjects are offered on an equal basis to girls and boys.

In particular, they have been instructed to halt the practice whereby girls are only given the opportunity to study "boy's" subjects if they make a special request to do so.

Ms Pamela Montgomery, a Labour councillor from Brighton, found her daughter Nicola was being offered one term of needlework and two terms of domestic science in her first year at Dorothy Stringer school, a 12–16 comprehensive. Boys in her class were being offered one term of metalwork and two of woodwork.

Nicola was keen to study metalwork. Three girls in her year had already made a special request for metalwork and had arranged "swops" with boys who wanted to take a "girl's" subject.

After complaining about the arrangement, her daughter was allowed to take metalwork for one term without having to "swop" with a boy. She is currently taking domestic science for one term and, following a change in the school's curriculum, she will study woodwork next term.

A spokeswoman for East Sussex said the education committee voted last week to remove unequal opportunities in the craft curriculums of schools.

from THE TIMES 22nd January 1982

Girls stick to typing and boys dominate the sciences

Pupils shunning their chance to be equal

by David Shaw

BOYS WILL be boys and girls will be girls when it comes to choosing subjects at school, says an Equal Opportunities Commission report today.

Although schools have stuck to the letter of the law and opened up subjects to both sexes, both boys and girls show a reluctance to take up the opportunities.

A report commissioned from North-East London Polytechnic said there had been very little change since the Sex Discrimination Act in 1975, with boys still dominating the sciences and girls languages and commercial subjects such as typing and office practice.

The survey showed that pupils have strongly stereotyped attitudes. For example, although more girls believed they should be encouraged to consider taking jobs normally done by boys, boys were hostile to the idea that they should consider traditional girls' jobs and were considerably less enthusiastic than girls at the thought of girls entering "their" jobs market.

Teachers were often at fault in not encouraging pupils to switch subjects. Subjects were sometimes linked in such a way as to make the choice of options less attractive to girls – for example, making physics a requirement for taking craft subjects.

The study showed that at some schools the complexity and lay-out of option forms were such as to discourage choice. There was evidence of collusion with employers to channel pupils into traditional jobs.

Although three-quarters of schools conformed to the letter of the law in opening up subjects to the opposite sex, one in six showed evidence of "bad practice."

from THE STANDARD 9th October 1984

Girls 'face fight for equality in schools'

By Wendy Berliner, Education Correspondent

Nearly half the teachers questioned in a survey were unsympathetic to equal opportunities policy according to research presented yesterday. It analysed the views of 850 teachers in 50 schools in England and Wales.

The least sympathy came from teachers of subjects such as mathematics and physical sciences in which girls are under-represented and in technical crafts, including domestic and secretarial studies.

Mr John Pratt, director of the Centre for Institutional Studies at the Anglian Regional Management Centre, who undertook the research for the Equal Opportunities Commission, described a number of the conclusions as disturbing.

Mr Pratt said in a paper presented to a Manchester conference on "Girl-Friendly Schooling" backed by the EOC, that the majority of teachers surveyed appeared to be in favour of equal opportunities in principle but were less committed to them in practice.

"The attitudes of maths teachers suggest that girls' reluctance to study that subject, and by association physical sciences, is unlikely to be recognised as a matter of concern by those teachers."

Teachers of English and social studies were most in favour of equal opportunities. Women teachers responded most positively towards equality.

from THE GUARDIAN 13th September 1984

Film 'reinforces' male bias on heavy crafts

by Hillary Wilce

A teacher at an Oldham comprehensive school is to complain to the Equal Opportunities Commission over two strips of slides which her school plans to purchase.

Mrs Joan Frost, a teacher in design and technology at the 1,500 pupil Saddleworth School, claims that the films reinforce the prejudice that heavy crafts are only for boys.

The slides, called *Health and Safety at School*, deal with metalwork, woodwork, machine work and general workshop hazards. They show only boys being taught by all-male staff.

Although much of the material was "excellent", Mrs Frost said that it will not help to encourage girls to take up practical subjects. "At this school all first- and second-year pupils attend classes in all practical subjects offered", Mrs Frost said.

"When a choice is made at third year level, however, many pupils still polarise towards formerly traditional 'male' and 'female' choices."

At Saddleworth only three girls out of 10 forms of fourth- and fifth-year pupils are taking heavy craft subjects.

Mrs Frost will take the matter up with officers from the Equal Opportunities Commission when they pay the school a previously-arranged visit next week.

Mr William Dorset, managing director of Camera Talks, the firm which produced the slides, said Mrs Frost was right. "This was not done intentionally," he said. "It was just one of those mistakes for which I take full responsibility.

"We filmed it at a Croydon boys' school and though there was a girls' school adjacent they were not keen to co-operate in making the films. We might correct it in a subsequent edition, but you can never please everyone."

The films, which have been on the market for about a year, have been bought be "several hundred" schools, Mr Dorset said.

from THE TIMES EDUCATIONAL SUPPLEMENT 5th February 1985

Mathematics bias for the boys

by Virginia Makins

Many school mathematics books show that maths is for boys, says a survey of five mathematics schemes for children aged 3 to 13.

Ms Jean Northam of Rolle College, Exmouth, looked at the pictures and problems in the five schemes. For the youngest children the books were Nuffield guidelines designed for teachers. Their illustrations did not differentiate between girls and boys. However, many children were shown looking passive and dependent and not taking the sort of initiative and exploration suggested as desirable for infant mathematicians.

In primary books, the active and exploring children are almost always boys. Most adults are male. Women, when they appear, are passive and expressionless.

At the junior stage, women virtually disappear. A few girls are still around – but an analysis of one scheme, *Maths Adventure*, showed that boys set problems and solve them, while girls keep records, practise skills dutifully, and comment on the boys' behaviour.

Pictures and problems in a scheme for older children, *Discovering Mathematics*, showed even more bias. Far fewer women were pictured than men. When they do appear, women sit in vehicles driven by men and watch men at work. The men use telescopes, make calculations, build houses and mend roads. There is even a male chef, demonstrating cake baking on television and being copied by four women.

In problems, boys and men appear far more often than girls (women appear only once). Jean Northam finds a close parallel between research results about girls' declining involvement in maths between the ages of 7 and 16, and their gradual disappearance from maths textbooks.

from THE TIMES EDUCATIONAL SUPPLEMENT 30th April 1982

The Hidden Curriculum

As the children grow older, their ideas of sex roles begin to be influenced by factors beyond the home, the most significant of these influences being the school, the peer group and the media. Since the only factor controlled by teachers is the school, every effort should be made to present a non-discriminatory environment. Many small but significant procedures can affect the development of a non-discriminatory environment and teachers need to give consideration to the following points.

- Do boys and girls line up separately to move about the school?
- Are girls more often given the unexciting, monotonous tasks requiring more patience and concentration?
- Are boys more often given the unattractive, heavy, messy jobs requiring little sensitivity?
- Do boys always carry the milk crates?
- Do girls always put out the paints etc?
- Are girls ever encouraged to operate the school's audio-visual or other mechanical aids?
- In thematic work, do girls always investigate clothes, food, home-life etc. while the boys research into weapons, building techniques, space travel, engines etc?
- Are boys and girls segregated in classroom and assembly seating arrangements?
- Do you invite workpeople in non-traditional jobs to talk to pupils, e.g. female bus driver, male nurse, etc?
- Are girls and boys treated the same? Care should be taken to not react like the teacher who told a boy who could not knock a nail in to "get on with it", but responded to a girl in the same situation by taking the wood, nail and hammer and doing it for her.
- Do the boys usually cover areas of work such as traffic surveys while the girls always do the work connected with plants, trees and pets?
- Are out-of-school activities organised so that the football club and the recorder club meet at the same time, thus becoming mutually exclusive?

Home Economics Education for All

In some schools, boys still do not have the opportunity to study home economics. In other schools the subject is not studied by all girls, but the gross under-representation of boys in home economics once subject choices have been made should give cause for concern.

Attention has been drawn repeatedly to sex differentiation in subject choice in the secondary school (DES 1975, 1979, 1980). Girls are under-represented in physical science and craft, design and technology and boys are under-represented in home economics. Pupils of both sexes are consequently denied important educational experiences and their vocational opportunities are restricted to traditional sex-stereotyped occupations.

Most boys and some girls will leave school ill-equipped for personal independence and for taking shared responsibility in home and family life unless home economics forms part of a compulsory core, not necessarily examinable, whether or not it is also offered as an optional subject.

There are many thousands of girls studying a whole range of Craft, Design and Technology (CDT) subjects in years one to three in secondary schools in this country, but very few remain with the subject area in years four and five.

In 1979 there were a total of 305,095 candidates – entries for CDT subjects at CSE and GCE 'O' level. Of those 7,478 were girls; a mere 2.45% of the total subject entry.

WHY DO SO FEW GIRLS CONTINUE WITH THEIR STUDY OF CDT?

WHAT CAN BE DONE TO CHANGE THE CURRENT SITUATION?

from a leaflet published by the Equal Opportunities Commission

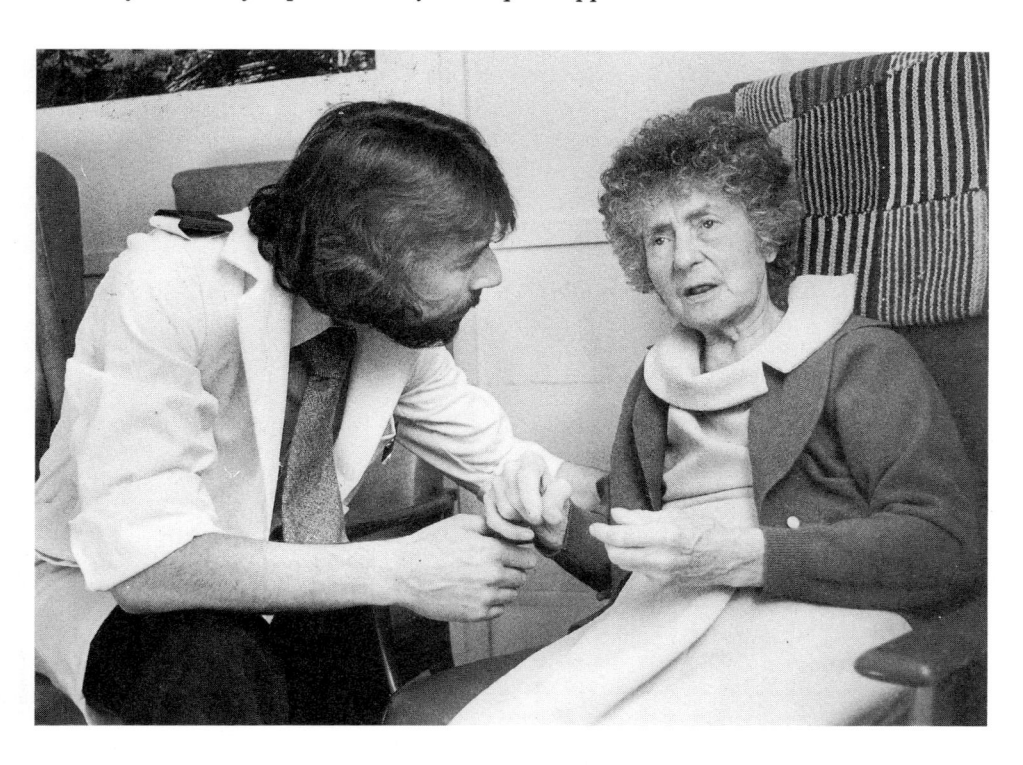

Percentages of Boys/Girls taking particular 'A' Level Courses (1975)

Subject	% of Boys	% of Girls
Mathematics	41	15
Further Mathematics	9	3
Physics	41	9
Chemistry	30	13
Biology	16	21
English Literature	23	53
French	8	24
German	3	9
Geography	27	22
History	23	28
Economics	22	8
Art	9	15
Music	2	4

Source: Curricular Differences for Boys and Girls, DES, Education Survey 21, HMSO 1975

Secondary School Staffing Survey: Subject of Highest Qualification Analysed by Sex. 1977

| England and Wales | Full-time teachers | | |
	Men	Women	All
Main subject of highest qualification	Percentages		Thousands
English	44	56	26.2
Mathematics	64	36	21.2
Physical education	53	47	19.2
History	59	41	18.6
Geography	65	35	16.3
Art/craft	58	42	15.2
Craft, design and technology	99	1	14.3
Home economics	1	99	12.8
French	38	62	12.5
Biology	48	52	12.1
Chemistry	82	18	8.9
Music	50	50	7.9
Physics	88	12	7.3
Religious education	49	51	5.8
Other subjects:			
Other languages	56	44	7.4
Other sciences	76	24	6.1
Any other subject	59	41	21.7
All subjects	57	43	233.6

Source: DES Statistical Bulletin 5/82

9 WAR-TIME

During an air raid, children of hop pickers in Kent take refuge in an open trench for emergency shelter.

This Unit explores aspects of life (mostly in Britain) during the Second World War.

Before you read the various materials, have a look at the following quiz. How many of the questions can you answer?

About the War

1. What was an evacuee?
2. Food was rationed in the War. What else was rationed?
3. There was no television during the War. What were the two main forms of entertainment?
4. What was the 'Black Market'?
5. At what age were men conscripted to the armed forces?
6. At what age were women conscripted?
7. For what purpose were men conscripted other than to fight with the armed forces?
8. For what other purposes were women conscripted?
9. What is a refugee?
10. How frequent were air raid warnings? And what was the warning?

True or False?

11. There was no unemployment during the War.
12. Manufacturers were ordered to stop making long socks, and to stop making trousers with pockets.
13. More civilians than soldiers were killed during the War.
14. Many children had no schooling at all.
15. Many women were compelled to work in factories.
16. Everyone had to have an Identity Card and keep it with them all the time.
17. Jams, margarine and treacle were rationed to 8 oz per person per month.
18. Soap was rationed to 3 oz per month.
19. Men and women workers were given equal pay.
20. The average child was healthier during the War than before it.

The War Begins

In her autobiography, *Rose Gamble* describes growing up in London in the 1930s. Here she recalls the days leading up to the outbreak of the War.

I had little time for anything other than working for the School Certificate examinations, in which I was not to distinguish myself. Quite suddenly, in the middle of the term, new girls came to the school. They spoke hardly any English, and we soon discovered that they were Jewish refugees from Germany.

On the newsreels I watched Hitler making speeches to thousands of people, and I saw rows of soldiers in steel helmets. In the newspapers there were photographs of shabby old men cleaning the gutters in German streets, and they wore marks on their clothes to show that they were Jews. Germany was a long way away, and I was sorry for the old men, but I had things nearer home to worry about. Now it was different. Seeing Elsa and Güdrun – who had been driven from their homes – every day at school made me realise what terrible and wicked things were happening. And nobody seemed to be doing anything to stop it!

Dodie and I went to the pictures one Saturday afternoon, and for sixpence each we sat through two films, a cartoon, the organist and a newsreel. In addition to all this, they screened a recruitment film for the Territorial Army. It was called 'The Gap', and it showed what would happen if the gap in our anti-aircraft defences was not filled by urgently needed volunteers. I sat and watched an aeroplane bombing a row of defenceless little houses, over and over again. The walls and windows crumpled in the blasts and roofs fell into the rooms. Nothing was there to stop the aeroplane, and I just could not believe it. It couldn't be as dreadful as that! War happened abroad, in Spain and Abyssinia. It happened to foreigners, to them, not to us. Dodie must have been as shocked as I was, because a couple of days later she volunteered for classes in air-raid precautions.

The war came a step nearer when Mum took Joey and me to queue up outside the Town Hall to receive our gas masks. Dad didn't come with us. He never conformed with any public duty in case they put his name on a list. It was growing dusk and people around us talked quietly, asking each other questions and knowing no answers. Newspaper sellers ran about shouting headlines, adding stabs of anxiety to the tension. 'The Gap' was still vivid in my mind, and the rubbery smell of the mask when I tried it on was suffocating. 'There won't be a war, will there Mum?' I asked, longing for reassurance.

'A' course not love.' Mum smiled, and added confidently, 'They won't let it happen!'

'Who do you mean by "they"?' I wanted to know.

'God,' she replied, 'an' the newspapers, an' the Gover'ment.'

For once Mum's magic formula of three didn't work, because there was a war and we were separated, never again to live together as a family. We were sent away, each in turn to survive alone, for which we had been well prepared. Georgie went straight into the Merchant Navy and Dodie to a munitions factory. Lu was to have her first baby while Teddy was in an army training camp. Joey joined the Royal Air Force in 1941 and I wanted to be a Wren. I thought I was well qualified to handle a boathook and row Admirals out to the fleet. But they wouldn't have me because my measly old eye was just about sightless. I finished up in a boy scout's hat and more bloody boots, up to my knees in Welsh cow-dung. It was the Land Army for me.

Joey had only just arrived home on leave on the night the buildings were bombed. Mum was making him a cup of cocoa when the whistling crunch of the bombs fell in a line across the four blocks. Many of our neighbours were killed, but Dad staggered through the smoke and dust into the glare of the burning gas main in his long underpants, clutching two bits of salvage – the canary in its cage and a bottle of beer.

Nothing was ever the same again. The war swept away life as we had known it and it disappeared for ever. When I drank my tepid mug of tea in a freezing cowshed before dawn, and dismally contemplated the value of my war effort, I always thought fondly of Mum, just 'popping the kettle on'. Tea, I reflected, had seen us through every crisis, and would see us through plenty more. I thought of her faith in 'God, the newspapers and the Government', and wondered which of the three had failed her. She would battle on through, it would take far more than a war to defeat Mum. After all, she had been fighting one all her life – single-handed.

from *Chelsea Child: an autobiography* **by Rose Gamble**

For discussion

1. Who were Elsa and Güdrun?
2. What evidence, if any, is there in this part of the writer's memoirs that the government was seriously preparing for war?
3. What did the writer do in the War?
4. Who worked harder for the family, Mum or Dad? What is the evidence in this passage?
5. Discuss any unusual words. For instance, Rose Gamble wanted to be a 'Wren'. What does that mean?

Personification

6. In paragraph 4, Rose Gamble writes: 'The war came a step nearer'. This is an example of a figure of speech: *personification*, in which a thing or an idea is referred to as if it is a person. Find another example of personification in this extract.

Under the Counter

Most goods were difficult to get during the War, and almost everything was rationed. This led to a very active 'Black Market' – the illegal sale of almost anything that people were prepared to pay high prices for. Here is an extract from a social history of the War, describing how the Market operated.

With rising prices and tight controls on trade there developed speculation and profiteering. Paradoxically many people were earning more money than they had during the Depression through compulsory drafting into the services or factory war-work, but with rationing and shortages they had only a limited amount of spending power. The government encouraged people to save with War Bonds, a system to invest money in the war effort and prevent speculation, to be repaid at a certain percentage after the war. But if people chose not to invest there was a certain amount of money about.

People talked of 'knowing a man' who might have spare parts for radios, alcohol, rubber tyres, petrol, or even dolls, nylons and perfumes – known to be illegally acquired. The grey market was a more individual process of being in the right place at the right time, whether shop or lorry depot. Many tradespeople, much to their irritation, found their supplies already nibbled away on arrival. This meant a painstaking reorganisation of rationed amounts and sometimes tedious explanations to the rampant Ministry inspectors. Some people would regularly tip, or try to tip, shop assistants in the hope of getting something under the counter when stocks did arrive, and shopkeepers who knew which side their bread was margarined would keep rare consignments like salmon or peaches for their richer customers. A lorry driver, saving for Christmas, might leave the cab door open during a tea break, after a wink and a nod, and return to find a few crates missing and a fiver on the seat.

Attitudes were very mixed to these dealings. They varied from moral outrage at even a whiff of Black Market dealings to the view that if sharp dealing was the only way to provide for a family and friends at a time of stress, then it was the obvious course to take.

In 1942 *War Illustrated* wrote:

> *Not a day has passed but somebody has been prosecuted or imprisoned. The small fry have paid their fines or gone to gaol but the big bosses behind the scenes have not infrequently managed to escape ... To what end are our seamen facing death night and day to bring in the food necessary to our salvation if such vermin as the Black Market dealers are allowed to wax fat upon this scandalous business?*

But the grinning spivs, the 'wide boys', the barrow boys and the 'wheelers' gradually endeared themselves to the general public. The archetypal spiv wore yellow shoes, a wide-lapelled suit and wide tie, and sported a shifty little trilby pulled rakishly over the forehead. He symbolised a flashy flaunting of authority and petty regulations – especially towards the end of the war when people were long tired of self denial and the many wartime restrictions.

The inconsistent fines inflicted by magistrates only added to the feeling of irritation: a woman was fined twelve shillings for feeding her own bread to birds; workers were sent all the way home from their factories to collect forgotten gas masks; a shopkeeper was fined five pounds for selling homemade sweets out of his own sugar ration; farmers were subject to ludicrous penalties for slaughtering a pig a day late or in the wrong building – even if the kill had been witnessed by the right inspector.

A mass of petty bureaucratic rules failed to meet the spirit of a people who by 1944 were bursting with resentment. The Defence Regulations dominated daily life – the Home Secretary, from 22 May 1940, had the right to imprison anybody he believed 'likely to endanger the realm'. These regulations, among other things, banned chinks of light in the blackout, wasting of food, talking of your fighting son's whereabouts in public or making inessential journeys, and enforced compulsory check-ups of those suspected of venereal disease. In 1943 187,000 people were found guilty of breaking Defence Regulations. About one in every fifty were found guilty of infringing the lighting regulations, and 300,000 were prosecuted in 1943. In industry 30,000 were prosecuted for breaking regulations, and 12,500 under the Control of Employment Act. In such conditions, which must always have seemed stressful, and sometimes unfair, it was not surprising that some turned all the more readily to the luxury-laden spiv.

One family in Chalk Farm, drawn to the forbidden fruit, remembers 'never going short'. As soon as the air-raid sirens sounded, their uncle was 'off on the loot'. While families abandoned their houses for the safety of the air-raid shelter, pilfering was as easy as robbing a piggy-bank. Their gran often had steak, and no questions asked, while toys and clothes were never a problem, and the booty was always shared with neighbours. A Stepney child, accustomed to a single toy car, remembers dashing home from the air-raid shelter during a lull in the bombing to fetch his cat (although pets were illegal in shelters) and discovering a toyshop blasted open to reveal a wealth of pre-war stock. He set to and collected everything he could, and 'Me and my mates had a good old time in the shelter after that.'

from *Bombers and Mash* **by Raynes Minns**

For discussion

1. Make a note of any unusual or difficult words, and work out what you think they probably mean. Compare your answers and then check them in a dictionary.
2. Is there a modern equivalent of the *Black Market?*
3. Is there a modern equivalent of the *spiv?*
4. The writer talks of the 'archetypal' spiv. What does this mean?

The Leaders

The leaders of the opposing sides are usually portrayed as they were during the War itself. But what kinds of lives had they lived when they were young?

Here are two extracts. The first is from Alan Bullock's *biography* of Hitler; the second is from Winston Churchill's *autobiography*, My Early Life.

Hitler's Youth

Hitler was born in 1889 and went to Vienna as a young man in the hope of making a living as an artist. In fact, it was difficult for him to make any kind of living at all and he experienced acute hardship and poverty. This extract from the biography explores Hitler's life at this time.

A few others who knew Hitler at this time have been traced and questioned, amongst them a certain Reinhold Hanisch, a tramp from German Bohemia, who for a time knew Hitler well. Hanisch's testimony is partly confirmed by one of the few pieces of documentary evidence which have been discovered for the early years. For in 1910, after a quarrel, Hitler sued Hanisch for cheating him of a small sum of money, and the records of the Vienna police court have been published, including (besides Hitler's own affidavit) the statement of Siegfried Loffner, another inmate of the Home in the Meldemannstrasse who testified that Hanisch and Hitler always sat together and were friendly.

Hanisch describes his first meeting with Hitler in the doss-house in Meidling in 1909. "On the very first day there sat next to the bed that had been allotted to me a man who had nothing on except an old torn pair of trousers – Hitler. His clothes were being cleaned of lice, since for days he had been wandering about without a roof and in a terribly neglected condition."

Hanisch and Hitler joined forces in looking for work; they beat carpets, carried bags outside the West Station, and did casual labouring jobs, on more than one occasion shovelling snow off the streets. As Hitler had no overcoat, he felt the cold badly. Then Hanisch had a better idea. He asked Hitler one day what trade he had learned. " 'I am a painter,' was the answer. Thinking that he was a house decorator, I said that it would surely be easy to make money at his trade. He was offended and answered that he was not that sort of painter, but an academician and an artist." When the two moved to the Meldemannstrasse, "we had to think out better ways of making money. Hitler proposed that we should fake pictures. He told me that already in Linz he had painted small landscapes in oil, had roasted them in an oven until they had become quite brown and had several times been sucessful in selling these pictures to traders as valuable old masters." This sounds highly improbable, but in any case Hanisch, who had registered under another name as Fritz Walter, was afraid of the police. "So I suggested to Hitler that it would be better to stay in an honest trade and paint postcards. I myself was to sell the painted cards, we decided to work together and share the money we earned." This arrangement is confirmed by Hitler's statement to the police court in 1910.

Out of the fifty crowns secured from his half-sister (which was probably part of Hitler's share in the proceeds of the sale of their father's house), Hitler bought cards, ink and paints. With these he produced little copies of views of Vienna, which Hanisch peddled in taverns and fairs, or to small traders who wanted something to fill their empty picture-frames. In this way they made enough to keep them until, in the summer of 1910, they quarrelled over the division of their earnings. Hanisch sold a copy which Hitler had made of a drawing of the Vienna Parliament Building for ten crowns. Hitler, who was sure it was worth far more – he valued it at fifty in his statement to the police – was convinced he had been cheated. When Hanisch failed to return to the Home, Hitler brought a lawsuit against him, which ended in Hanisch spending a week in prison and the break-up of their partnership.

This was in August, 1910. For the remaining four years before the First World War, first in Vienna, later in Munich, Hitler continued to eke out a living in the same way, acting as his own salesman in place of Hanisch. Some of Hitler's drawings, mostly stiff, lifeless copies of buildings in which his attempts to add human figures are a failure, were still to be found in Vienna in the 1930s, when they had acquired the value of collectors' pieces. More often he drew posters and crude advertisements for small shops – Teddy Perspiration Powder, Santa Claus selling coloured candles, or St. Stefan's spire rising over a mountain of soap, with the signature "A. Hitler" in the corner. Hitler himself later described these as years of great loneliness, in which his only contacts with other human beings were in the Home where he continued to live and where, according to Hanisch, "only tramps, drunkards and such spent any time."

After their quarrel Hanisch lost sight of Hitler, but he gives a description of Hitler as he knew him in 1910 at the age of twenty-one. He wore an ancient black overcoat, which had been given him by an old-clothes dealer in the Home, a Hungarian Jew named Neumann, and which reached down over his knees. From under a greasy, black derby hat, his hair hung long over his coat collar. His thin and hungry face was covered with a black beard above which his large staring eyes were the one prominent feature.

Hanisch depicts him as lazy and moody, two characteristics which were often to reappear. He disliked regular work. If he earned a few crowns, he refused to draw for days and went off to a café to eat cream cakes and read newspapers. He had none of the common vices. He neither smoked nor drank and, according to Hanisch, was too shy and awkward to have any success with women. His passions were reading newspapers and talking politics. "Over and over again," Hanisch recalls, "there were days on which he simply refused to work. Then he would hang around night shelters, living on the bread and soup that he got there, and discussing politics, often getting involved in heated controversies."

When he became excited in argument he would shout and wave his arms, until the others in the room cursed him for disturbing them, or the porter came in to stop the noise. Sometimes people laughed at him, at other times they were oddly impressed. "One evening," Hanisch relates, "Hitler went to a cinema where Kellermann's *Tunnel* was being shown. In this piece an agitator appears who rouses the working masses by his speeches. Hitler almost went crazy. The impression it made on him was so strong that for days afterwards he spoke of nothing except the power of the spoken word." These outbursts of violent argument and denunciation alternated with moods of despondency.

from *Hitler, a Study in Tyranny* by **Alan Bullock**

For discussion

1. Is there anything in the extract that you either do not understand or wish to question?
2. What does the incident of the lawsuit tell us about Hitler's character?
3. What was Hitler's attitude to work?
4. Is there anything about Hitler's behaviour in this part of his life that in any way suggests he might later become a national leader?

Churchill's Youth

This extract from Churchill's autobiography concerns an incident that occurred while he was at Sandhurst training to be an army officer. He and his friends were frequent visitors to the Empire Music Hall in Leicester Square. A member of the London County Council, a Mrs Ormiston Chant, disapproved of the promenade and bars at the rear of the theatre and wanted them closed, on the grounds that they encouraged too much 'merrymaking'. Churchill and his friends considered this a disgraceful interference with people's liberties, and decided to fight back. The authorities decided on a compromise.

It was settled that the offending bars were to be separated from the promenade by light canvas screens. Thus they would no longer be technically "in" the promenade; they would be just as far removed from it in law as if they had been in the adjacent county; yet means of egress and ingress of sufficient width might be lawfully provided, together with any reduction of the canvas screens necessary for efficient ventilation. The music-hall proprietors for their part, after uttering howls of pain and protest, seemed to reconcile themselves quite readily to their lot. It was otherwise with the Sandhurst movement. We had not been consulted in this nefarious peace. I was myself filled with scorn at its hypocrisy. I had no idea in those days of the enormous and unquestionably helpful part that humbug plays in the social life of great peoples dwelling in a state of democratic freedom. I wanted a clear-cut definition of the duties of the state and of the rights of the individual, modified as might be necessary by public convenience and decorum.

On the first Saturday night after these canvas obstructions had been placed in the Empire promenade it happened that quite a large number of us chanced to be there. There were also a good many boys from the Universities about our own age, but of course mere bookworms, quite undisciplined and irresponsible. The new structures were examined with attention and soon became the subject of unfavourable comment. Then some young gentleman poked his walking-stick through the canvas. Others imitated his example. Naturally I could not hang back when colleagues were testifying after this fashion. Suddenly a most strange thing happened. The entire crowd numbering some two or three hundred people became excited and infuriated. They rushed upon these flimsy barricades and tore them to pieces. The authorities were powerless. Amid the cracking of timber and the tearing of canvas the barricades were demolished, and the bars were once more united with the promenade to which they had ministered so long.

In these somewhat unvirginal surroundings I now made my maiden speech. Mounting on the debris and indeed partially emerging from it, I addressed the tumultuous crowd. No very accurate report of my words has been preserved. They did not, however, fall unheeded, and I have heard about them several times since. I discarded the constitutional argument entirely and appealed directly to sentiment and even passion, finishing up by saying, "You have seen us tear down these barricades to-night; see that you pull down those who are responsible for them at the coming election." These words were received with rapturous applause, and we all sallied out into the Square brandishing fragments of wood and canvas as trophies or symbols. It reminded me of the death of Julius Cæsar when the conspirators rushed forth into the street waving the bloody daggers with which they had slain the tyrant. I thought also of the taking of the Bastille, with the details of which I was equally familiar.

It seems even more difficult to carry forward a revolution than to start one. We had to catch the last train back to Sandhurst or be guilty of dereliction of duty.

It remains only for me to record that the County Council Elections went the wrong way. The Progressives, as they called themselves, triumphed. The barricades were rebuilt in brick and plaster, and all our efforts went for nothing. Still no one can say we did not do our best.

My course at Sandhurst soon came to an end. Instead of creeping in at the bottom, almost by charity, I passed out with honours eighth in my batch of a hundred and fifty. I mention this because it shows that I could learn quickly enough the things that mattered. It had been a hard but happy experience. There were only three terms, at the end of each of which one advanced almost automatically from junior to intermediate, and then to senior. The generations were so short that in a year one was a senior. One could feel oneself growing up almost every week.

In December 1894 I returned home fully qualified to receive the Queen's commission. In contrast with my school days, I had made many friends, three or four of whom still survive. As for the rest, they are gone. The South African War accounted for a large proportion not only of my friends but of my company; and the Great War killed almost all the others. The few that survived have been pierced through thigh or breast or face by the bullets of the enemy. I salute them all.

I passed out of Sandhurst into the world. It opened like Aladdin's cave. From the beginning of 1895 down to the present time of writing I have never had time to turn round. I could count almost on my fingers the days when I have had nothing to do. An endless moving picture in which one was an actor. On the whole Great Fun! But the years 1895 to 1900 which are the staple of this story exceed in vividness, variety and exertion anything I have known – except of course the opening months of the Great War.

When I look back upon them I cannot but return my sincere thanks to the high gods for the gift of existence. All the days were good and each day better than the others. Ups and downs, risks and journeys, but always the sense of motion, and the illusion of hope.

from *My Early Life* by Winston S. Churchill

For discussion

1. Is there anything in this extract that you either do not understand or wish to question?
2. What does the incident tell us about Churchill's character?
3. Mrs Ormiston Chant disapproved of the merrymaking in the music halls and wanted to stop it. Can you think of any similar attempts today to stop people from 'merrymaking'?
4. Is there any similarity, judging from these two extracts, between Hitler and Churchill as young men?

For individual work

Questions on the two extracts

1. Why did Churchill object so strongly to the setting up of the screens to separate the bars from the promenade, at the back of the theatre?
2. Why did his speech produce little real effect?
3. Churchill says he made his 'maiden speech' at the back of the theatre. What is a maiden speech?
4. Setting up the screens was a 'compromise'. Explain what this means.
5. What was the business arrangement that Hitler made with Hanisch?
6. In what way, according to Hitler, did Hanisch break their agreement?
7. Later, Hitler made a living from drawings of a different kind. What were they?
8. When he achieved power, Hitler persecuted the Jews. Is there anything in this passage which suggests that he ought not to have disliked the Jews at all?
9. Hitler was fascinated by a film showing an 'agitator' at work. What does this word mean?
10. Churchill thought the plan to put up the screens was an example of 'hypocrisy'. Explain what this means.
11. Judging from these two passages, what do you think is the main difference between Hitler's life as a young man, and Churchill's life as a young man?
12. Using the evidence of these two passages, was there any similarity in their lives as young men?

War Criminals (1)

Thomas Keneally's novel *Schindler's Ark* tells the story of Oskar Schindler, a German industrialist, who repeatedly risked his life to save Jews from the Nazi concentration camps. The novel keeps so closely to the historical facts, that it has been spoken of as *faction* – a new genre of fiction.

In this extract, a group of Polish Jews have attempted to escape from a concentration camp, and have been caught. They are all executed, but the Commandant of the Camp, Amon, wants someone to type up his report on the escape. He sends for a boy who is suspected of having been part of the conspiracy.

> Frau Kochmann was too slow for such late work, and so the commandant had Mietek Pemper roused from his barracks and brought to the villa. In the front parlour, Amon stated in a level voice that he believed the young man was party to the escape attempt. Pemper was astounded and did not know how to answer. Looking around him for some sort of inspiration, he saw the seam of his trouser leg, which had come unsewn. How could I pass on the outside in this sort of clothing? he asked.
>
> The balance of frank desperation in his answer satisfied Amon. He told the boy to sit down and instructed him how the typing was to be set out and the pages numbered. Amon hit the papers with his spatulate fingertips. "I want a first-class job done." And Pemper thought, That's the way of it – I can die now for being an escapee, or later in the year for having seen these justifications of Amon's.
>
> When Pemper was leaving the villa with the drafts in his hand, Goeth followed him out on to the patio and called a last order. "When you type the list of insurgents," Amon called companionably, "I want you to leave room above my signature for another name to be inserted."
>
> Pemper nodded, discreet as any professional typist. He stood just a half-second, trying for inspiration, some quick answer that would reverse Amon's order about the extra space. The space for his name. *Mietek Pemper*. In that hateful torrid silence of Sunday evening in Jerozolimska, nothing plausible came to him.
>
> "Yes, Herr Commandant," said Pemper.
>
> As Pemper stumbled up the road to the Administration Building, he remembered a letter Amon had had him type earlier that summer. It had been addressed to Amon's father, the Viennese publisher, and was full of filial concern for an allergy which had troubled the old man that spring. Amon hoped that it had lifted by now. The reason Pemper remembered that letter out of all the others was that half an hour before he'd been called into Amon's office to take it down, the commandant had dragged a girl filing clerk outside and executed her. The juxtaposition of the letter and the execution proved to Pemper that, for Amon, murder and allergies were events of equal weight. And if you

told a tractable stenographer to leave a space for his name, it was a matter of course that he left it.

Pemper sat at the typewriter for more than an hour, but in the end left the space for himself. Not to do that would be even more suddenly fatal. There had been a rumour among Stern's friends that Schindler had some movement of people in mind, some rescue or other. But tonight rumours meant nothing. Mietek left in each report the space for his own death.

When both typescripts were word perfect, he returned to the villa. Amon kept him waiting by the french windows while he himself sat in the parlour reading the documents. Pemper wondered if his own body would be displayed with declamatory lettering. *So Die All Jewish Bolshevists!*

At last Amon appeared at the windows. "You may go to bed," he said.

"Herr Commandant?"

"I said, you may go to bed."

Pemper went. He walked less steadily now. After what he had seen, Amon could not let him live. But perhaps the commandant believed there would be leisure to kill him later. In the meantime, life for a day was still life.

The space, as it proved, was for a prisoner who had let it be known he had a cache of diamonds somewhere outside the camp. While Pemper sank into the sleep of the reprieved, Amon had the man summoned to the villa, offered him his life for the diamonds' location, was shown the place and, of course, executed him and added his name to the reports.

from *Schindler's Ark* **by Thomas Keneally**

For discussion

1 Why is Pemper so amazed by Amon's letter to his father?
2 What different things do you learn from this extract about Amon's character?
3 What has happened that might still lead to Pemper's execution?
4 Discuss any difficult vocabulary. Work out what the words probably mean from the way they are used. Then check their meaning in a dictionary.
5 What might happen next?

War Criminals (2)

Rudolf Hoss was the commandant of the concentration and extermination camp at Auschwitz. This is part of his own account of his childhood and youth.

I had been brought up by my parents to be respectful and obedient towards all grown-up people, and especially the elderly, regardless of their social status. I was taught that my highest duty was to help those in need. It was constantly impressed upon me in forceful terms that I must obey promptly the wishes and commands of my parents, teachers, priests, etc., and indeed of all grown-up people, including servants, and that nothing must distract me from this duty. Whatever they said was always right.

These basic principles on which I was brought up became part of my flesh and blood. I can still clearly remember how my father, who, on account of his fervent Catholicism, was a determined opponent of Hitler's Government and its policy, never ceased to remind his friends that, however strong one's opposition might be, the laws and decrees of the State had to be obeyed unconditionally.

From my earliest youth I was brought up with a strong awareness of duty. In my parents' house it was insisted that every task be exactly and conscientiously carried out. Each member of the family had his own special duties to perform.

And of his role as mass murderer for the Nazis:

I had nothing to say. I could only say Jawohl! We could only execute orders without thinking about it. From our entire training the thought of refusing an order just didn't enter one's head, regardless of what kind of order it was.

I am completely normal. Even while I was carrying out the task of extermination I led a normal family life and so on. Let the public continue to regard me as the bloodthirsty beast, the cruel sadist and the mass murderer; for the masses could never imagine the commandant of Auschwitz in any other light. They could never understand that he, too, had a heart and that he was not evil.

from *The Face of the Third Reich* **by Joachim Fest**

For discussion

1. What reason does Hoss give for his actions in the War?
2. We quite often mean different things when we use the word *normal*. What does Hoss mean when he says, 'I am completely normal'?
3. In 1947 Hoss was tried before the Polish Supreme People's Court for his crimes in the War. He was found guilty and executed at Auschwitz. Is there anything in his statements quoted here that you would have accepted as a good defence?
4. Think of any situation where you consider somebody to have done something very wrong (for example, a murder, a robbery, an act of treason). Discuss it with the class. Then, in role-play, speak as if you are that person and in his or her defence, while the rest of the class interview you.

Herman Goering (on the left in the front row of chief defendants) listening to the summary at the Nuremberg trials, 1946

Four Poems

Home

The people have got used to her
they have watched her children grow
and behave as if she were
one of them – how can they know
that every time she leaves her home
she is terrified of them
that as a German Jew she sees
them as potential enemies

Because she knows what has been done
to children who were like her own
she cannot think their future safe
her parents must have felt at home
where none cared what became of them
and as a child she must have played
with people who in later life
would have killed her had she stayed

Karen Gershon

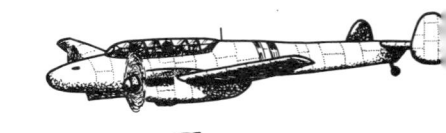

Song of the Bomber

I am purely evil;
Hear the thrum
Of my evil engine;
Evilly I come.

The stars are thick as flowers
In the meadows of July;
A fine night for murder
Winging through the sky.

Bombs shall be the bounty
Of the lovely night;
Death the desecration
Of the fields of light.

I am purely evil,
Come to destroy
Beauty and goodness,
Tenderness and joy.

Ethel Mannin

Lament

We knelt on the rocks by the dark green pools
The sailor boy and I,
And we dabbled our hands in the weed-veined water
Under a primrose sky.
And we laughed together to hide the sorrow
Of words we left unsaid;
Then he went back to his dirty minesweeper
And I to a lonely bed.
O the anguish of tears unshed.

And never again on this earth shall we meet,
The sailor boy and I,
And never again shall I see his face
Framed in a primrose sky,
For the sea has taken his laughter and loving
And buried him dark and deep
And another lad sleeps on the dirty minesweeper
A sleep that I cannot sleep.
O that I could forget and weep.

Frances Mayo

War Widow

I have grown old and dull, and out of date.
The children – but they are not children now –
They have run on so fast that I am tired,
Left, like a runner who could not stay the course,
Lagging behind.

They don't remember you: they think they do.
They were too young to know you never shared
Their baby world: that your keen, questing mind
Had other fields to travel.

You are not old and dull and out of date!
You are the spare young soldier who looks down
From the tall picture, painted that last leave
They look at you, and shrug, and their eyes say:
'He would have understood!'

I wonder... would you?

Had we grown old together,
I might have slid more gently into age;
You would have altered: touched by autumn's frost
To a more sober russet. As it is, you live
In the shrill green of youth, forever young,
As I last saw you – fifteen years today –
When you went back... to that:
And spring-time fled away.

Margaret Hamilton Noël-Paton

For discussion

1   What do you think is the main mood of each poem?
2   Is there a contrast in the moods of any, or all, of the poems?
    Re-read the poems to each other.
3   What do you think is the main idea, or thought, of each of the poems?

Advertising in War-time

WOMEN OF BRITAIN
COME INTO THE FACTORIES
ASK AT ANY EMPLOYMENT EXCHANGE FOR ADVICE AND FULL DETAILS

For discussion

1 Who has issued each of the advertisements?
2 All advertisements try to persuade people to do something. What different things are these persuading people to do?
3 Which of the advertisements actually *says* less?
4 Many advertisements make a direct appeal to our emotions. What emotions do these advertisements appeal to?
5 Which of these do you find the more effective advertisement?

The End

Nella Last kept a diary throughout the War. This is the last entry.

Tuesday, 14 August, 1945

I set the table with a bowl of marigolds I'd picked in the early morning, and with the windows flung wide to allow any little breeze to blow across it. We had cheese and tomatoes, apples in jelly and custard, wholemeal bread and butter, plum jam and cake. We listened eagerly to the six o'clock news – still nothing tangible. I thought of a remark I'd heard: 'Perhaps Japan, too, has a mystery bomb and is playing for time.' We went down to the Library, and then to sit by the seat at Walney. Lads were gathering anything burnable off the seashore, and dragging it off in little carts, presumably to bonfire heaps. I wished again we had a wireless in the car, and could hear any news that might come through, but we came home before nine o'clock, as a thick sea-mist rolled in, and we heard thunder over the sea. When there was nothing on the nine o'clock news, I said that I was going to bed, as my back ached badly.

Today, a shop had fireworks for sale, and hundreds of excited children, some with parents or older people, queued up in the longest queue I've ever seen except at a railway station. By the sounds everywhere, they cannot wait to hear definite news; they are frapping and popping all round. Little boys had been round begging for any salvage or dry stuff off garden piles; and on every bit of waste-land there seems to be a pile of light rubbish, ready for a bonfire.

1.00 a.m.

I woke with a start from my half-awakeness, slightly alarmed at the shouting and noise of ships' sirens and church bells. Then I realised the longed-for news of peace had come through on the last news. I got out of bed and looked through the window. Cars were rushing down Abbey Road into the town. My neighbour, Mrs. Helm, who is very excitable, was half-screaming 'God Save the King', seemingly knowing all the verses or singing what she did know over and over again. I remembered her words that she had a bottle of champagne and one of gin, and intended opening them both and drinking a tumbler full of each! My husband woke and came in. He said, 'Sounds as if it's all over.' Chidren's voices came from open bedroom windows; everywhere was chatter and noise, the sound of opening doors and people telling each other they had been in bed and asleep. I went into the back room and looked out over the town. I could see by the glow that bonfires had been lit. Rockets and searchlights went up from all the ships in the dock, and there were sounds of feet hurrying as if to go and see all that there was to be seen. Mrs. Helm sounded as if she had done as she intended, and her daughter and son-in-law rushed up in their car. Both seemed to be 'well lit up': they are the type who howl and shriek if they are happy – or sad. They all sounded as if they were letting themselves go.

My husband has gone back to bed, wishing there was not so much noise. I don't feel like getting dressed and going out myself, either. Even the dogs are barking crazily, as if the fireworks and noise have excited them. The ship's hooters seem to have been turned on and forgotten, and now the sound of fireworks is coming out of little back gardens, and there are shrill childish voices and shrieks from older girls, as if fire crackers are being tossed round.

I feel disappointed in my feelings. I feel no wild whoopee, just a quiet thankfulness and a feeling of 'flatness'. Dear God knows what I'd imagined it would be like. I think I'll take two aspirins and try and read myself to sleep.

from *Nella Last's War*

For discussion

1 What kind of person does the husband seem to have been?
2 Is there a contrast of moods in Nella Last's experiences as the War ends?
3 Is there a contrast in the earlier account by Rose Gamble of the outbreak of the War? (p. 135)
4 What kind of person does Nella's neighbour, Mrs Helm, seem to have been?
5 What differences are there in the ways Nella Last and Rose Gamble have written their accounts?

Punctuation: the dash

6 Nella Last twice uses a dash. The first is in the first paragraph. The second is near the end of the third paragraph. What seems to be the function or purpose of the dash in these two instances?
When you have discussed this, look also at the way Rose Gamble uses the dash in her final sentence.

Punctuation: two dashes

7 Rose Gamble uses two dashes in the penultimate sentence of her second paragraph. What seems to be their function?

Review of all the material in this Unit

To answer these questions, you will need to re-read all the materials in this Unit and look at all the illustrations.

1. What did Rose Gamble want to do in the War? And what job did she actually do?
2. Why, according to Raynes Minns, did some people come to approve of the spivs?
3. Why did Hitler sue Hanisch?
4. How did the authorities deal with the complaints that there was too much 'merrymaking' in the bar and the promenade at the Empire Music Hall?
5. The Commandant left a space at the bottom of the list of names for execution. For whose name did he leave this space?
6. What evidence does Hoss use to show that he is normal?
7. Which if any poems are written in the first person?
8. At whom are the different advertisements aimed?
9. Why does Nella Last end her account by saying she is disappointed?

According to the evidence given in the materials in this Unit, which of these statements are true? Write *true* or *false*, and refer to the evidence on which you base your answer.

10. Jewish refugees were coming to Britain just before the War.
11. Women were expected to do many essential jobs in the War, such as working in factories and on the land.
12. The Government could imprison anyone suspected of being dangerous, whether or not there was any proof.
13. Most people took part in the Black Market.
14. Hitler was fascinated by the cinema, just as Churchill was fascinated by the music hall.
15. The British Government wanted people to feel guilty when they spent money during the war.
16. Everyone was very excited when the war ended.
17. In the county of Kent, the only air raid shelters were open trenches.

Punctuation

18. Explain why the *dash* is used in the last sentence of the extract from Rose Gamble.
19. Explain why the *hyphen* is used in the same sentence.
20. Find and write out a sentence in *Under the Counter* where a dash is used in a similar way to the one you noted in question 18.
21. Explain all the different marks of punctuation in the first sentence of the second paragraph of *Under the Counter*.

Figures of Speech

22. Rose Gamble writes that news headlines caused people 'stabs of anxiety' (fourth paragraph). What figure of speech is this, and what does it mean?
23. In *Under the Counter*, the magazine *War Illustrated* is quoted as talking of 'the small fry'. What figure of speech is this, and what does it mean?
24. Find an example of *personification* in any of the advertisements, and explain what it means.
25. Find an example of a *simile* in any of the materials in this Unit.

Prefixes

Various prefixes are used to mean *not* (as in *incredible*, meaning *not credible*). Rewrite each of these words with the appropriate prefix so that they mean *not* legal, *not* perfect, and so on.

26. legal
27. conditionally
28. perfect
29. regular
30. eligible

For group work

Research

Choose a topic on which you can do research. Preferably choose one where you can talk to people of their own experiences as well as read accounts in books and magazines. Possibilities might include:

- memories of war
- experiences of immigration
- starting work
- unemployment
- holidays abroad
- fifty years ago

If possible, invite one or two people to come to be interviewed by the whole class.

Later, prepare a written report on your topic, perhaps including different kinds of writing in the report, such as first person narrative, extracts from letters, statistical data, report of a discussion, poetry and newspaper stories.

10 FIVE POEMS

A class of students began their study of a set of poems by talking about poetry in a general way. They were asked to talk about three topics:
> what they think poetry is;
> their memories of actual poems;
> what they think makes a good poem.

Here is a transcript of their discussion.

What is Poetry?

Michael It's like a short story or paragraph that may be in rhythm or rhyme, which is about something you feel strongly about, and that you feel you want to write down.

Sarah It's an expression of feeling.

Brenda It's something so short that it catches your imagination.

Jane There are different categories of poems, for example funny poems – and these usually have strong rhythms.

Sukhvir They're a description of something or someone and how you feel about them.

Brenda Many poems are about people who are left anonymous, they're not named.

Michael It's a way of people realising your inner feelings, or it may just be to entertain someone.

Jatinder It's like a story but with no specific introduction, but it ends like a story would end.

Robert Like a short story, but not directed at any particular reader.

Hasmukh The way a writer tries to put you in a particular mood.

Jane Poets are usually biassed.

Robert Do poems have to have a particular rhythm or rhyme?

Andrew Biassed? Why?

Jane Exploring one side only.

Hasmukh Do poems have to be in verses?

Mike Do poems have to make sense to anyone else but the writer?

Brenda Is there such a thing as an ideal poem?

Robert Does there have to be a certain length?

Sukhvir Does it have to have more than one meaning?

Michael Does it have to have meaning?

Memories of Specific Poems

Julie I can always remember a poem from my junior school days by Spike Milligan. 'On the ning nang nong' – why? Just unusual.

Michael I remember in a general way various limericks. 'There was an old lady...'

Brenda	I remember a poem about a girl getting depressed.
Ian	I remember having to learn off 'The Inch Cape Rock' – seventeen rocks!
Dyan	I remember a poem about gypsy life and ancestors.
Andrew	I remember *Responsibility* – a poem about war and bomb raids.
Michael	I remember *Dulce et Decorum Est* – a good poem with good imagery.
Sukhvir	I remember a poem on a birthday card. I think it went:

> 'You can make others happy
> By showing you care,
> By the warmth of your nature,
> So willing to share.
> You can make others happy,
> And each time you do,
> Some of that feeling
> Will rub off on you!'

Robert	I remember a couple of rugby songs on a cassette when I was about seven.
Brenda	Are they poems though?
Robert	Yes, sort of like a poem. They had a flow. One was called *The Mayor of Bayswater*, and the other, *Dinah, show us a leg*.
Andrew	I remember a poem made into a song, *My four-legged friend*, sung by Billy Connolly.
Jatinder	I remember a poem of a picture of girls doing homework:

> 'First I meant to write to mum
> Then I changed and did a sum
> You couldn't read it, I suppose,
> But mumma could –
> She always knows.'

Brenda	A poem engraved on a plaque on the wall:

> 'God chose our relatives:
> Thank God we can choose our friends!'

Steven	Poem called *If* – goes: if you can do this and you can do that, ending up, 'You'll be a man, my son!'

What makes a Good Poem?

Daniel	When it doesn't bore you.
Ian	That it makes your imagination flow.
Robert	All depends on you, the reader.
Jane	I like short funny ones, or nonsense.
Sukhvir	I like poems with good imagery.
Brenda	I like a poem that makes you read it again.
Michael	The shorter the better.
Jatinder	One that leaves you thinking about it.
Steve	One with a strong rhythm.

Andrew	Short rhythmic verses.
Michael	One that, like Jatinder, you remember many years after you've read it.
Brenda	The actual printing and decorating of it.
Andrew	The title of the poem.
Hasmukh	The description.
Michael	The topic.
John	The writer himself. A certain poet may make the poem interesting.
Ian	The characters in the poem.
Robert	The particular kind of poem, such as romance.
Michael	The language, such as the use of old English.
Sukhvir	A surprise ending.
Anne-Marie	One that you can compare with your own experiences.

For discussion

What is poetry?

1 Are there any answers that you would strongly agree or disagree with?

2 The students finish their discussion with a series of questions. How would you answer their questions?

Memories of specific poems

3 Are there any poems that you remember especially well?

What makes a good poem?

4 Are there any answers you would especially agree or disagree with?

5 Overall, what do you think makes a good poem?

What makes a poem interesting?

In effect, in their discussion the class suggest various aspects of a poem that can make it interesting to a reader or listener:

- the subject-matter of the poem – what it is about;
- the language of the poem, including its imagery;
- the form of the poem, including its rhythm and rhyme;
- the mood or feeling of the poem;
- the theme, or overall idea or meaning of the poem.

Each of these five points will be looked at more closely in relation to the set of poems that follow.

This is an extract from a long narrative poem. Two friends have an argument and decide to resolve it by fighting.

The Everlasting Mercy

From the beginning of the bout
My luck was gone, my hand was out.
Right from the start Bill called the play,
But I was quick and kept away
Till the fourth round, when work got mixed,
And then I knew Bill had me fixed.
My hand was out, why, Heaven knows;
Bill punched me when and where he chose.
Through two more rounds we quartered wide
And all the time my hands seemed tied;
Bill punched me when and where he pleased.
The cheering from my backers ceased,
But every punch I heard a yell
Of 'That's the style, Bill, give him hell.'
No one for me, but Jimmy's light
'Straight left! Straight left!' and 'Watch
　his right.'
I don't know how a boxer goes
When all his body hums from blows;

I know I seemed to rock and spin,
I don't know how I saved my chin;
I know I thought my only friend
Was that clinked flask at each round's end
When my two seconds, Ed and Jimmy,
Had sixty seconds help to gimme.
But in the ninth, with pain and knocks
I stopped: I couldn't fight not box.
Bill missed his swing, the light was tricky,
But I went down, and stayed down, dicky.
'Get up,' cried Jim. I said, 'I will.'
Then all the gang yelled, 'Out him, Bill
Out him.' Bill rushed... and Clink, Clink, Clink.
Time! and Jim's knee, and rum to drink.
And round the ring there ran a titter:
'Saved by the call, the bloody quitter.'
They drove (a dodge that never fails)
A pin beneath my finger nails.
They poured what seemed a running beck
Of cold spring water down my neck;
Jim with a lancet quick as flies
Lowered the swellings round my eyes.
They sluiced my legs and fanned my face
Through all that blessed minute's grace;
They gave my calves a thorough kneading,
They salved my cuts and stopped the bleeding.
A gulp of liquor dulled the pain,
And then the two flasks clinked again.
Time!
    There was Bill as grim as death.

from The Everlasting Mercy **by John Masefield**

For discussion

1. **What is going to happen next?**
2. **What is the mood or feeling of the poem?**
3. **Whose side, if any one's, does the poet want you to be on?**
4. **What is the importance of the rhythm in this poem?**

The Song of the Shirt

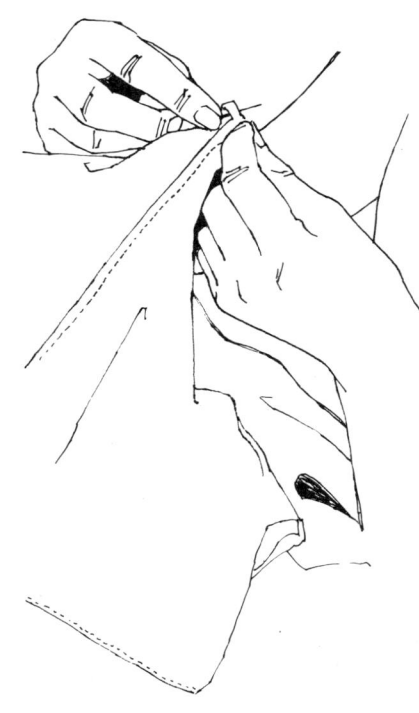

With fingers weary and worn,
   With eyelids heavy and red,
A woman sat, in unwomanly rags,
   Plying her needle and thread –
     Stitch! stitch! stitch!
In poverty, hunger and dirt,
   And still with a voice of dolorous pitch
She sang the 'Song of the Shirt'!

   'Work – work – work
Till the brain begins to swim;
   Work – work – work
Till the eyes are heavy and dim!
Seam, and gusset, and band,
   Band, and gusset, and seam,
Till over the buttons I fall asleep,
   And sew them on in a dream!

'O! men, with sisters dear!
   O! men! with mothers and wives!
It is not linen you're wearing out,
   But human creatures' lives!
     Stitch – stitch – stitch,
In poverty, hunger, and dirt,
Sewing at once, with a double thread,
   A shroud as well as a shirt.

'But why do I talk of death?
   That phantom of grisly bone,
I hardly fear his terrible shape,
   It seems so like my own –
   It seems so like my own,
   Because of the fasts I keep,
Oh! God! that bread should be so dear,
And flesh and blood so cheap!

   'Work – work – work!
My labour never flags;
And what are its wages? A bed of straw,
   A crust of bread – and rags.
That shattered roof – and this naked floor –
   A table – a broken chair –
And a wall so blank, my shadow I thank
   For sometimes falling there!

   'Work – work – work!
From weary chime to chime,
   Work – work – work –
As prisoners work for crime!
   Band, and gusset, and seam,
   Seam, and gusset, and band,
Till the heart is sick, and the brain benumbed,
   As well as the weary hand.

'Work – work – work,
 In the dull December light,
   And work – work – work,
 When the weather is warm and bright –
 While underneath the eaves
   The brooding swallows cling
 As if to show me their sunny backs
   And twit me with the Spring.

   'Oh! but to breathe the breath
 Of the cowslip and primrose sweet –
   With the sky above my head,
 And the grass beneath my feet,
 For only one short hour
   To feel as I used to feel,
 Before I knew the woes of want
   And the walk that costs a meal!

 'Oh but for one short hour!
   A respite however brief!
 No blessed leisure for love or hope,
   But only time for grief!
 A little weeping would ease my heart,
   But in their briny bed
 My tears must stop, for every drop
   Hinders needle and thread!'

 With fingers weary and worn,
   With eyelids heavy and red,
 A woman sat in unwomanly rags,
   Plying her needle and thread –
     Stitch! stitch! stitch!
   In poverty, hunger, and dirt,
 And still with a voice of dolorous pitch,
 Would that its tone could reach the rich!
   She sang this 'Song of the Shirt'!

from *The Song of the Shirt*
by Thomas Hood

For discussion

1   What is the importance of the rhythm to this poem?
2   What is the importance of repetition in this poem? What different parts of the poem are repeated?
3   What do you see as the moods of the poem?

Platform Goodbye

My hand waving from the window
Felt still the touch of your fingers:
Sorrow that made me dumb
Becomes pride in your love: and now,
As you turn the key in the door,
Or enter the room where our lives
Are still touched by the cushions and cards,
The tea gone cold in the cups,
My train takes me as though through sleep
To an empty room and the night.

I cannot delude my sense. The cards
Through my fingers slip. Loneliness
Brings you near, a tear's reach from my hand:
But from the flower at your neck
The colours already fade.

It is not these tangible things
That give me strength to endure,
But the echo still of your voice
In the deep abyss of my heart:
The way you stare through my eyes,
The intimate touch of your hand
On this pencil with which I write;

The years we have shared will give
To the hive of our senses both,
Honey to sharpen the taste
Of the years while our bodies lie
Lonely and separately.

The hammering in my heart
Forges from sorrow pride
As the train draws us apart.
Though the hurt under the flesh
Spreads like the numbness of snow,
My love is in all you do,
Yours with me wherever I go.

H. B. Mallalieu

For discussion

1. The poem expresses a mood of sorrow. Is there any other contrasting mood it also expresses?
2. What is the most moving picture or image that the poem creates?
3. What do you see as the main theme or idea of the poem?

The Companion

She was sitting on the rough embankment,
her cape too big for her tied on slapdash
over an odd little hat with a bobble on it,
her eyes brimming with tears of hopelessness.
An occasional butterfly floated down
fluttering warm wings onto the rails.
The clinkers underfoot were deep lilac.
We got cut off from our grandmothers
while the Germans were dive-bombing the train.
Katya was her name. She was nine.
I'd no idea what I could do about her,
but doubt quickly dissolved to certainty:
I'd have to take this thing under my wing;
– girls were in some sense of the word human,
a human being couldn't just be left.
The droning in the air and the explosions
receded farther into the distance,
I touched the little girl on her elbow.
'Come on. Do you hear? What are you waiting for?'
The world was big and we were not big,
and it was tough for us to walk across it.
She had galoshes on and felt boots,
I had a pair of second-hand boots.
We forded streams and tramped across the forest;
each of my feet at every step it took
taking a smaller step inside the boot.
The child was feeble, I was certain of it.
'Boo-hoo,' she'd say. 'I'm tired,' she'd say.
She'd tire in no time I was certain of it,
but as things turned out it was me who tired.
I growled I wasn't going any further
and sat down suddenly beside the fence.
'What's the matter with you?' she said.
'Don't be so stupid! Put grass in your boots.
Do you want to eat something? Why won't you talk?
Hold this tin, this is crab.
We'll have refreshments. You small boys,
you're always pretending to be brave.'
Then out I went across the prickly stubble
marching beside her in a few minutes.
Masculine pride was muttering in my mind:
I scraped together strength and I held out
for fear of what she'd say. I even whistled.
Grass was sticking out from my tattered boots.
So on and on
we walked without thinking of rest
passing craters, passing fire,
under the rocking sky of '41
tottering crazy on its smoking columns.

Yevgeny Yevtushenko

For discussion

A group of students discussing this poem commented:
1 'It's like a small story.'
2 'The poet has a vivid imagination.'
3 'I picture a big flat waste land with craters around and these two in a vast expanse of land by themselves.'

Would you agree with any of these comments?

The Responsibility

I am the man who gives the word,
If it should come, to use the Bomb.

I am the man who spreads the word
From him to them if it should come.

I am the man who gets the word
From him who spreads the word from him.

I am the man who drops the Bomb
If ordered by the one who's heard
From him who merely spreads the word
The first one gives if it should come.

I am the man who loads the Bomb
That he must drop should orders come
From him who gets the word passed on
By one who waits to hear from *him*.

I am the man who makes the Bomb
That he must load for him to drop
If told by one who gets the word
From one who passes it from *him*.

I am the man who fills the till,
Who pays the tax, who foots the bill
That guarantees the Bomb he makes
For him to load for him to drop
If orders come from one who gets
The word passed on to him by one
Who waits to hear it from the man
Who gives the word to use the Bomb.

I am the man behind it all;
I am the one responsible.

Peter Appleton

For discussion

1 The poem is written in the first person ('I . . .'). How many different first persons are there in the poem?
2 What do you think is the main idea or theme of the poem?

Group Discussion

A group of four students, Pratish, Ravi, Samsur and Sanjay, talked about their interpretation of the poem *The Responsibility*. Here is part of their discussion.

Sanjay It's about the one who's got control of the bomb, isn't it. About a bloke who's a president or a prime minister. Who's got the power to control the bomb that's going to be used.

Ravi If you look at the one part here:
   I am the man that drops the bomb
   If ordered...

Samsur It portrays the way a person passes on responsibility.
   I am the man who gives the word
   If it should come...
In other words, it's passing the buck.

Ravi Then who do you think is talking?

Pratish Who's talking?

Ravi Is it the person who's going to drop the bomb talking? Is he trying to do whatever he's told to do? Has he got authority over the bomb?

Pratish What's the theme, right?

Sanjay I think it's all the people involved, right?

Pratish I reckon the underlying idea is to get through that we don't know who is responsible for the bomb.

Sanjay Yeah, putting everyone into it.

Pratish It could be just two people at a conference, saying – right we've got war.

Ravi It could be a sequence of events but then it's only one event, isn't it.

Samur It's one event, right. A sequence of small events leading up to it.

Pratish Then who do you reckon is responsible? Is it each person or all of them together, or what?

Sanjay Can't blame one person.

Pratish Is it the person who says, right, we're going to drop the bomb? Or is it all the people involved?

Sanjay I reckon it's all the people who make the bomb and buy the bomb. 'Cos that's what people buy a bomb for.

Pratish What about the people who make the bomb?

Samsur That's what I said. They're responsible as well.

Ravi I think you're getting off the topic of the bomb. We're not talking about nuclear bombs. We're just talking about this one poem.
[*after a pause*] If we talk about the theme? The theme literally is war. Some kind of war is about to take place.

Samsur The theme, right, the generalised theme is war. But the theme, what it is actually about, is the responsibility.

Sanjay	Looks at all the people who could be responsible. There is the person who makes it. Person who buys it.
Ravi	Person who pays the tax.
Sanjay	All these people. So you can't really blame one person.
Ravi	So what we're trying to say is the title really is the theme.
Pratish	Exactly.
Ravi	Responsibility. Who is responsible?
Samsur	The chain, all the people in order of superiority handling the bomb, literally handing the bomb down.
Pratish	To who?
Sanjay	The person who gives the word. He's the one to blame for starting it.
Ravi	I agree with Samsur. They all say what they do, until they get to the one responsible. Until they get on to the one responsible.
Pratish	Each person doesn't know what is going on. He just does his job.
Samsur	If I get into trouble, right, I could pass the blame to you.
Pratish	It's everybody's fault.
Samsur	So he's taking a look at aspects of society.
Ravi	Each person as the bomb passes down says, 'I'm not responsible.'
Pratish	What's the poem trying to symbolise then?
Sanjay	Life. People. You can't really blame them.
Ravi	The responsibility extends to everyone.
Samsur	Any questions then? – Like this poem: let's generalise a bit more. What aspects of life does it actually cover?
Pratish	What I'm trying to say is, are we saying that everyone is responsible? Or one person is responsible?
Samsur	I don't think it's one person.
Ravi	I think we're agreed that everyone is responsible.
Samsur	It goes round and round, like. A vicious circle. So this does portray – a society.
Samsur	Can I just bring you to just one point? Can you look at the last two to three lines, right? 'I am the one responsible?' Who do you think that is – 'I'?

For discussion

1 Is there any point made here that you would strongly agree with?
2 Is there any point you would disagree with?
3 What is your answer to Samsur's final question?
4 What are some of the good things about the ways these four speakers talk together?

Writing about Poetry

Here is part of a student's essay on one of the poems in this Unit:

This extract from John Masefield's *The Everlasting Mercy* tells a simple but dramatic story. Two friends have argued and are fighting. The story-teller is losing to his friend, Bill, and all the people around them are backing Bill and urging him on to victory:

'That's the style, Bill, give him hell.'

The story-teller is nearly dead with exhaustion but is briefly saved by the bell. His mates revive him by driving a pin beneath his nails, but then the break is over, the bell sounds again and the fight continues.

In a sense, everything about the poem is simple. The form itself is simple: the whole poem is written in rhyming couplets, which means that the first line rhymes with the second, the third rhymes with the fourth, and so on. Each line has a strong rhythm, with four stresses to the line, and this is repeated throughout the poem. The repetition of the rhythm seems to give an impression of the fight going on and on, and of the pain of the story-teller going on and on also.

The language is simple too. It is everyday language, the language that anybody might speak. But it builds up a powerful image or picture of the pain that the story teller experiences. The poet portrays the victim's body and the victim's feelings as the opponent bears down upon him:

'his body hums from blows . . .
. . . I seemed to rock and spin . . .
. . . I stopped: I couldn't fight nor box.'

But perhaps the most moving image of pain is created when,

'They drove . . .
A pin beneath my finger nails.'

And this is followed by the list of various remedies applied to him to restore him for the next round. Each of these reinforces the picture of the man's suffering – whether it be the swellings round his eyes or the attempts to heal the cuts and stop the bleeding.

The image of pain is so vivid that the reader experiences the pain of the fighter. The crowd's lack of sympathy for the loser makes this pain even worse. So a mood or feeling of suffering runs right through the poem. Perhaps this is made even more effective because the story is told in the first person. The poem might be less moving if it were told in the third person; for it might be harder then to feel for the man's pain and defeat.

The underlying idea or theme of the poem seems to be the foolishness of fighting, the foolishness of trying to settle a quarrel between friends by deciding to have a fight. Whatever the cause of their quarrel, nothing can justify the suffering that is inflicted. As this extract ends, the bell sounds and the two opponents return to face each other. The narrator has only just about revived from the licking that Bill has already given him, and now, once again,

'There was Bill as grim as death.'

Julie Wilson

For discussion

1. Is there anything in the essay that you would question or disagree with?
2. Suggest a heading for each paragraph.
3. Julie Wilson writes about various aspects of the form (or structure) of this poem. What different aspects of the form of *The Song of the Shirt* do you notice?
4. She writes about the way the poet builds up the image of pain and suffering. What do you feel is the key image of *The Companion*? (Or do you feel there is more than one 'key' image?) How is this imagery built up throughout the poem?
5. In many poems, there is a contrast between two different images running right through them.
   Is this the case with any of these five poems?
6. Similarly, in many poems there is a contrast between two different moods running right through them.
   Is this the case with any of these five poems?

For group discussion

Choose the two poems that you find the most interesting.

Make a list of two or three statements that you would make about them; about their subject-matter, language, imagery, form, mood or theme.

Turn your statements into questions.

Then, working in groups, discuss your various questions.

Keep notes of your discussion, so that later you can report back to the whole class.

Before your group discussion, briefly revise with the class the various rules or techniques that help to make a good discussion possible, and see how far you can keep to these.

Suggestions for writing

1. Choose a theme for yourself and write some poems of your own.

2. Write about your response to the poems which were discussed in your groups. Perhaps write about just one or two of them. Before you write, discuss with the class the ways in which you will plan or structure your essay.

3. Choose a piece of music or a painting (or any kind of picture) and write a poem to accompany it.

11 THE END OF THE STORY

Paris **by Jean Mohr**

One of the most important features of any story is its ending. As children, we read or hear stories in which all the good characters go on to live happily ever after. Later, our taste in stories changes, as does our sense of what constitutes a good or acceptable ending. We may, for example, like the way a story ends because:

- it shows very clearly what has happened and what is going to happen to all the main characters;
- it is a surprise;
- it can be interpreted in more than one way;
- it leaves questions unanswered; the readers or the audience are left wanting another instalment to tell them more;
- it is a mere formality; it tells us what we have known all along; the story could not possibly have ended in any other way.

For discussion

1 Which of these qualities do you (in general) like the end of a story to possess?
2 Suggest examples of stories, from films, plays or novels, whose endings have any of these qualities.

The four stories in this Unit illustrate different kinds of endings. Read them and discuss them first in groups, and then report back to the rest of the class.

I Spy

Charlie Stowe waited until he heard his mother snore before he got out of bed. Even then he moved with caution and tiptoed to the window. The front of the house was irregular, so that it was possible to see a light burning in his mother's room. But now all the windows were dark. A searchlight passed across the sky, lighting the banks of cloud and probing the dark deep spaces between, seeking enemy airships. The wind blew from the sea, and Charlie Stowe could hear behind his mother's snores the beating of the waves. A draught through the cracks in the window-frame stirred his nightshirt. Charlie Stowe was frightened.

But the thought of the tobacconist's shop which his father kept down a dozen wooden stairs drew him on. He was twelve years old, and already boys at the County School mocked him because he had never smoked a cigarette. The packets were piled twelve deep below, Gold Flake and Players, De Reszke, Abdulla, Woodbines, and the little shop lay under a thin haze of stale smoke which would completely disguise his crime. That it was a crime to steal some of his father's stock Charlie Stowe had no doubt, but he did not love his father; his father was unreal to him, a wraith, pale, thin, indefinite, who noticed him only spasmodically and left even punishment to his mother. For his mother he felt a passionate demonstrative love; her large boisterous presence and her noisy charity filled the world for him; from her speech he judged her the friend of everyone, from the rector's wife to the "dear Queen", except the "Huns", the monsters who lurked in Zeppelins in the clouds. But his father's affection and dislike were as indefinite as his movements. Tonight he had said he would be in Norwich, and yet you never knew. Charlie Stowe had no sense of safety as he crept down the wooden stairs. When they creaked he clenched his fingers on the collar of his nightshirt.

At the bottom of the stairs he came out quite suddenly into the little shop. It was too dark to see his way, and he did not dare touch the switch. For half a minute he sat in despair on the bottom step with his chin cupped in his hands. Then the regular movement of the searchlight was reflected through an upper window and the boy had time to fix in memory the pile of cigarettes, the counter, and the small hole under it. The footsteps of a policeman on the pavement made him grab the first packet to his hand and dive for the hole. A light shone along the floor and a hand tried the door, then the footsteps passed on, and Charlie cowered in the darkness.

At last he got his courage back by telling himself in his curiously adult way that if he were caught now there was nothing to be done about it, and he might as well have his smoke. He put a cigarette in his mouth and then remembered that he had no matches. For a while he dared not move. Three times the searchlight lit the shop, while he muttered taunts and encouragements. "May as well be hung for a sheep," "Cowardy, cowardy custard," grown-up and childish exhortations oddly mixed.

But as he moved he heard footfalls in the street, the sound of several men walking rapidly. Charlie Stowe was old enough to feel surprise that anybody was about. The footsteps came nearer, stopped; a key turned in the shop door, a voice said: "Let him in," and then he heard his father. "If you wouldn't mind being quiet, gentlemen. I don't want to wake up the family." There was a note unfamiliar to Charlie in the undecided voice. A torch flashed and the electric globe burst into blue light. The boy held his breath; he wondered whether his father would hear his heart beating, and he clutched his nightshirt tightly and prayed, "O God, don't let me be caught." Through a crack in the counter he could see his father where he stood, one hand held to his high, stiff collar, between two men in bowler hats and belted mackintoshes. They were strangers.

"Have a cigarette," his father said in a voice dry as a biscuit. One of the men shook his head. "It wouldn't do, not when we are on duty. Thank you all the same." He spoke gently, but without kindness: Charlie Stowe thought his father must be ill.

"Mind if I put a few in my pocket?" Mr Stowe asked, and when the man nodded he lifted a pile of Gold Flake and Players from a shelf and caressed the packets with the tips of his fingers.

"Well," he said, "there's nothing to be done about it, and I may as well have my smokes." For a moment Charlie Stowe feared discovery, his father stared round the shop so thoroughly; he might have been seeing it for the first time. "It's a good little business," he said, "for those that like it. The wife will sell out, I suppose. Else the neighbours'll be wrecking it. Well, you want to be off. A stitch in time. I'll get my coat."

"One of us'll come with you, if you don't mind," said the stranger gently.

"You needn't trouble. It's on the peg here. There, I'm all ready."

The other man said in an embarassed way, "Don't you want to speak to your wife?" The thin voice was decided: "Not me. Never do today what you can put off till tomorrow. She'll have her chance later, won't she?"

"Yes, yes," one of the strangers said and he became very cheerful and encouraging. "Don't you worry too much. While there's life . . ." and suddenly his father tried to laugh.

When the door had closed Charlie Stowe tiptoed upstairs and got into bed. He wondered why his father had left the house again so late at night and who the strangers were. Surprise and awe kept him for a little while awake. It was as if a familiar photograph had stepped from the frame to reproach him with neglect. He remembered how his father had held tight to his collar and fortified himself with proverbs, and he thought for the first time that, while his mother was boisterous and kindly, his father was very like himself, doing things in the dark which frightened him. It would have pleased him to go down to his father and tell him that he loved him, but he could hear through the window the quick steps going away. He was alone in the house with his mother, and he fell asleep.

from *The Collected Stories* **by Graham Greene**

For discussion

1. When and where does this story take place? How do you know?
2. In most stories, characters change as a result of what happens to them in the story. In what way, if at all, does Charlie change in this story?
3. What different things do you learn about Charlie's mother?
4. The writer does not make clear what is happening to Charlie's father. Why do you think he does not make it clear?
5. What do you think is happening to Charlie's father?

Vedi

This is an extract from Ved Mehta's autobiographical account of his early schooldays in an Indian orphanage for blind children.

In this part of his story, he writes about two other boys in his dormitory, *Ramesh* and *Jaisingh*.

Ramesh was two years older than I was, but he was smaller than I was. He spoke as if he had clusters of sweets inside his cheeks, and he dragged his feet and always walked in a crooked line. He seemed to be all bones and no skin. Whenever he went to bed, he cried, as if the wooden planks pained his body. I remember that once I told Mrs. Ras Mohun he should have a soft bed, like mine, and she said, "He's not a special student from a cultured home." Ramesh was slow in classes; everything had to be explained to him several times. He was also touchy; if anyone pulled his shirt, he got badly upset. But he didn't know how to fight back, so the boys were constantly going up to him and pulling his shirt.

Jaisingh sounded like a big boy and had fuzz on his cheeks, though he was only four years older than I was. He could neither hear nor see, and could speak very little. He had come to our school straight from the hospital, at the age of four, and for the next three years he was so sick that Mr. Ras Mohun let him stay in bed all the time and excused him from all the classes. Then Mr. Ras Mohun got an audit-tube, a sort of horn, and while Jaisingh touched Mr. Ras Mohun's throat Mr. Ras Mohun shouted through the tube into Jaisingh's ear. He found that Jaisingh could hear a little after all. After that, Mr. Ras Mohun came regularly to the boy's dormitory and gave Jaisingh a talking-class in his bed. Jaisingh slowly learned to follow a few commands and recognize a few objects. Mr. Ras Mohun used to call him the Dadar School's Helen Keller. We didn't know who Helen Keller was, but we imagined that she was an American Jaisingh. Jaisingh had to be helped everywhere. Two or three times a day, the Sighted Master took him out to the back courtyard, and Jaisingh showed great interest in going up the climbing bars and jumping down. As he hit the ground he would laugh uncontrollably. If we happened to be playing in the back courtyard, too, and one of us tried to take a turn at the climbing bars, Jaisingh would shriek.

Jaisingh couldn't even go to the bathroom by himself; in fact, he couldn't even say "small bathroom" or "big bathroom." When he was trying to be a good boy, he would make noises as if he wanted to go to the bathroom. He would grunt and bleat, and then the Sighted Master would run to him and take him to the boys' common bathroom. But sometimes in the night he would do his small bathroom and big bathroom in bed, and then, instead of being sorry about it, he would let out a howl. The howl was so loud that it would wake up the Sighted Master. The Sighted Master would run to him, and when he found out what Jaisingh had done he would beat him, with an old, discarded shoe of Mr. Ras Mohun's that the Sighted Master kept under his bed. "Why didn't you make your bathroom noises?" he would shout, forgetting that Jaisingh couldn't hear him. Often, Jaisingh had made those noises and the Sighted Master had slept through them, but Jaisingh would be beaten anyway. We never dared to tell the Sighted Master that Jaisingh had made the noises, no matter how much we wanted to, because if any of us talked back – or even cried – we would be beaten, too. So whenever we heard poor Jaisingh being beaten we would feel sad.

Ramesh and Jaisingh would cry in the middle of the night. The Sighted Master would shout from his bed "Stop it!" and Ramesh would generally stop, but Jaisingh would go on crying until the Sighted Master got up and took the shoe to him. Actually, we got so used to Jaisingh's crying, to his eerie moans and wails, that we were aware of the sounds only when they suddenly stopped.

One night, both Ramesh and Jaisingh began crying, and neither would stop. I heard the Sighted Master curse and get up. I waited for the scraping sound that I always heard when he was fumbling around for the shoe, but I didn't hear it. "The blind devils!" he muttered. "I would rather break stones, but there are no jobs to be had. The damned blind devils."

He stubbed his toe on the foot of my long bed and cursed some more.

I heard him walk slowly, in his bare feet, to Jaisingh's bed. "I will finish Ras Mohun's Helen Keller," he said.

Two beds over from Jaisingh's, Bhaskar was snoring slightly. On the other side of Bhaskar, Abdul was grinding his teeth.

I heard the Sighted Master struggling with a bed plank. The plank slipped off the iron frame and bounced on the floor like the end of a seesaw. I knew that it was a plank from either Ramesh's or Jaisingh's bed, but I couldn't tell which, because I wasn't sure exactly where the Sighted Master was. I heard the plank banging and reverberating on the floor and against the iron frame. All at once, Bhaskar stopped snoring and Abdul stopped grinding his teeth. I curled up at the bottom of my bed, trying to make myself as small as I could, and breathed as silently as I could. I repeated to myself, "Heavenly Father, Thou wilt hear me." Then Ramesh stopped crying. I thought that Jaisingh would also decide to be a good boy, and that the Sighted Master would go back to his bed. But Jaisingh continued crying.

Then I heard a swishing noise that reminded me of Sher Singh raising an axe to chop a piece of wood. After that, I heard a sound that was hard to remember later. It could have been like the swatting of a fly or the slam of a screen door or the beating of a coat with a coat brush. But it was very penetrating. Jaisingh's crying abruptly stopped, and everything became completely still. Then there was the clatter of the plank being replaced on the iron frame.

The Sighted Master started walking back toward his bed. I thought he paused a second at the foot of my bed, but then I heard him hurrying on and fumbling to get back into his own bed.

I stayed awake for a long time, waiting to hear a sound from Jaisingh. Finally, I thought I heard him begin to moan in a sustained manner, like the motor of an old car that won't start. I immediately fell asleep.

The next day, when I came back from having breakfast with Mr. and Mrs. Ras Mohun the boys were whispering about Ramesh and Jaisingh.

"Their beds are empty," Abdul said. "They're gone."

I went over and felt all around Ramesh's and Jaisingh's beds. The thin sheets that had covered them had been removed, but all the planks were intact – they felt dry, like kindling wood.

"He killed them last night," Abdul said. "Both of them. The Sighted Master did, with two blows of a plank."

"There was only one blow," Reuben said.

"I heard Jaisingh cry afterward," I said.

"No, you didn't," Abdul said. "You were dreaming. The Sighted Master took a plank off the bed and cracked first one head and then the other. I heard it with my own ears."

"No, he didn't kill Ramesh," Bhaskar said. "I saw it with my good eye. He killed Jaisingh."

"No, I think Jaisingh has gone off to a new, deaf-and-dumb school," Tarak Nath said.

"Good riddance to bad rubbish," Abdul said.

"They didn't die," Reuben said. "I think they have been taken to the hospital for throat operations."

We were confused about precisely what had happened that night and some of us waited for Ramesh or Jaisingh – or both – to come back. But neither of them came back, and in due course their beds were given to two new boys.

I wanted to ask Mr. Ras Mohun what had happened to Ramesh and Jaisingh, but I was afraid of the Sighted Master

from *Vedi* by Ved Mehta

For discussion

1 This is an extract from an autobiography. Could it be an extract from a novel? (Is there anything in the way it is written that shows it could *not* be?)

2 What seem to be the differences between Vedi and the other boys in the dormitory?

3 Ved Mahta never learns any more about the fates of Ramesh and Jaisingh. What do you think happened to them? On what evidence do you base your ideas?

4 In what ways do Vedi and his friends seem to be like any other chidren?

At sea off the Falklands, 1982: a survivor from HMS Sheffield *being carried to the sick bay of* HMS Hermes.

Falklands victims the army tried to forget

Seumas Milne meets an officer who was shot in the head in the South Atlantic. He says the sniper who hit him was doing his job but believes the military establishment and Civil Service have not done theirs. He was kept out of the way at the St Paul's service of remembrance, had to pay for a 'free' car and was told nothing about how to start a new life.

LIEUTENANT Robert Lawrence was a 21-year-old Scots Guards officer with five years' army service when he was sent to the Falklands on the QE2 in April 1982.

A few days before his 22nd birthday, and $1\frac{1}{2}$ hours before the Argentinian surrender, he was shot in the back of the head by a sniper during the assault on Tumbledown Mountain. For his part in that action, he was awarded the Military Cross.

The high-velocity bullet tore through his brain and shattered his skull. He was the only soldier, British or Argentinian, to survive such an injury. Now he is paralysed down the left side of his body, is occasionally incontinent and regularly gripped by searing pains from fused vertebrae in his neck. He has lost 45 per cent of his brain and part of his skull is now made of acrylic.

But Robert Lawrence feels little bitterness about his injury. "That's war. The guy who shot me was doing his job, and so was I.

"I could tell you stories about the cock-ups during the Falklands war that you would hardly believe. But I wouldn't want to. The public would get the wrong idea. They would blame the Government and it would have been the same with any government."

Less seriously injured men return to a welcome at Brize Norton, Oxfordshire.

He is, however, bitter about the way he and other war victims were treated once they were back in Britain. His prosperous public school background had not prepared him for the insensitivity and bureaucratic niggling that would greet the returning Falklands war heroes.

The first thing that angered him was the embarrassed secrecy surrounding the arrival in Britain of the most seriously injured survivors.

"A few days before I was flown into Brize Norton from Montevideo there had been a press reception for the guys with the slings and head bandages with blobs of tomato ketchup. When we came back, the press was kept away.

"They put a tent round the plane and drove the ambulances inside to pick us up, so that no one would see the burn disfigurements or the blokes with half a head. Then they cleaned us up as best they could and gave us 10 minutes with our families."

Similar efforts were made on later occasions to avoid spoiling a good show with unpleasant spectacles. "The worst casualties were kept out of the St Paul's remembrance service.

"We had to turn up out of uniform more than an hour early and leave from the back after everyone else had gone. We weren't even invited to the victory parade. But people should be shown what war really means."

Other indignities were to dog his slow and partial recovery. He was confined for three weeks in a ward with 15 mentally disturbed patients in the Maudsley Hospital while recovering from neurosurgery.

Weeks later, he managed to drag himself away from Woolwich army hospital and took a taxi to his old haunts in Chelsea, where he was eventually found by police, still carrying his drip-feed.

When Lt Lawrence arrived at the army rehabilitation centre at Headley Court, no-one knew anything about him. "They didn't seem to know whether I could speak or move. The army just couldn't cope with us. They're used to dealing with accidents on the sports field and guys in their fifties with heart problems."

It was a difficult period in other ways. He split up with his girlfriend. "She couldn't handle it." And after leaving the centre he was mugged and kicked repeatedly in the head in Guildford. The boot of his assailant, whom he suspects was a soldier, missed the exposed part of his brain.

Even while still too ill to move, Lt Lawrence was buoyed up by the idea that, although he would never be able to walk properly again, he might at least be able to drive. He asked the army to help him take a disabled driving test.

"They knew nothing about it. They didn't want to know. Eventually my mother found out the details and drove me to the Queen Elizabeth mobility centre, Banstead. The trials cost me £60, but I passed."

The Swansea Licensing Centre, nevertheless, refused to issue him with a licence. "They told me there was no way I'd be allowed to drive if I'd had a bullet in my head."

His parents helped him to secure an interview with the junior transport minister Mrs Lynda Chalker. "She told me she would authorise the licence if three Harley Street specialists said I was fit enough. The first two said no, the third yes. Then I went back to the first two and they changed their minds."

The battle to be allowed to drive seemed worthwhile when the Scots Guards told Lt Lawrence that, along with a group of other Falklands casualties, he was to be given a free car as a mark of the nation's gratitude and to help him move around more easily.

The regiment said it would have to be a British car and arranged for them to try some models at a BL dealer in Barnes, south-west London.

Members of the armed forces parade down Moorgate, London, in 1982.

The four veterans were invited to a celebration to mark the launch of the Maestro in March 1983, at which the actor Derek Nimmo presented them with symbolic keys to their new cars for the benefit of the press. Lawrence's car was a Rover 2300.

A few weeks later he was sent a bill. Most of the cost of the converted car (£10,500 minus BL's 17 per cent disability discount) was deducted from advances on his South Atlantic Fund settlement, to which no strings were supposed to be attached. In disgust, he traded the BL car for one of his choice.

A Ministry of Defence spokesman said he was surprised Lt Lawrence was bringing up the matter after all this time.

Lt Lawrence's fund settlement was relatively generous but using cash from the £15 million fund for free telephone calls home for garrison troops on the island rankles with him.

Since November, he has received a war disablement pension of £8,000 a year. But only a few days ago, he received a letter from the Department of Health and Social Security advising him that his pension is being reviewed. "They're worried I'm getting better.

"When I was in the Falklands I was sure that if we were wounded we would be looked after once we got back to Britain. Others thought the same.

"But even though we were just a handful compared with the World War casualties, the army wasn't prepared for us and the civil servants were even worse.

"No one told us we could claim a mobility allowance, or what sort of money we would get from our pension or the South Atlantic Fund. No one gave us any advice on how to start a new life."

When Lt Lawrence was discharged from the army, he received a letter assuring him he would be useful in the reserve. "They hadn't bothered to find out I was disabled.

"But if you complain, the reaction is: 'Who the hell does this guy think he is?' Disabled people are supposed to sit quietly and be grateful. I did complain and fight back. The guys who didn't got a very raw deal."

from THE GUARDIAN *17 August 1984*

For discussion

1. Robert Lawrence says the Army 'didn't want to know' about him. What evidence is there of this in the news report?

2. If a novel was written, based on this story, how do you think it would begin?

3. Choose any two of his complaints and discuss how you think the Army would answer them.

4. Like many newspaper reports, this is an 'unfinished' story. What would you need to be told if you now wanted to find out how the story 'ends'?

Questions on all three stories

To answer these questions, you will need to re-read all three stories in this Unit.

Before you answer them, talk with the class about any further aspects of the stories that you feel unsure of, including the vocabulary and punctuation as well as overall meaning and interpretation.

Also, briefly revise the work in Unit 4 on *conventions of storytelling* and in Unit 6 on *conventions of news reports.*

In writing your answers:
- use your own words as far as possible. When you quote from the text, show this by the use of speech marks;
- write sentences, unless the question specifically indicates otherwise;
- remember that in many cases there is more than one good answer – everything depends on the care with which you explain your answer and the evidence you give;
- keep your answers reasonably short, but note that sometimes the question clearly requires extended writing. The art and difficulty of this kind of work lie in keeping a balance between being *economical* (avoiding unnecessary elaboration or repetition) and being *precise* (writing exactly what you mean).

1. In *I Spy*, what are the three main things you learn about the father's character?
2. In the last paragraph, Charlie mentions one way in which he is like his father. Is he like him in any other ways?
3. What is the most important example of irony in the story?
4. What do you think is the writer's main aim in his telling of the story?
5. Mrs Ras Mohun tells Vedi he is 'a special student from a cultured home.' What does this probably mean?
6. What different explanations do the boys put forward to explain the disappearance of Ramesh and Jaisingh? Examine each one in the light of the evidence in the story itself.
7. How does the story show the storyteller himself in a sympathetic light?
8. What do you think is the writer's main aim in his telling of the story?

9. What are the three most important things you learn about Lieutenant Robert Lawrence's character in the newspaper story?

10. What is the most important general criticism levelled at the Army in this story?

11. What is ironic about Lawrence's story, as told in the first part of this report?

12. What do you think is the writer's main aim in his telling of the story?

13. Does Graham Greene use any particular conventions of storytelling in *I Spy*?

14. In Unit 6, page 89, a journalist's advice to news reporters is quoted. Has the writer (Seumas Milne) of the Falklands story observed or disregarded any of this advice?

15. The third story is a news report. Could it be a fictional short story? (Is there anything in the way it is written that shows it could *not* be?)

16. Many people like stories to end with all the questions answered. Show briefly how each of these three stories might have ended so as to satisfy such readers.

Punctuation

17. Explain the use of the colon in a) the last paragraph of the Falklands story, and b) the sixth paragraph of *I Spy*.

18. Explain the use of the brackets in the middle section of the Falklands story in the paragraph beginning, 'A few weeks later' (p. 186).

19. Explain why the 'Sighted Master' (in *Vedi*) is always printed with a capital **S** and capital **M**.

20. In the introduction to the Falklands story, the 'military establishment' is printed with a small **m** and a small **e**, but the 'Civil Service' has a capital **C** and capital **S**. Explain why.

21. Graham Greene uses the semi-colon three times in the second paragraph of *I Spy*. Explain why he uses it.

22. In the opening section of the Falklands story, why are there speech marks round the word *free* in 'a "free" car' (p. 183)?

The Great Wall of China, completed in the third century BC, and stretching for over 1,500 miles.

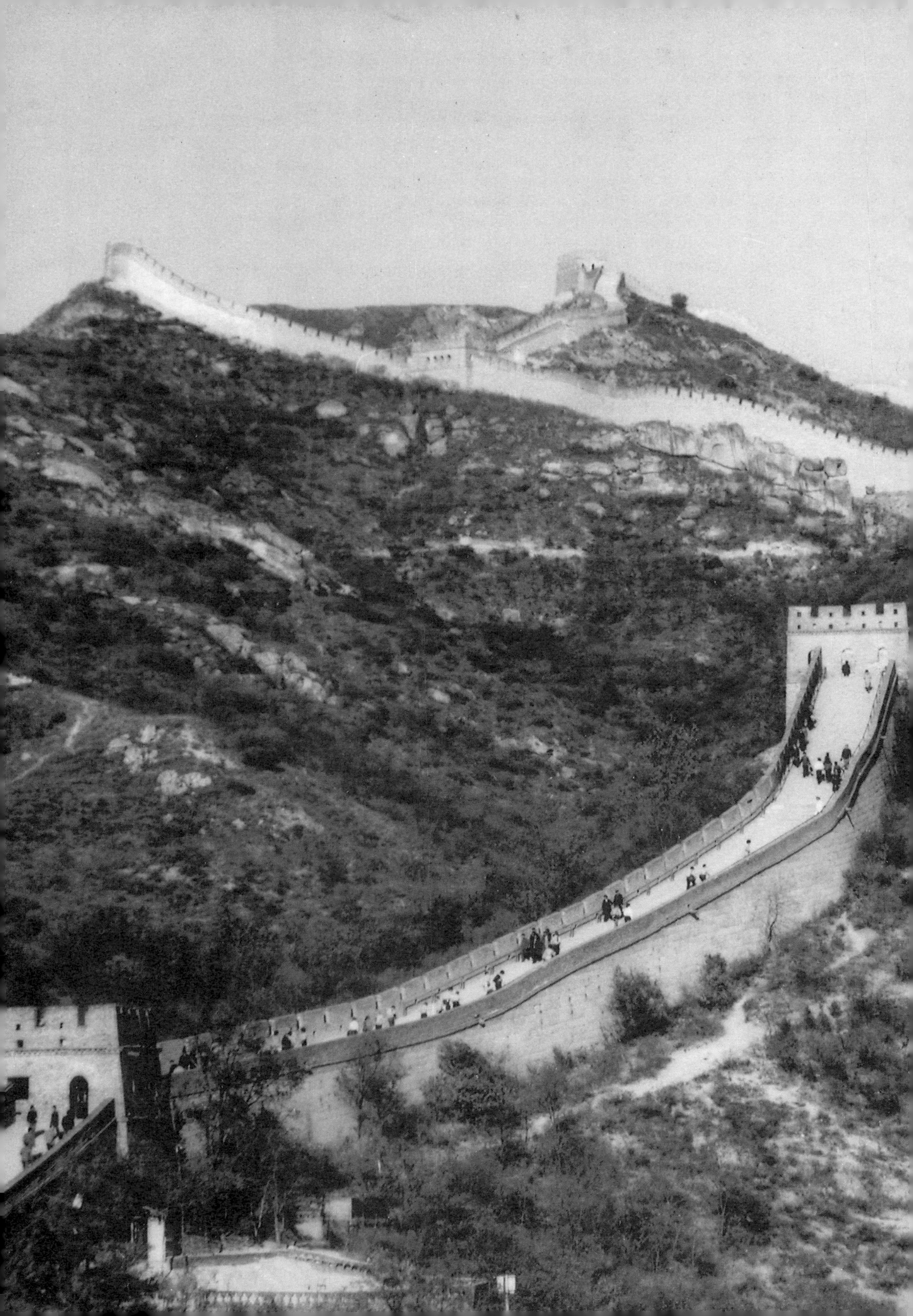

Dramatic Irony

The way any story ends depends, of course, on the ability or inability of the various characters to achieve what they set out to do – to fulfil their intentions. Sometimes these intentions are defeated by other characters. Sometimes they never even surface.

One of the pleasures of watching a play (or a film) is in watching and anticipating the ways in which characters pursue what they want. Often the audience know more about the different intentions of the different characters than the characters themselves do. This is dramatic irony.

For example, *we* may know that the landlady intends to lace the lodger's tea with arsenic, but the lodger does not know this.

Briefly think back to any plays or films you have seen recently. Discuss any scenes where there was dramatic irony.

For improvisation

This time you will need to recruit three students to take part. On this occasion, the instructions for each character will be given in front of the class while the other two characters are out of the room. So the audience will know what is happening right across the drama, while the individual characters will know very much less.

The basic situation, to be given to all three characters, is as follows: the three of you have recently formed a pop group that has performed with great success at a number of parties and discos locally. You have also made a fair amount of money, about £500, which the father of one of you (who is a bank manager) has been looking after. You have recently been invited to perform for 15 minutes at a big talent contest organised by a major recording company. If you win this, you will also win a contract to make records.
Today you agree to meet at the home of one of the group to discuss exactly what you will do at the contest and how you will prepare for it.

The three members of the group:
    Character A was the brains behind the setting up of the group; is the group's drummer; father is the bank manager.
    Character B is the group's lead singer; the group rehearses and also meets now at **B**'s home.
    Character C is the group's electric guitarist; has written and composed all the songs performed so far by the group.

    Before you start the improvisation, you should all invent the titles of the three most popular numbers that **C** has composed.

    Your teacher will give you further details.

For discussion

After the improvisation:

1. How far does each of the three players now understand the intentions of the other two characters?
2. The three should now reveal their original instructions to each other. Did any of the characters' intentions not surface?
3. Which (if any) of the characters actually succeeded in getting what they wanted?
4. At which points in the improvisation did the audience experience dramatic irony?

Punctuation

Rewrite these extracts from a story with the correct punctuation:

> Kay knew that danger was imminent the look in everybodys faces told her so martin was suddenly very quiet and still george was even quieter than usual somethings wrong i know it she said dont move said eleanor suddenly this was followed by a pause a pause that seemed to last for ever.

And this is a little later in the same story:

> She thought about it carefully she even thought briefly that it was a good idea if i accept your suggestion she said would you also accept and this is important that i have the right later to change my mind in other words you want to be able to act think and behave however you wish whenever you wish said martin.

Suggestions for writing

1. Find and cut out an interesting and fairly lengthy story or feature article in a newspaper. Devise a set of comprehension questions to go with the writing, and then exchange your work with each other. Answer the questions and then return the work for marking and discussion. In devising the questions, consider matters such as:
   - vocabulary,
   - style,
   - the author's intentions,
   - theme and interpretation, and
   - punctuation.

2. Write a story of your own in which you experiment with the ending. It might for instance leave some of the major questions unanswered. Perhaps experiment also with the *form* in which the story is written. For example, you might write it in the form of a diary, or of letters, or of memoranda. You might even write it twice over in two different forms. If you wish, you could use the pictures on pages 175 or 189 as if they are designs for the cover page of your story.

3. Instead of writing a story, write a play. Perhaps begin by writing out the instructions for each character together with an introductory note for all the characters. Perhaps ask a group of students to improvise these in front of the class before you write the play itself.

12 PERSUASION (1) ADVERTISING

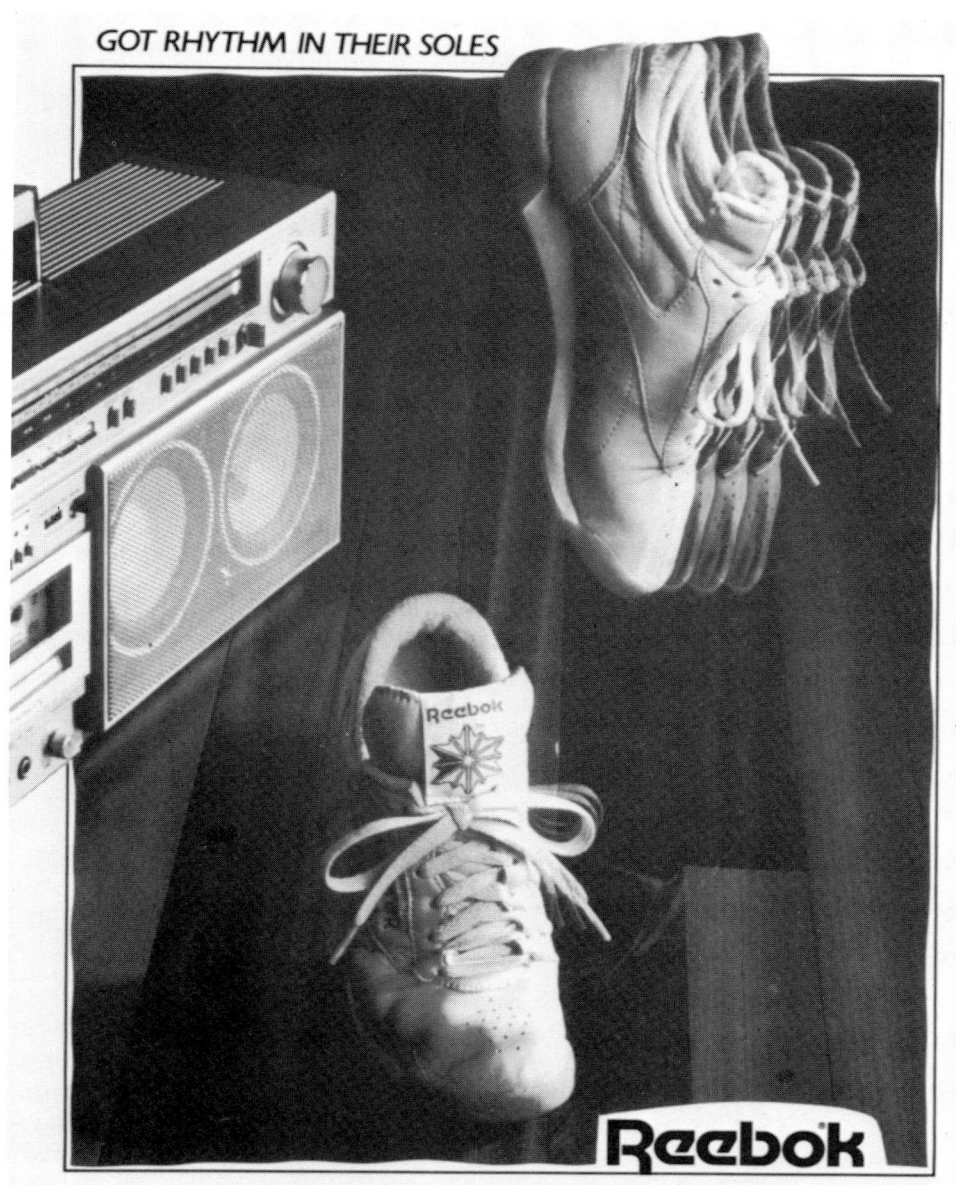

GOT RHYTHM IN THEIR SOLES

Reebok
· CATCH US IF YOU CAN ·

This Unit looks at some of the issues raised by advertising.

Before you read the first text, discuss:

- What do you think are the main advantages, to society in general, of advertising?
- What do you think are the main disadvantages?

Make a note of the main points raised in your discussion, and compare them later with the two writers below.

The case for . . .

These are the views of an American economist.

The marked expansion in our national economy during the past quarter of a century has been accompanied by a sevenfold rise in total advertising expenditures. Such expenditures have more than kept pace with national economic growth so that advertising has been a larger proportion of personal consumption expenditures since the mid-1950s than in the pre-World War II period.

After adjusting for price changes, advertising expenditures in real terms more than tripled in the postwar period as compared with the doubling of real personal consumption expenditures. It seems far more probable that the rise in economic activity has caused the rise in advertising than the reverse.

The rise in relative importance of advertising reflects several developments including: the new product explosion, the development of television as a major advertising medium, the sharp rise in discretionary incomes, and the increasing intensity of competition. The phenomenal expansion of industrial research and development has led to vast improvements in older products and to an increasing array of new ones. A relatively high advertising cost often is required to launch new and improved products. The simultaneous increase in discretionary incomes has meant a marked expansion in the market for such products.

There is no way to determine a cutoff point above which "advertising is too high" either in dollars or as a per cent of sales volume. The situation in each company and industry must be evaluated separately. The relative importance of new products, the role played by other marketing tools, the nature of the product (consumer's good v. industrial product), competitive pressures – these and other factors determine the meaningfulness of any level of advertising expenditures.

Without high advertising expenditures, the new products which contribute so significantly to the well-being of consumers and to national economic growth would not develop mass markets, and in the absence of the possibility of such markets, there would be little incentive for large-scale research and development. Thus, national economic activity and advertising act and interact to induce higher levels for both.

Advertising does not take place in a vacuum. It is one of several marketing alternatives which may be selected at the option of a company, although competitive pressures may result in greater emphasis upon one or more of these alternatives. The abandonment of advertising could not represent a net saving to a company or to the economy. Instead, such a development would require a shift to alternative marketing techniques, some of which undoubtedly would be less efficient than advertising, since companies do not deliberately adopt the least effective marketing approach. Such a shift would indeed be wasteful.

There is wide agreement that advertising provides very useful information which plays a significant role in our highly complex economy. Although precise data are not available, it appears that the charge that advertising represents economic waste refers to substantially less than half of all advertising expenditures. Most types of competition involve duplication and waste. Competition in advertising is no exception. But if the accent is placed solely on the negative, a distorted picture is obtained. On balance, the contribution of competition to our economy has more than overbalanced the wastes, and the same is true for competition in advertising. The charge of large-scale waste in advertising appears to reflect in part a yearning for an economy with standardized, homogeneous products which are primarily functional in nature.

The effectiveness of advertising depends upon the characteristics of an industry's products. Many more advertising dollars are spent on consumer goods than for industrial products. The proportions spent for advertising vary widely among consumer goods and even for the same product as companies adopt different marketing strategies. It is most widely used for relatively low-priced brand-name items available from many retail establishments and subject to frequent repeat purchases. These are brutally competitive markets in which new products and new brands become available frequently.

Total consumer disposable income rather than advertising is the major determinant of aggregate consumer demand. However, advertising may affect total demand through its contribution to the launching of new products. Advertising together with other factors (for example, relative prices, packaging, changes in composition of the population, distribution facilities, tastes, religion, geography, and customs) helps to influence the extent to which companies and industries will receive some share of the consumer's dollar.

from *Advertising and Competition* by Julius Backman

For discussion

1 What is the main point made by the writer in his first paragraph?
2 What does the writer mean by 'high advertising expenditures' in paragraph five? And what does he see as their justification?
3 Why does he think that the 'abandonment of advertising' (paragraph six) would be bad for the country's economy?
4 The first sentence in the last paragraph contains some difficult and technical language. What does it mean?
   Talk about it until you can put it into your own words.
5 Overall, what does Backman see as the two main arguments in favour of advertising?

FREE LUXURY SHOWER WITH YOUR SERVOWARM CENTRAL HEATING

Install a Servowarm Central Heating system this summer worth £1,500 or more, and we'll fit you a £350 luxury shower absolutely free.*

And the Servoflow is a superb shower, with an automatic thermostat and fully adjustable height control.

We'll install it at the same time as your central heating, usually ready for use in only four days.

Send the coupon to have your free shower, and your Servowarm Central Heating fitted without delay. It's first come first served while stocks last. Offer must close 24 August 1985.

SERVOWARM
DON'T SETTLE FOR LESS THAN THE BEST.

To: Servowarm, FREEPOST, 199 The Vale, London W3 7BR (no stamp required) or dial 100 and ask for FREEFONE SERVOWARM.

Please tell me more about your free luxury shower offer.
☐ I'm interested in having a full central heating system.
☐ I'm interested in having a boiler replacement.

Mr/Mrs/Miss _____
Address _____
Postcode _____ Tel. No. _____

*Installed in same household, subject to survey. Servowarm are Licensed Credit Brokers. Written details on request. Offer applies to orders confirmed by 24/8/85 and installed by 14/9/85. SD/14/7

ARE YOU A POOR TALKER?

A NOTED international publisher reports that there is a simple technique of everyday conversation and writing which can pay you real dividends in both social and professional advancement. It works like magic to give you added poise, self-confidence, and greater popularity.

The details of this method are described in a fascinating book, "Adventures in Speaking and Writing," sent free on request.

Influence

According to this publisher, many people do not realise how much they could influence others simply by what they say and how they say it. Those who realise this radiate enthusiasm, hold the attention of their listeners with bright, sparkling conversation that attracts friends and opportunities wherever they go. Whether in business, at social functions, or even in casual conversation with new acquaintances, there are ways in which you can make a good impression every time you talk.

After all, conversation has certain fundamental rules and principles – just like any other art. The good talkers whom you admire know these rules and apply them whenever they converse. Learn the rules and make your conversation brighter, more entertaining, and impressive. Then you will find yourself becoming more popular and winning new friendships in the business and social worlds.

Free

To acquaint more readers of *The Guardian* with the easy-to-follow rules for developing skill in everyday conversation and writing, we, the publishers, have printed full details of this interesting self-training method in a fascinating book, "Adventures in Speaking and Writing," sent free on request. No obligation. Simply complete and return the coupon on Page 3 (you don't even need to stamp your envelope).

WHAT THIS FREE BOOK WILL SHOW YOU

- How to talk easily and effectively!
- How to overcome self consciousness!
- How to win friends – and impress people!
- How to succeed in your job and social life!
- How to increase your word power!
- How to develop poise, charm and personality!
- How to say the right thing always!

Listening Comprehension

The case against...

The passage for listening comprehension is from a psychologist's study of *The Techniques of Persuasion*.

Most ad-men would claim that there is a genuine science of advertising psychology. The first text-book on the subject to arrive in Britain was written by Professor Walter Dill Scott, Director of the Psychological Laboratory at the North-Western University in Chicago. This appeared in 1909, and the writer enunciated a number of principles, most of them obvious to the point of platitude, of which the most fundamental was the long-familiar principle of association; not only should words come to be associated together so that 'Pears' comes to stand for soap and 'Hoover' for a vacuum-cleaner, but an attempt should be made to associate the product with the individual's basic motivations. These included the maternal instinct, greed, emulation, the desire for health and good looks, the desire to be appreciated by others, and so on. Advertisements should not be ugly or show, even in jest, unpleasing figures, and the wealthy and prosperous should be depicted rather than the poor and undistinguished.

However, whether or not advertising is a 'science', the advertising agency employing trained psychologists, sociologists, psychoanalysts, and social anthropologists is now an established reality in the United States and rapidly invading Europe.

That skilful advertising produced dramatic results even before the advent of these more subtle methods is beyond doubt, but those concerned with the modern profession, apparently from some latent sense of guilt or perhaps embarrassment (there is something a little shaming in the picture of an adult writing drivel about 'yummy' sweets and similar baby-talk), must needs justify their actions by an appeal to the social benefits conferred upon the rest of us by advertising.

Thus it is claimed that advertising cheapens goods by increasing the sale of an article which in turn lowers prices. This, of course, does not apply to basic goods and services; but in the case of non-essentials such as cigarettes it often happens that the product could be sold more cheaply if wasteful competition between firms did not cause the cost of advertising to be passed on to the public. *Which?* (the journal published by the Consumers' Association Ltd) has pointed out that aspirin, unbranded, can be had for twenty-five for 4p whereas the same formula, advertised at a cost of half a million pounds a year, costs 40p for twenty-seven. Elizabeth Gundrey (*Your Money's Worth*, Penguin Books) quotes the case of a kettle which went up in price from £1 to £3; when the manufacturer was asked the reason, he wrote: 'An extensive national advertising campaign is being conducted on it, and the price has been lifted mainly owing to the advertising charges.' In fact advertising may either raise or reduce prices.

Secondly, it is contended that advertising justifies itself economically by its function of bringing knowledge of desirable goods to the customer, and it is, of course, useful to know what is on at the local cinema, the date of a sale, or even that certain types of goods are available. Unfortunately the great bulk of advertising is much more than merely informative and a good deal is positively misleading. This is especially true in the case of patent medicines: to say, for example, that glucose gives you energy is not entirely untrue, since glucose is indeed the body's natural source of energy – what is not true is the advertiser's claim that people are tired because of lack of glucose, since nobody under any conceivable natural conditions suffers from any such deficiency.

When advertising seeks to give specific information about factual matters, it is very often misleading or lying. This is almost as true of the detergent manufacturers as of those who make patent medicines. It would take a pretty stupid person to believe that all the detergent 'tests' carried out on television were genuine; and television advertisements often deceive the public in other ways. Thus, in a polish advertisement black glass was used instead of wood to give the effect of gloss; and in a cats' food advertisement, fresh liver, because the cat refused to oblige by eating the tinned product. A. S. J. Baster (*Advertising Reconsidered*) comments:

The major part of *informative* advertising is, and always has been, a campaign of exaggeration, half-truths, intended ambiguities, direct lies, and general deception. Amongst all the hundreds of thousands of persons engaged in the business, it may be said about most of them on the informative side of it that their chief function is to deceive buyers as to the real merits and demerits of the commodity being sold.

Finally, it is said that advertising brings about an improvement in the quality of goods and a sustained reliabilty. By and large this may be true, but it would be an optimistic person who would be ready to claim that the quality of, say, groceries, has improved over the years, that packed and branded cheese let alone 'processed' cheese is as good as the unwrapped product, or canned or frozen vegetables as good as fresh ones. Poor quality goods *can* be sold.

Many advertisers are willing to admit that their work consists largely in the creation of imaginary differences between products which are, for all practical purposes, the same. Thus only a small minority of cigarette smokers are capable of distinguishing between one brand and another when they are blindfolded and the cigarette is smoked through a holder. Moreover, the emotions to which they appeal are by no means the most pleasant: fear, social embarrassment, greed, hypochondria, emulation in keeping up with the Joneses, and the rest. There is the appeal to social embarrassment in advertisements relating to bad breath, body-odour, facial blemishes, the state of one's W.C., and so on; the appeal to greed of the football pools and the food (especially confectionery) advertisements; the pseudo-scientific nonsense of patent medicines, 'health' foods, or 'tonic' wines which trade on hypochondria and personal insecurity ('By the time I left the office, I felt finished ... younger men than me were coming on in the firm', etc.); and the desire for emulation in buying an unnecessary new car or living in a house in a particular part of the country which is regarded as being in accordance with one's social status.

from *The Techniques of Persuasion* **by J. A. C. Brown**

Multiple choice questions

Each item consists of a question or an incomplete statement followed by four suggested answers or completions.

You should select the most appropriate answer in each case. (Do not write out the question. Just write down the number of the question together with the letter of the appropriate answer.)

1. The writer of this article is a psychologist. This means that he or she has studied
   a the behaviour of people who are mentally disturbed.
   b the behaviour of people.
   c the behaviour of animals.
   d the effects of advertising on people.

2. The writer says that most ad-men claim there is a 'genuine science of advertising psychology'. If there is such a science it would mean that
   a all advertisements would have their desired effect.
   b all advertisements devised by psychological experts would have their desired effect.
   c there have been many careful studies of the factors that make advertisements successful or unsuccessful.
   d advertisers employ scientists to devise their advertisements.

3. The writer of this article thinks that
   a it is nonsense to suggest there is a science of advertising.
   b there may be a science of advertising.
   c there is a science of advertising.
   d there is not a science of advertising.

4. The writer says that most of the old principles of advertising were 'obvious to the point of platitude'. A platitude is
   a something that is too obvious to be worth saying.
   b something that is obviously absurd.
   c something that is too absurd to be worth thinking.
   d something that is too good to be true.

5. The writer thinks that advertisers talk about the social benefits of advertising because they are
   a irritated by their critics.
   b embarrassed by the money they earn.
   c embarrassed by some of the silly things they say in their advertisements.
   d keen to show how clever they are.

Go On...
Give 'em a Ginsters

Ginsters "Cornwall's Pride" Pasties are baked fresh every day in Cornwall.
Only the finest lean beef and fresh vegetables are blended to an original Cornish recipe to give that distinctive Ginsters flavour.
The delicious puff pastry is still crimped by hand in the traditional way giving Ginsters their unique home-made appearance.
Insist on Ginsters for the assurance of all that's wholesome, fresh and Cornish.

Fresh from Cornwall

6. According to the writer, advertisers have defended their work on all the following grounds except that
   a advertising keeps down the cost of goods.
   b advertising improves the quality of goods.
   c advertising entertains people.
   d advertising keeps people well informed.

7. According to the writer, the information in advertisements is
   a generally misleading.
   b often irrelevant.
   c misleading.
   d misleading and irrelevant.

8. According to the writer, advertisements
   a may lead to an improvement in the quality of goods.
   b rarely lead to an improvement in the quality of goods.
   c never lead to an improvement in the quality of goods.
   d have no effect on the quality of goods.

9. The writer thinks that advertisers are able to sell
   a very expensive goods.
   b rubbish, if they try hard enough.
   c goods that nobody wants.
   d very unattractive goods.

10. The writer says that hypochondria can induce people to buy goods they see advertised. Hypochondria is
    a anxiety about the unknown.
    b anxiety about being inferior to your neighbours.
    c anxiety about being thought stupid.
    d anxiety about being ill.

11. The writer says that advertisers appeal to emotions such as
    a embarrassment, greed and fear.
    b embarrassment, fear and unhappiness.
    c greed, fear and unhappiness.
    c unhappiness, fear and hypochondria.

12. The writer says that advertisements can play on people's 'personal insecurity'. An example of this feeling would be
    a wanting to be rich.
    b wanting to be clever.
    c feeling you are unlikeable.
    d feeling you are not paid enough.

13. The writer says that emulation is an important factor in advertising. Emulation means
    a looking alike.
    b conceit.
    c ignorance.
    d copying.

14. The writer mentions the 'pseudo-scientific nonsense' of some advertisements. Pseudo means
    a clever.
    b silly.
    c impressive.
    d false.

15. Many advertisements, says the writer, play on the individual's sense of his or her 'social status'. Social status can refer to all the following except

    a one's place in society.
    b one's position in a company of profession.
    c one's intelligence.
    d one's qualifications.

16. The writer quotes other writers who

    a agree with him or her.
    b disagree with him or her.
    c show that advertising is partly good and partly bad.
    d are psychologists like himself or herself.

17. According to this passage, advertisers generally

    a think people's emotions outstrip their intelligence.
    b think people are very stupid.
    c think people are difficult to persuade.
    d think people are too emotional.

18. Social anthropologists are often employed by advertising agencies. Social anthropologists principally study

    a the psychology of advertising.
    b advertising.
    c primitive peoples.
    d psychology.

19. The writer says that many advertisements create 'imaginary differences' between products. So we can infer that

    a advertisements often tell lies.
    b the public will believe anything.
    c advertisers are very clever.
    d advertising helps people to recognise superior products.

20. The writer's tone in this passage could best be described as

    a ironic.
    b critical.
    c mocking.
    d sarcastic.

When villains start working 9 to 5, so will we.

Like most other white collar workers, police officers work at least eight hours a day, five days a week.

18.10 HARROW: An old lady hasn't been seen for a few days and the milk is piling up on her doorstep. A Woman Police Constable breaks in and finds her dead on the floor. Foul play? The Inspector and Police Surgeon are called in.

There the similarity ends.

In a place like London, accidents, football matches, demonstrations, crime, tourists, and the like keep us busy twenty four hours a day, seven days a week.

And since quite a lot of our work involves dealing with London's anti-social elements, anti-social hours are what we tend to work.

You could find yourself up well before the lark on Early Turn, 6 am to 2 pm.

Or you could be putting in a hard day's night while most law-abiding folk are comfortably parked in front of the television.

20.00 BERMONDSEY: The Community Liaison Officer visits a local youth club to talk about the dangers of drugs and glue-sniffing. The kids complain about being 'picked on', so the message doesn't get through this time.

Look on the bright side, though. While everyone else is slaving away at work, you can spend an afternoon in the garden or at the squash club.

So much for routine.

There's not much chance of anyone settling into a comfortable routine in the Metropolitan Police.

It's one of the few occupations where you can turn up for work and not have an inkling of what the day holds in store for you. You could be called to the scene of a fatal accident, or an armed robbery.

Or you could spend the afternoon in a community centre helping to sort out old people's problems.

21.00 COVENT GARDEN: A man is seen trying to feed an American Express card into a bank's all-night cash dispenser. It turns out he's high on LSD and the card is high on our stolen list. That won't do nicely at all sir.

Every day, you'll find yourself in situations that demand something different from you.

By turns, you'll be a tourist guide, marriage guidance counsellor, diplomat, child psychologist, criminologist, self defence expert, first aid specialist, lawyer and speaking clock.

Every one of these jobs requires different individual qualities.

23.05 FULHAM: A bomb reported in a shop doorway. Chief Inspector and C13, Anti-Terrorist Branch called out to assess the situation. The Explosives Officer confirms our worst suspicions were unfounded. Better safe than sorry.

You need them all to get into the Metropolitan Police Force.

How do you measure up?

First of all, you must be at least 168 cms tall if you're a woman and at least 172 cms if you're a man.

Ideally, the academic qualifications we're looking for are around five good 'O' levels.

Nevertheless, people who've got a string of 'A' levels won't get in if they don't possess all the right personal qualities.

You'll need a lot of common sense, a genuine concern for people, a strong sense of fair play, an agile mind in a fit body and a well developed sense of humour.

03.15 SOHO: Two officers spot a man climbing the scaffolding outside an office block. He claims he's looking for his football. They offer to help him look and find all the signs of a break-in on the second floor. The phantom footballer gets booked.

And as these aren't the sort of things we can discern from an application form, you'll have to go through our two-day selection process.

A copper earns every penny.

The pay is very good. Considering some of the things we'll ask you to do for it, it has to be. At 18½ (our minimum age), the least you'll start on is £8,520, including London allowances.

04.30 CLAPHAM: An officer in a Panda Car spots a suspiciously parked van. He investigates and finds three men doing a clothes shop. He gives chase and with assistance nabs two of them. A good night's work.

If you're a bit more mature, you'll be better equipped to help us. So over 22's start on more.

As you gain experience and make progress in the Force, your salary will keep pace.

Although you can be sure the hours won't get any easier.

For further information, phone (01) 725 4575. Write to the Appointments Officer, Careers Information Centre, Dept. MD145, New Scotland Yard, London SW1H 0BG. Or visit us at our Careers Information Office in Victoria Street.

*These incidents are based on real events, but for legal reasons the locations have been changed.

Group work for research and writing   205

The Psychology of Advertising

The remaining materials in this Unit are either advertisements from newspapers or magazines, or news stories about advertising. Read them through and:

1. devise a list of rules for advertisers. Collect examples of advertisements from newspapers and magazines to illustrate each rule. Choose your examples from advertisements of entirely different commodities, perhaps two for each rule.

2. show these advertisements to three of four different people and get them talking about their effectiveness: does the advertisement work for them? If so, why? If not, why not? If possible, show them to people who are unconnected to each other.

3. write a report on the psychology of advertising, using:
   a) your rules and the advertisements illustrating them;
   b) the comments of the people you have spoken to, using them to qualify or illustrate the rules;
   c) any of the news stories in this Unit in so far as they cast light on the psychology of advertising and on the various points you make;
   d) some reference to and perhaps a quotation or two from the texts by Backman and Brown in this Unit.

Girls fall for advertising puffs

More teenage girls than boys are now regular smokers, according to research carried out in Sheffield.

A survey of more than 4,000 school-children suggests that, by the age of 15, one in four girls, compared with one in six boys, smoke at least one cigarette a week.

The author of the study, Ms Pam Gillies, lecturer in community medicine at Nottingham University Medical School, believes that the media image of smoking as glamorous and sexy is to blame for the fact that more adolescent girls than boys are smoking regularly in many areas of the country. "The seductive young heroine in the film *Flashdance* was recently seem by millions of young women to smoke and 'get her man,'" she said.

She also accuses magazines like *Company* and *Cosmopolitan* of trying to resurrect the view that smoking and passionate sex go together.

Another influence on young girls is cigarette advertising. Ms Gillies says that, since the decline of smoking among men, tobacco companies are trying to make smoking more appealing to women and girls.

Many children experiment with smoking between 11 and 12 years of age, according to the study. But, contrary to popular belief, they do not usually start in the school toilets. More than 60 per cent have their early experiences of smoking in the open air, and most smoke with their friends.

Peer group pressure is the main reason why teenagers continue to smoke regularly. One in four children said they smoked because their friends did.

But 16 per cent said they smoked to calm their nerves. "It's disturbing that so many young people feel nervous, anxious or emotionally disturbed in some way and use cigarettes in the belief that they will calm them down," commented Ms Gillies.

Schemes like the Health Education Council's "My Body" project, however, seem to be reducing the risk of school-children smoking. One in three younger smokers said they had given up because of the effects to health.

Parents also play an important part in deterring their children. One in ten ex-smokers said they had stopped because their parents disapproved.

from THE TIMES EDUCATIONAL SUPPLEMENT *14 September 1984*

Amplex brings you closer.

Fresher breath. The confidence that comes with Double Amplex capsules.

Aiming at Children

Television commercials aimed at children work. Manufacturers of toys, sweets, breakfast cereals and crisps spend millions on them because they know how effective they are, not only during the run up to Christmas but all the year round as well. The sales figures prove it.

It's harder to say whether or not this sort of advertising is in any way harmful. The only time there is any concerted protest is in the run up to Christmas. Then, the army of toy and game advertisements, marching shoulder to shoulder during commercial breaks on ITV, elicit squeals of protest from parents beset by nagging children. A poll of mothers at a primary school revealed that each had been asked for something their offspring had seen advertised on TV.

In 1977, this form of advertising seemed in jeopardy. Lord Annan's Committee of Enquiry into the Future of Broadcasting announced: "The majority of us believe that children should not be exposed during their own programmes to the blandishments and subtle persuasiveness of advertising. The majority of us therefore recommend that no advertising should be shown within children's programmes or between two programmes for children."

The recommendation was never adopted. The Independent Broadcasting Authority countered it by saying that their Code of Advertising Standards and Practice was equal to the task of protecting children from the excesses of TV advertising...

Christmas advertising seems to cause annual concern, not so much because of their content and style but because of their sheer bulk, particularly on Saturday morning television, where programmes tend to be short and episodic. In 1982, the IBA commissioned National Opinion Polls to do some pre-Christmas research. A sample of parents were asked whether children asking for the purchase of toys was the cause of family argument: 26 per cent said yes. Only 3 per cent blamed TV, others were far more ready to blame peer group pressure. How do these pressures start?

"One of the principal objectives of advertising to children", says Glen Smith, "is to get a product talked about in the child's peer group as well as at home with parents." So can children be affected by television advertising without even watching television?

from THE TIMES EDUCATIONAL SUPPLEMENT 7 December 1984

Campaign agreed for ban on alcohol advertising

Twin assault by BMA on beer and cigarettes

By David Hencke,
Social Services Correspondent

A campaign to ban the advertising and promotion of alcohol is to be launched by the British Medical Association in tandem with a series of measures to strengthen its campaign against the tobacco industry.

The BMA's annual meeting at Plymouth yesterday carried by large majorities eight motions which will transform the association's stance on the two products.

As well as committing itself to a ban on advertising the association is pledged to press government ministers for a substantial rise in alcohol duty, and to demand that the specific gravity of draught ales and beer should be declared in public houses and shops.

The association is also pledged to press for a ban on tobacco advertising, and on arts and sports sponsorship by tobacco companies. The association will also seek substantial increases in fines for shopkeepers who sell cigarettes to children, and a ban on the sale of new nicotine snuff products such as Skoal Bandits and Tobacco Teabags.

The tobacco campaign will be intensified as Department of Health ministers and Mr Neil Macfarlane, the sports minister, start to renegotiate voluntary agreements on tobacco advertising and sports sponsorship. The BMA will seek a new tobacco act to impose a complete advertising and sponsorship ban, and with the power to prosecute companies who ignore it.

The BMA's interest in tackling the alcohol industry has been stimulated by the part drink plays in soccer hooliganism, and Mr Stuart Horner, a community physician, who moved the motion, said yesterday: "Even a Tory government has been forced to introduce a ban on the sale of alcohol in this instance."

He claimed that alcohol is partly responsible for child abuse and child battering, for accidents after the pubs have closed, and for domestic violence. Advertisements were increasing in quantity, quality, and subtlety as they tell the public that alcohol is part of a sophisticated lifestyle.

Dr John Dawson, BMA undersecretary for the Board of Science, said at a press conference that alcohol was thought to be responsible for about 15,000 deaths a year, compared with 100,000 deaths attributed directly or indirectly to cigarette smoking. This emphasis is expected to be reflected in the weight given to the two campaigns by the BMA.

The BMA also decided to campaign for compulsory rear seat belts in cars after persuading the Government to make front seat belts compulsory. It will also publish a report on the effects of a nuclear winter after a number of nuclear bombs have dropped.

All this, plus yesterday's votes supporting the principle of surrogate motherhood and embryo research, was too much for one speaker. Mr Richard Greenwood, a consultant, told conference members: "We are now a pill-pushing rent-a-womb mob of unilaterally disarming hippies. The BMA is not the organisation I joined."

from THE GUARDIAN 27 June 1985

SPOT THE SUN

Enter the New Zealand Lamb "Sun Seekers" Competition

NEW ZEALAND LAMB SUN SEEKERS COMPETITION

£10,000 MUST BE WON

When you buy tender, top value New Zealand Lamb you get more than a great deal – you could win a great deal too.

The prize in our sensational "Sun Seekers" Competition is £10,000 in cash. You can use this advertisement as an official entry form.

Use your skill and judgement to decide where the exact centre of the sun is located – and mark it clearly with a cross. Each cross must be accompanied by a competition pack sticker, Price/Weigh label or till receipt for New Zealand Lamb. **Here's a special bonus. Collect 5 "Proofs of purchase" in any combination – and you can have 5 extra goes at spotting the sun.** (Maximum entry per form is ten crosses.)

So the more you collect, the more your chances of winning. To enter, fill in your name and address, securely attach your "proofs of purchase", and post the complete picture and coupon section off – **to arrive no later than 31.8.85.**

RULES & CONDITIONS

1. The "Sun Seekers" Spot the Sun Competition is open to all UK residents. It is not open to employees of the New Zealand Meat Producers Board, the TV Times, participating stores, their families, agents or anyone connected with the competition in any way whatsoever.

2. The winner of the £10,000 national prize will be the entrant who matches or most closely matches the centre of the sun as determined by a panel of independent judges. In the event of a draw, the money will be equally divided amongst the winners.

3. Entries received after the closing date of 31.8.85 will not be considered. Neither will entries that are illegible, altered, incomplete, contain more than 10 crosses or are not accompanied by the correct number of any combination of competition pack stickers, Price/Weigh labels or till receipts for New Zealand Lamb.

4. The judges' decision is final and no correspondence can be entered into. Winning details can be obtained by sending a stamped and addressed envelope to: New Zealand Lamb "Sun Seekers" Winner, P.O. Box 14, Horley, Surrey after 30.9.85. "Sun Seekers" is promoted by the New Zealand Meat Producers Board, Chancery House, 53/64 Chancery Lane, London WC2A 1RX.

To: New Zealand Lamb "Sun Seekers" Competition (TVT), P.O. Box 14, Horley, Surrey.

I enclose _____ (No.) "Proofs of purchase" for New Zealand Lamb.
(5 "Proofs of purchase" entitles you to the maximum entry of 10 crosses)

Name _____

Address _____

Please use BLOCK CAPITALS. Competition closes 31.8.85.

Mealmakers from New Zealand Lamb

Advertisers enlist fear as selling aid

By Rosemary Collins

Advertisers are increasingly trying to frighten customers into buying goods, the Advertising Standards Authority suggests.

In its latest monthly report the authority's investigators uphold six complaints against firms using fear as an advertising ploy.

A blatant example was the Huddersfield shop selling locks, bolts, and invisible marking pens which delivered a circular leaflet to households in the area claiming: "This is not an advertisement," and signed "A very frightened man."

The leaflet referred to local burglaries, personal attacks, and the danger to children before pointing out that B & S of Moldgreen, Huddersfield, could sell all kinds of security accessories to make homes safer.

The Home Office complained recently to the authority about a leaflet advertising domestic fire-fighting equipment with claims that "domestic fires increased by a third in the UK during 1982," when the true increase was less than 1 per cent.

The leaflet, from Ashwin Fire and Safety Equipment of north London, also claimed that 80 per cent of fire engines called out in the UK attended domestic fires, when the true figure is around 10 per cent. And it tried to tell potential customers that almost 1,000 people died in house fires in London alone during 1983. The Home Office pointed out that figures for 1983 are not yet available, but that in recent years the death rate in house fires in Greater London has not exceeded 158.

Burglar alarm firms are most often guilty of "terror tactics", but this month the ASA also accuses a windscreen washer manufacturer, Decosol of Halifax, of playing upon people's fears that methanol, a chemical commonly used in washers, might be present in toxic levels in rival products.

The authority reminds advertisers that it is against the industry's code of practice to arouse fears on health matters.

from THE GUARDIAN 17 October 1984

13 PERSUASION (2) ARGUMENT

In this Unit there are examples of three different kinds of argument, in all of which the speaker's principal aim is to persuade the listener to take a specific course of action. They are:

- the examination and cross-examination of a witness in a court case;
- a parliamentary debate;
- a lawyer's summing-up for his client at the end of a court case.

In looking at all this material, you should especially consider:

1. the various techniques used by the speakers to achieve their purpose.
2. the importance of the actual *form* of the argument. In an ordinary private argument or discussion, people can sulk, walk out, stamp their feet and so on. In formal arguments the people involved are supposed to keep to the appropriate rules, and these may oblige them, for example, to:

   a) address their opponents by *specific titles*, such as 'my learned friend' (barristers in court) and 'the honourable member' (Members of Parliament in the House of Commons);

   b) *speak only once*. For example, in a parliamentary debate the main speakers for and against a motion open and also close a debate, but other speakers can speak only once;

   c) keep their argument to very specific matters; they cannot raise any topic they wish. For example, in a criminal court case, it is not generally permitted to discuss other offences that the accused may or may not have committed, or to discuss the possible guilt of people other than the accused.

For discussion

1 What do you think is the importance of such rules? Consider each one in turn.

2 What do you think are the possible disadvantages of any of them? In other words, could any of these rules hinder the achievement of a fair argument?

COURT MARTIAL:
A Case of Desertion

In John Wilson's play *Hamp* a young soldier runs away from the battlefield at Passchendaele in the First World War. It is pleaded in his defence that he has fought bravely in many earlier battles and has never previously tried to desert. But these pleas are of no use to him. According to military law, if he deliberately deserted he is guilty of a capital offence and must be shot. So everything depends on whether or not he can be held *to have intended to desert*.

In this extract from the play, the defending officer (Hargreaves) and the prosecuting officer (Midgley) examine and cross-examine the accused about his intentions.

Characters: **Hamp** (the accused)
President of the Court
Hargreaves
Midgley

Hargreaves	Did you realise what you were doing when you left the battalion that night?
Hamp	(*unconvincing, because he doesn't really understand*) No, sir. I don't think so, sir. I ——
Hargreaves	D'you mean that you weren't fully in your right mind?
Hamp	(*loyally*) That's what it was, sir.
Hargreaves	(*desperately*) Were you worried about your wife?
Hamp	Yes, sir.
Hargreaves	Will you tell the Court why?
Hamp	Well, I — I got a letter.
President	Yes?
Hamp	Well, it were to tell me she's been carrying on a bit — with some other chap, like.
Hargreaves	(*after waiting*) And this was preying on your mind?
Hamp	Well, it were a bit, like, sir.
Hargreaves	When you were absent, were you really conscious of what you were doing? Or was it as if you were being compelled to do it?
Hamp	Yes, sir. I think it were — same as you said.
Hargreaves	I mean, it's not true, is it, to say that you *decided* to desert, deliberately decided — prepared to risk the consequences, but hoping to get away with it?
Hamp	I weren't thinking much at the time, sir.

Hargreaves No, exactly. And ——
Hamp (*remembering the phrase*) Didn't have no plan in my mind.
Hargreaves (*more hopefully*) Had you any idea where you were going?
Hamp I were only wantin' to get left alone for a bit, sir, that's all.
Hargreaves Did you —— ?
President You say you wanted to be left alone 'for a bit'. Does that mean you intended to go back to the battalion?
Hamp (*after looking helplessly at* Hargreaves) I don't know, sir.
President This is a very important question, Private Hamp. I can't emphasise too much how important it is. Did you intend to return to the battalion?
Hamp (*in great difficulty*) Honest to God, sir, I — I can't say.
Hargreaves (*sudden outburst*) My God, can't you see it's because he didn't know what he was doing. He doesn't know how to lie to you. (*Then he turns to* Hamp, *and asks very gently*.) Wasn't it simply because you can't clearly remember?
Hamp That's right, sir.
Hargreaves And likewise you can't clearly remember why you went absent — because, as you say, there wasn't any clear reason or plan in your mind at all, was there?
Hamp That's right, sir. Didn't have no plan. It were same as I just started goin', sir, makin' tracks, because I couldn't stop myself.
President Did you try to stop yourself?
Hamp I couldn't sir, that's all. (*To* Hargreaves.) Same as you told me to say; sir, I couldn't help it. It were same as some way — I were made to —(*Then, after struggling*.) That's all I can say, sir. I can't think of no more.
President Have you any other questions, Mr. Hargreaves?
Hargreaves No, thank you, sir.
President Mr. Midgley?
Midgley (*to* Hamp) Did you know you were doing wrong when you deserted?
Hamp I never thought much on it, sir.
Midgley But you must surely have been aware of it all the time at the back of your mind?
Hamp If anybody'd tried to stop me I'd have stayed, sir.
Midgley But didn't you wait till you'd made sure there was nobody there to stop you?
Hamp I think I were just lucky, sir, getting away, like.
Medgley (*rather sadly*) That's very much a matter of opinion — whether you were lucky or not in being allowed to desert your duty. But what I'm asking is this. You did know, didn't you, that it was your duty to stay with the battalion?
Hamp Yes, sir.

Midgley	And you must have been quite aware of that in your mind during all the time when you were absent — from the very first moment when you deserted?
Hamp	I don't know, sir. It's a long while ago.
Midgley	I'm asking you to remember, and tell the truth about it.
Hamp	But I told them already, sir. It were same as I couldn't stay. I can't tell it no different. I can't remember nothing else in my mind, and that's the God's truth, sir.
Midgley	But you could walk, and speak, and think, like anybody else. And you managed to get quite a long way away before you were captured.
Hamp	Same as I said, though, sir — I were only lucky.
Midgley	Let me put it to you quite simply. Did you know what you were doing?
Hamp	Yes, sir. But I couldn't help myself.
Midgley	And you knew your comrades were staying at their posts, prepared to do their duty while you were deserting them? Didn't you? Didn't you?
Hamp	(*after a pause — beaten*) I never did the like of this before, sir, never. This were the very first time.
Midgley	(*to President*) That's all, sir.

from *Hamp* by John Wilson

For discussion

1. According to Hargreaves, what was Hamp's intention when he ran away?
2. According to Midgley, what was his intention?
3. Why does Hargreaves introduce the point about the letter?
4. Why do you think Midgley does not make any reference to the letter?
5. Do you think Hamp intended to desert? Why?

Read the scene again. *Then discuss*:

6. What different rules or conventions are observed by the members of the court martial?
7. What is the importance of the President's question to Hamp: 'Did you intend to return to the batallion?'?
8. How do you think Midgley would have responded if Hamp had said he *did* intend to return?
9. What do you think is the most important point that Midgley makes?
10. Now repeat your discussion of question 5, but this time imagine you are all members of the court martial. Discuss it informally, disregarding the formal rules of a court. Choose players for the roles of Hamp, Midgley and Hargreaves. Permit yourselves to ask any questions that you think are relevant and also to change your minds if you feel genuinely persuaded to do so. At the end of the discussion, compare your opinions (and verdict) now with your earlier opinions.

Postscript

In the play, as in the many real-life cases from the First World War which inspired it, Hamp was found guilty and was executed.

Corporal Punishment Debate
The House of Lords 1985

In 1985, the British Government sought to introduce legislation that would have made it unlawful for a state school to administer corporal punishment to any pupil unless the pupil's parents agreed to the punishment. The main reason for the decision to change the law in this way was an earlier decision by the European Court of Human Rights (binding on all members of the Common Market) that it was a breach of the European Convention on Human Rights to administer corporal punishment to a child if that child's parents disapproved.

In the House of Lords, Baroness David introduced an amendment to the Government's proposed legislation which sought to abolish corporal punishment in schools altogether. This led to the following debate.

Before reading the extracts below, discuss your own views on corporal punishment in school and also on the government's proposal. Make a note of your main arguments for and against.

Baroness David:
> I do not think that I need again to go into the case for the abolition of corporal punishment which I put very fully at Committee stage. I should like to emphasise just two points. The first is that as a deterrent it does not work. The same children get beaten over and over again and frequently for the same offence. The second is that it is degrading for both the giver and the receiver and that a school which relies on that form of punishment will not have the sort of atmosphere conducive to good education and good relationships between teacher and taught. I would remind your Lordships of what the noble Lord, Lord James of Rusholme, said back in 1973 when speaking in the debate on the Protection of Minors Bill of my noble friend Lady Wootton. He said that,

> *"the harm of corporal punishment goes a good deal further than its effect on the frightened child. I am referring to the more subtle damage to the atmosphere of an educative community and to the proper development of the individuals in it when authority has to rest on the infliction of physical pain". — [Official Report, 10/12/73; col. 947].*

> If that was true 12 years ago, it is even more true today. Since some people who were not here at Committee stage may not be aware of it, I should say that all the teacher organisations are against the Bill, even the three which have not yet an explicitly abolitionist policy. All would prefer abolition to this Bill. The very important and influential Society of Education Officers argues against the Bill in strong terms. It takes,

> "the view that any form of exemption scheme, though one might be devised and made to work, would be unsatisfactory, unfair and divisive. If one were introduced, it could, by creating a sense of injustice, be very damaging to the ethos of a school and could eventually undermine a school's discipline".

That is not, I imagine, what the Secretary of State wants.
The society goes on:

> "It would be preferable for the Government to grasp the nettle immediately and issue a policy statement announcing the abolition of corporal punishment within a specified timescale".

We would agree that a specified timescale is necessary in order to give those schools that still rely on corporal punishment as a method of discipline time to phase it out. For this reason we have put down Amendment No. 61 to Clause 8 which would enable the Secretary of State to appoint the day on which the Act would come into force. A year to 18 months should be ample time.

Lord Beloff:
My Lords, I have listened with growing amazement to the self-styled voice of reason and progress, and I find it impossible to reconcile what has been argued with the fact (which was admitted by the noble Baroness) that of the teachers' organisations, three have not gone on record as being in favour of abolition. Yet abolition is to be the keynote of a Bill which was designed for a rather different purpose.

I remind your Lordships that our proceedings this afternoon will be interrupted by a Statement on the highly regrettable pay dispute involving the teaching profession, and I would point out that one of the reasons which has been advanced by the teachers' organisations for extra remuneration is the greater degree of physical risk and strain which some of them now face in some schools. It seems that if those teachers themselves believe that the existence, as a final sanction, of corporal punishment is to some extent a protection for them, it is not for your Lordships to remove that protection.

The Earl of Onslow:
Most of the time I am longing to thrash my children, but that may be an unhealthy reaction. I think we have all wanted to thrash our children, and I quite understand the schoolteachers who want to thrash the children in their class. However, to be able to thrash Johnny but not Fred would be a ridiculous and unfair system; and, against my will, I shall be forced to vote for the noble Baroness, Lady David.

4 p.m.

Lord Boothby:
My Lords, very briefly, I want to support this amendment. The date of 4th August 1914 is a day that will always be imprinted on my mind. On that date I was beaten for the first time as a schoolboy, and on that date the First World

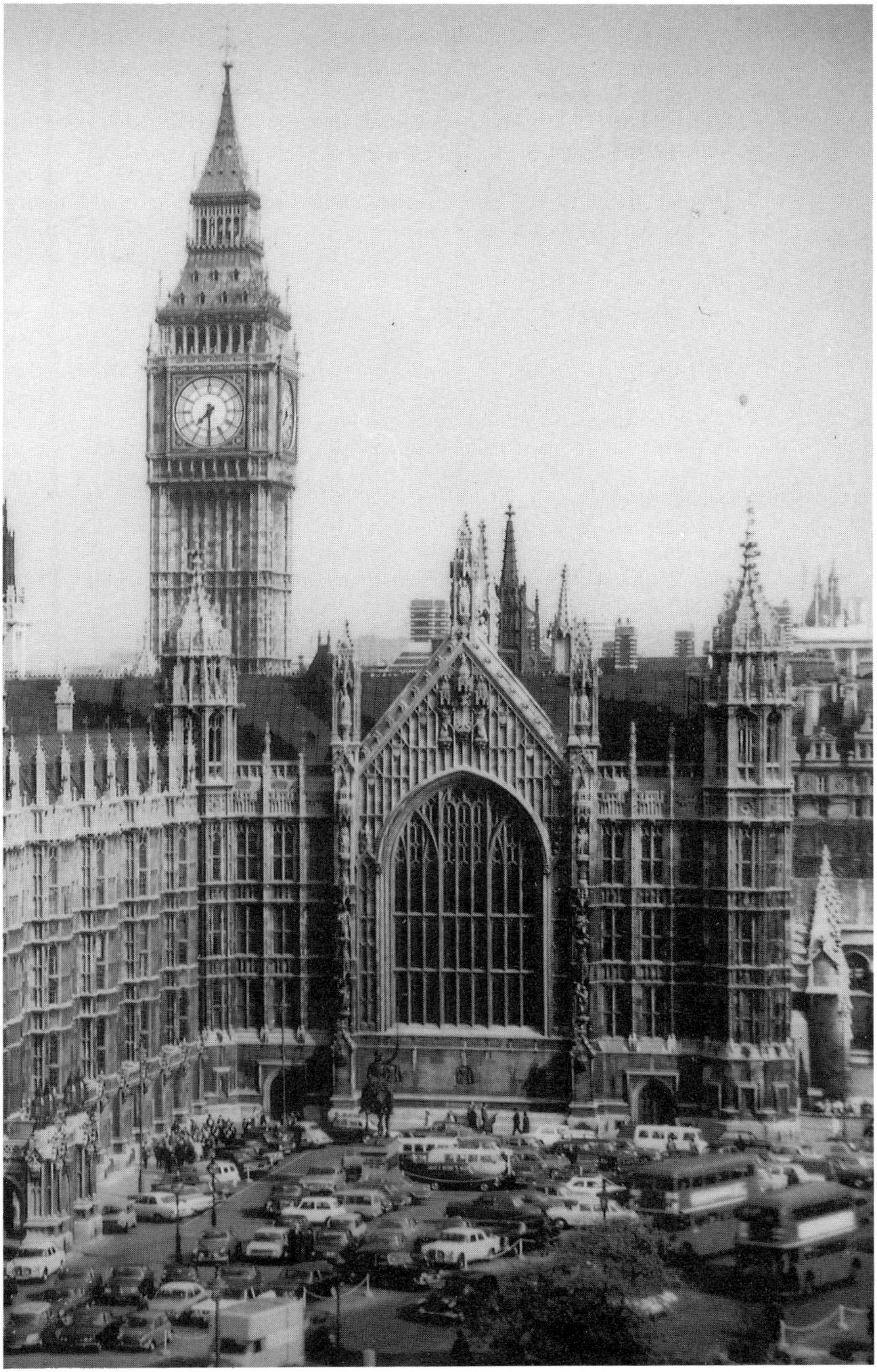

War broke out! I shall never forget it. In those days the houses at Eton – for that was my school, which was then regarded as a very posh school – were governed by a select group of five or six senior boys called the library, of whom two, the captain of games and the captain of the houses (and my noble friend Lord Home was both) were allowed to beat other boys with a cane. It was called tanning. That happened every Saturday night in my house, and the consent of the whole library had to be obtained. When I was put into the library by the housemaster I used my vote to veto all tanning, and that lasted for about four weeks. There were no beatings in the house during that period. I took the view that the house was very much happier at the end of that time.

My housemaster, however, took a different view. He said that all discipline had been undermined, and replaced by anarchy. He therefore decided to make a new rule, which was that my vote on this question should be disregarded. Therefore, every Saturday night when tanning was to take place I was reduced to walking out in protest, and tanning was restored. But even at that time I realised that more damage was being done to the beaters and the watchers than to the beaten, because very soon you could see that they began to enjoy it.

Whichever way we look at it, and however much the noble Lord who has just spoken may maintain that beating is an essential part of the Christian religion, I nevertheless say that corporal punishment, however administered in nurseries and schools, is to legalise physical assault upon unprotected children. As such it condones violence, and even encourages it. This is extremely dangerous.

Violence should be a cause of great anxiety to all of us at the present time. I have never seen anybody turn on a television screen, or turned one on myself, at any hour of the day and for any programme, for the last five years, without my saying, "I bet ten to one that this is violent". If anybody had ever taken the bets I would be a rich man today. Violence is the greatest danger we have to face at the present time, and it is growing...

Violence, I repeat, is the greatest menace we have to face. We should make a better start putting an end to violence in nurseries and schoolrooms than we shall in the conference rooms of Geneva. I believe, therefore, that underlying this Bill and this amendment, which I quite agree lends itself to considerable jokes from time to time, is a problem which adds up to the greatest menace of our time.

Lord Henderson of Brompton:

I admit that the schoolboy concept of fairness is pretty crude. Recently I read these words of Sidney Smith, written in 1709:

"The morality of boys is generally very imperfect; their notions of honour extremely mistaken; and their objects of ambition frequently very absurd".

But there is this fundamental notion of fairness which we all recognise from our schooldays, and that concept of fairness is carried on into adult life and is one that we all share. Indeed, the schoolboy concept of what is fair now has statutory recognition and is incorporated into such concepts as fair trading. Surely we cannot impose on boys and girls at school something which we know they will consider to be unfair.

Baroness Wootton of Abinger:
My Lords, I think we should remind ourselves at this stage of the seriousness of the matter we are discussing. We are not discussing trifling things that happen and are not taken much notice of, and that some schools have and some schools do not have. We are thinking of what would be a serious criminal assault if similar and equal force was applied to an attack made upon a grown adult of one's own size.

I have always believed that the principle of justice was that one never attacked a man who was not of one's own size. It is not so long ago that we abolished corporal punishment for adults who were convicted of serious criminal offences. I believe that there has been some reason to suppose that this has had a beneficial effect upon the necessarily large number of criminal offences that were formerly dealt with in this way.

I suppose that we might retain corporal punishment in schools if we admitted that the aim of education is to teach children that force always wins in the end. Perhaps I might refer once again to my friends, the Russian children, who, when our English party arrived, greeted us all with a warm handshake and the moving words, "So you come from Britain, where they beat the children?" This has remained as a stain and a mark of guilt on my mind ever since. Wherever I go I have to say to myself, "I come from Britain where they beat the children" – and I carry this sort of mark of the devil about with me. And so do all of you who are equally to blame!

The Earl of Arran:
My Lords, having been beaten at school I shall no doubt be under deep suspicion in this House before I say anything. I scarcely thought that some 30 years after having been beaten for listening to a state funeral on a crystal set I should be in your Lordships' House discussing the merits of whether beating should be allowed at all. I have the feeling that many of your Lordships would agree that in those 30 years most of the Western world has become a considerably softer place in its attitude towards discipline. I dare to suggest, furthermore, that many of your Lordships will consider that to be not a good thing. Perhaps like myself – and it would appear others – some of your Lordships have experienced a beating and found that it did no harm; and indeed on reflection did some good.

The reason we are discussing this Bill at all, as we all know, is a result of the judgement given by the European Court of Human Rights, to which we are a party. As a result of this judgment the British Government have decided that it is better to allow some form of corporal punishment rather than none at all. It is on this issue that I am in agreement with the Government. The entire spectrum, the whole principle, of corporal punishment has for years been accepted as a part of our daily lives.

What is it that now causes us to doubt its relevance? Is it fashion? Is it 40 years of peacetime? If we are not to continue to include this particular form of discipline in our schools through the assistance of a short, sharp rap that may sting for a few seconds in our stern endeavour to teach that child at an early age the difference between right and wrong, to teach that child respect and kindness towards its elders, its fellow pupils, and property, then teachers, and parents, and children later to be adults may well be the poorer citizens for it.

If we deny the option of administering reasonable and moderate corporal punishment in our schools, how long will it be before the Paediatric Association, the Royal College of Psychiatrists and other such august bodies will be recommending that all forms of discipline should be outlawed in all schools? Furthermore, the fact that we are the only Western European country which does not prohibit corporal punishment in schools is really not an argument for abolition. How many times in the past have we had to go it alone against strong pressures from outsiders to acquiesce? The majority is not always right.

In conclusion, very few clauses of any Bill are ideal. Some of the clauses in this Bill may not be ideal. But I suspect that as much as the ideology, the rights and wrongs, behind this particular Bill there lies the natural anxiety over the unknown, the uncertainty, as to whether this Bill can be made to work. Given understanding and patience and time, I have little doubt that it will. I therefore urge your Lordships to support the noble Baroness, Lady Cox, and thereby the Government, and to vote against this amendment.

Lord Ritchie of Dundee:

My Lords, I shall not keep your Lordships more than just a minute. At the Committee stage, I said something which now feels rather like a public confession: that is, that many years ago when I was running a small school as headmaster, I felt it was necessary to use the cane. This was the feeling from the staff – and also, it may surprise you, from the boys themselves. This was their idea of justice and of seeing that justice was done. But it was 20 years ago. I would not do it now. It is not just because I have given up playing tennis. It is because times have changed. The climate of opinion has changed. In an increasingly violent world, I think all civilised educationists, and perhaps all civilised people, agree that violence breeds violence and that we are not likely to achieve any better purposes by putting the clock back.

Baroness Cox:

My Lords, the government prefers to leave the decision concerning the appropriateness of corporal punishment to those closest to the child and with responsibility for his or her well-being. I refer, of course, to the parents and the teachers. No one is requiring them to use corporal punishment, but the enforced abolition of corporal punishment implies a lack of trust in them and in their judgement; and, indeed, during the debate this afternoon, even worse, sadistic motives have been imputed to them. The Government therefore oppose this amendment as a matter of principle.

Baroness David:

My Lords, we have had a long discussion on this amendment and I have had a great deal of excellent support for it . . . I press the amendment.

4.54 p.m.

        On Question, Whether the said amendment (No. 1) shall be agreed to?

        Their Lordships divided: Contents, 108; Not-contents, 104.

extracts from the Parliamentary Debates
(Hansard) The House of Lords, 4 July 1985

For discussion

1. Refer back to the various points you made in your own discussion of this issue. How many of your points are also made in the House of Lords debate? How many of your points are not made?

2. In Unit 2 various techniques were outlined by which speakers or writers can seek to mislead an audience. One of them was *making a generalised claim without any hard evidence to back it up.* Can you find any example of this in this debate?

3. Another such technique is *jumping from an agreed fact to a very definite conclusion,* but without any intervening argument or discussion. Can you find any example of this in this debate?

4. Who do you think makes the most persuasive speech *in favour* of the amendment? Discuss the points that you would make *in reply* to that speech.

5. Who do you think makes the most persuasive speech *against* the amendment? Discuss the points that you would make *in reply* to that speech.

6. In general, do you find that a *discussion* is more likely to allow you to express a good range of opinions than a *debate*? Or do you feel that a debate is better in this respect?

7. What different conventions are employed by the speakers in this debate?

8. Choose one of the speeches and read it aloud persuasively until you find the right style and tone to fit a public debate. Talk about the ways you need to change your normal speaking voice in order to do this.

Postscript

Baroness David's success in moving her amendment to the Government's Bill meant that the Bill itself was now defeated. The Government responded by dropping the Bill altogether and announcing that they would introduce a new one in due course. This meant the end also of Baroness David's amendment.

The Loeb–Leopold Murder Trial

The accused

Richard Loeb, 18, and **Nathan Leopold**, 19, were arrested and charged in Chicago in 1924 for the murder of a 14-year-old schoolboy, Robert Franks. At first they protested their innocence, but at the beginning of the trial their lawyer persuaded them to plead guilty.

They were both students and both had brilliant academic records. Loeb was the youngest person ever to have graduated from the University of Michigan and was shortly to enrol for a law course. Leopold had already obtained brilliant marks as a student at the University of Chicago and was now taking a further course there in law. They also belonged to two of the richest families in Chicago.

The evidence

According to their own evidence, they had murdered Franks in order to prove to themselves that the perfect crime was possible. They planned it and executed it without any particular feelings or motives. They knew Franks slightly – he lived near to them and was also a distant relative of Loeb. They chose him as their victim 'at random', gave him a lift home in a car they had rented, battered him to death with a chisel, and later disposed of the body in a swamp outside the city. Then they telephoned the boy's father and, using a false name, claimed to have kidnapped the boy. The next morning they sent a letter to the father demanding $10,000 in ransom money.

They remained convinced that their crime was perfect. Loeb offered his services to newspaper reporters looking for evidence in the neighbourhood, and Leopold asked questions in his law class that could have been taken to reveal an intense personal interest in the case. In fact, though, it was a very imperfect crime. The boy's body was found less than 24 hours after the killing, and Leopold's spectacles were found nearby. These led to Leopold's and then to Loeb's arrest, and both of them, when questioned separately, accused the other.

The defence

They were defended by one of the most brilliant lawyers of his time, Clarence Darrow. It was Darrow who told the accused they must plead guilty. It was the only way, he said, in which it might be possible to save them from hanging. This was because of the law in Chicago at that time, which allowed accused persons to give evidence on why they should not be hanged – but only if they pleaded guilty. In other words, by pleading guilty, there was just a chance that Darrow could persuade the judge not to hang the accused. He did not, though, attempt to plead that the accused were insane.

For discussion

Before reading the extract from Darrow's final speech to the judge, discuss:
1 What arguments and what techniques would you expect Darrow to have used? Note that he was addressing a judge and *not* a jury; since the accused pleaded guilty there was nothing for a jury to decide and so no jury was convened.
2 Note also the precise aim of Darrow's speech: to persuade the judge that the two accused, although guilty and although not insane, were nevertheless not sufficiently responsible for what they had done to deserve to hang.

Clarence Darrow's speech to the judge (adapted):

Your Honour, our anxiety over this case has not been due to the facts that are connected with this most unfortunate affair, but to the almost unheard-of publicity it has received. And when the public is interested and demands a punishment, no matter what the offence, great or small, it thinks of only one punishment and that is death.

This case has attracted publicity not because of the nature of the crime, but because the defendants are rich. If we fail in this defence it will not be for lack of money. It will be on account of money. I insist, your Honour, that had this been a case of two boys of these defendants' ages unconnected with families supposed to have great wealth, there is not a state's attorney in Illinois who would not have consented at once to a plea of guilty and a punishment in the penitentiary for life. Not one. My friend, Mr Savage [*one of the prosecuting lawyers*] in as cruel a speech as he knew how to make, said to the court that we pleaded guilty because we were afraid to do anything else. Your Honour, that is true. Your Honour will never thank me for unloading this responsibility upon you, but you know that I would have been untrue to my clients if I had not concluded to take this chance before a court, instead of submitting it to a poisoned jury in the city of Chicago.

The prosecution have called this a cold-blooded murder because they want to take human lives. But was it a cold-blooded murder? Was it the most terrible murder that ever happened in the state of Illinois? Was it the most dastardly act in the annals of crime? No. I insist, Your Honour, that under all fair rules and measurements, this was one of the least dastardly and cruel of any that I have known anything about.

Now let us see how we should measure it. I would say the first thing to consider is the degree of pain of the victim. Poor little Bobbie Franks suffered very little. There is no excuse for his killing. If to hang these two boys would bring him back to life, I would say let them hang, and I believe their parents would say so too. Robert Franks is dead and we cannot call him back to life. It was all over in 15 minutes after he got into the car, and he probably never knew it or thought of it. That does not justify it. It is the last thing I would do. I am sorry for the poor boy. I am sorry for his parents. But it is done.

Why did these brilliantly clever boys commit this crime? It is because they had an abundance of brains and a lack of feeling. This fact has been asserted by the psychiatrists called by the defence *and* by the prosecution. Neither boy is blameworthy. I know that they cannot feel what you feel and what I feel; that they cannot feel the moral shocks that come to men who are educated and who have not been deprived of an emotional system or emotional feelings. I know it, and every person who honestly studied this subject knows it as well. Is Dickie Loeb to blame, because out of the infinite forces that conspired to form him, the infinite forces that were at work producing him ages before he was born, that because out of these infinite combinations he was born without this emotional system? If he is, then there should be a new definition for justice.

We have heard that Leopold has studied philosophy at university, and that he has especially been drawn to the study of the German philosopher Nietzsche. He has been influenced and corrupted by Nietzsche's belief that some men are beyond the reach of morality. Such men, says the philosopher, are supermen. Is there any blame attached because somebody took Nietzsche's philosophy seriously and fashioned his life in it? And there's no question in this case that it is true. Then who is to blame? The university would be more to blame than he is. Your Honour, it is hardly fair to hang a nineteen-year-old boy for the philosophy that was taught him at the university.

from *Verdict* **directed by Sydney Lumet**

If I could ever bring my mind to ask for the death penalty, I would not do it boastfully and exultantly or in anger or in hate, but I would do it with the deepest regret that it must be done, and I would do it with sympathy even for the ones whose lives must be taken. This has not been done in this case. I have never seen a more deliberate effort to turn the human beings of a community into ravening wolves and take advantage of everything that was offered to create an unreasoning hatred against these two boys.

If these two boys die on the scaffold – which I can never bring myself to imagine – if they do die on the scaffold, the details of this will be spread over the world. Every newspaper in the United States will carry a full account. Every newspaper of Chicago will be filled with the gruesome details. It will enter every home and every family. Will it make men better or make men worse? I would like to put that to the intelligence of man, at least such intelligence as they have.

I can picture the execution scene. The boys are awakened in the grey light of morning, furnished a suit of clothes by the state, led to the scaffold, their feet tied, black caps drawn over their heads, stood on a trap door, the hangman pressing a spring so that it gives under them; I can see them fall through space and stopped by the rope around their necks.

[Here Darrow quoted a poem by A. E. Housman about a boy who is about to be hanged.]

> 'The night my father got me
> His mind was not on me
> He did not plague his fancy
> To muse if I should be
> The son you see.'

Your Honour may hang these boys. In doing it, you will turn your face toward the past. In doing it you will make it harder for every other boy who in ignorance and darkness must grope his way through the mazes which only childhood knows. You may save them and make it easier for every child that some time may stand where these boys stand. I am pleading for the future. I am pleading for a time when hatred and cruelty will not control the hearts of men; when we can learn by reason and judgement and understanding and faith that all life is worth saving, and that mercy is the highest attribute of man.

[Darrow concluded his speech by quoting from the Edward Fitzgerald translation of 'The Rubaiyat of Omar Khayyam'.]

> 'So I be written in the Book of Love,
> I do not care about the Book above.
> Erase my name or write it as you will,
> So I be written in the Book of Love.'

abridged and adapted from Clarence Darrow's final speech to the Judge, Chicago 1924

For discussion

1. Refer back to your earlier discussion. Does Clarence Darrow use any arguments that you had already suggested? Did you suggest any arguments that Darrow does *not* use?
2. Are there any techniques that you suggested that Darrow uses ? Or that he does not use?
3. Does Darrow at any point make a general claim with out giving any hard evidence to support it?
4. What do you think is the best point he makes?
5. Why does Darrow refer to the accused as 'boys'?
6. What different conventions does Darrow employ in this speech?
7. If you were the judge, would you sentence the accused to hang? Or would you sentence them to a long term of imprisonment? Why?

For individual work

8. Re-read the speech and make a note of a suitable sub-heading for each paragraph.

For discussion

9. Compare your sub-headings and briefly discuss whether you agree with the main point that Darrow makes in each paragraph.
10. Choose the most effective paragraph and practise reading it aloud. Talk about the ways you need to adapt the tone and style and also the volume of your speech in order to make Darrow's arguments effective.

Postscript

The two accused were spared the death penalty. The judge sentenced them to life imprisonment with the proviso that neither should ever be released on parole. In 1936 Loeb was stabbed to death in a fight in prison with another inmate. Leopold was released from prison in 1958 under a five year parole agreement. Five years later he was discharged from parole. For a time he worked as a nurses' assistant in a hospital in South America.

Questions on all three texts

To answer these questions you will need to re-read all three of the texts in this Unit and to keep on referring to them. You should work on your own.

1. Quote two or three things that Hamp says in *Court Martial: A Case of Desertion* to show most clearly the kind of person he seems to be.
2. What in particular does Midgley want Hamp to say?
   Does he succeed in getting Hamp to say it?
3. Explain in a paragraph or two whether or not you think Hamp should have been executed. Make some reference in your writing to what you consider to be the main point on the other side of the argument.
4. Write a reply to Baroness David's opening speech, as if you are opposed to her amendment. Limit your reply to a paragraph or two, but deal with each of her main points.
5. Write the first two paragraphs, with headlines, of two contemporary news reports of Clarence Darrow's speech. One of these should be a completely fair and neutral account. The other should be definitely but subtly prejudiced either for or against capital punishment for the accused. (The latter should not contain any flagrant lies!)
6. One of the most effective techniques in any argument is to take the arguments of the other side and use them again to your own advantage. Is there any example of this in any of these three texts?

For discussion

Choose a *controversial topic* about which the class feel strongly. Prepare for a discussion on it, making notes of the main points you wish to make.

1. Discuss it *informally* in groups, taking brief notes on the main points made by each speaker.
2. Discuss it *formally* as a class, as if for a parliamentary debate, with the topic debated as a motion to which speakers will express support or opposition. Again, take brief notes on the main points made by each speaker.
   Then vote on the motion.
3. Discuss the differences between informal and formal discussion. What are the advantages of each?

Punctuation

Find and explain examples of the use of

1. two dashes in one sentence (in Lord Boothby's speech);
2. one dash (in the dialogue in *Court Martial*);
3. one dash in a sentence (in Baroness Wootton's speech);
4. a stop, but not a full stop at the end of a sentence (in the final part of the report of the Lords' debate);
5. speech marks (in Clarence Darrow's speech);
6. the apostrophe, for two different purposes (in Clarence Darrow's speech).
7. For what other purpose can the apostrophe be used (in addition to those illustrated in question 6)?
8. For what other purpose can speech marks be used (in addition to that illustrated in question 5)?

For writing

1. Write the judge's reply to Clarence Darrow's speech, making close references to all his main points. If you wish, you can change the sentence from life imprisonment to capital punishment. In writing this, you should keep fairly closely to Darrow's own style and techniques.
2. Write a report of the discussion on your own choice of topic as if it has been a debate in the House of Lords.
3. Write a speech for the same debate, developing your arguments fully and at length. If you prefer you could write two speeches, one for and one against. Also, if you wish, change the topic to one of your own choice.

14 MAKING FILMS

The Home and the World **directed by Satyajit Ray**

My Ain Folk **directed by Bill Douglas**

All the materials in this Unit are concerned with the ways films are made, the kinds of films that are made, and the writing of film scripts.

Yield to the Night **directed by Lee Thompson**

For discussion

1. Who are the different personnel involved in the making of a film?
2. What are their jobs?
3. What different kinds of films are there?
4. What are the two or three most interesting films you have seen recently? What kinds, or genres, of films are they?

All the extracts that follow are taken from *An Introduction to Film-Making*, by Grace Matchett.

1 Who Makes Films?

If you ask someone, 'Who is the most important person in the making of a film?' the chances are they will reply, 'The actors!' In fact, nothing could be further from the truth. Sometimes, it is true, we go to see a film because a particular actor happens to star in it, but generally speaking, the actors (even the stars) have very little influence on how good or how bad a film happens to be. And as a matter of fact the actors may not even do much acting when they are making a film – but I'll explain that in a little while.

There are two important people in the making of any film – the producer and the director. And it's difficult to say which of these two is the more important, but I'll begin with the producer.

The producer is the person who finds the money for making the film. Generally, that means finding a great deal of money – more than most of us can ever imagine. For instance, very few films nowadays cost less than four or five million pounds. A new American film, *Raiders of the Lost Ark*, cost ten million pounds to make, and was considered cheap at that. It was produced by George Lucas, who made *Star Wars* – a film that has so far made no less than £250 million at box offices around the world.

What kind of people become producers? Well, like Lucas, they need to know a great deal about the business of making films, and especially of making successful films. They also need to know a lot of people who are willing to invest their money in the *idea* of a new film. And they also need to be very good at recognising a good idea for a film from a bad one.

Some people think it is easy to know a good idea when they see one but it isn't. The real difficulty is that the producer has to see how good or bad it is before the film is actually made, not after it. It is much easier, of course, to judge the film once it is actually on the screen. For example, the film *Heaven's Gate* cost £20 million and seems likely to lose every penny of it. But it must have looked a good idea originally.

What exactly, then, does the producer try to sell when he goes around inviting people to invest their money in his idea for a film? In a sense, he sells a package. The package consists of a number of different things, such as the name of the director (the man or woman who will actually make the film) plus the outline of the story, and the names of the star or stars who will probably appear in the film. Sometimes, the star or even the director will act as their own producers.

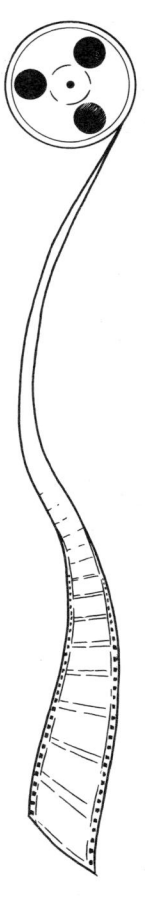

So the producer makes it possible for a film to be made. But he or she then hands over to the director, who is in complete artistic control throughout the making of the film. The director has the final say in every detail of the film: the actual shooting of scenes, the casting, the editing, even the script writing. He or she may not personally do any of these different jobs, but the director still retains the right to decide finally how such jobs are carried out. This does not mean, though, that the performing of these other jobs is in any sense unimportant. On the contrary, they are essential parts of the whole business of film-making, and a small number of individuals may become highly distinguished within the film maker's world as exponents of the various skills involved. A good editor is likely to be highly sought after, for he or she is the technician who puts together the final print of the film from all the shots and scenes that have been made. Equally important is the person in charge of continuity, whose job it is to ensure that there is perfect continuity from one shot to the next. At its simplest this may mean that the actor is wearing the same clothes in different shots in the same scene, but things are not generally so simple; for example, the continuity extends to questions of lighting, facial expression, scenery and sound.

Directors sometimes become famous. Sometimes, it is their names that sell the films to the public. Probably the best example of such a director was Alfred Hitchcock. More recently Steven Spielberg can be cited as a director in the same tradition: his films do not need to be graced by stars.

So although the quality of the acting may be an important ingredient in the making of any film, the actors themselves are not the central factor in the quality and impact of the final product. Indeed it is fair to say that many good films are good despite their actors – that the acting is nothing special. Also, there are many films in which the actors do very little: they pose, they move about, they smile, they prop up the scenery. Sometimes they do not know very much about what is happening. One famous actress recently confessed that many of the scenes in one of her most famous films were shot by the director without telling her that the cameras were rolling!

For discussion

1 Can you think of other famous directors? What films do you associate with them?

2 Can you think of any films in which the actor is the 'central factor in the quality and impact of the final product'?

3 Working in pairs, devise a short phrase to summarise each of the paragraphs. Then compare your summaries with the rest of the class.

4 Find an example from the article so far of each of the following marks of punctuation:
    colon, semi-colon, brackets, dash
Explain why each is used.

2 Kinds of Films

Broadly speaking, there are two kinds of films: the documentary film, which seeks to portray events more or less truthfully, and fictional films which seek to tell a story with a view to entertaining and perhaps enlightening the audience. Documentary films can themselves be divided into those that consist mostly of live film of the events themselves and those that consist mostly of reconstructed portraits of those events. A number of makers of documentary films have achieved distinction. For example, the Russian director Sergei Eisenstein made *The General Line* in 1928 about farming in the USSR. John Grierson, the British director, invented the word 'documentary' itself, and made one of the first such films in Britain (*The Drifters*, 1929) about the herring fleet. Robert Flaherty, an American director, was the most influential pioneer in documentary film-making, and followed his early study of Eskimo life, *Nanook of the North*, in 1920, with studies of life in the South Seas (*Tabu*, 1931), in Scotland (*Man of Arran*, 1934), and in India (*Elephant Boy*, 1937).

As the cinema has been overtaken by television, so the documentary has increased in popularity and dominance. Many news programmes are essentially documentary films and there can be little doubt that the particular ways in which television chooses to 'show' the news has an immense influence on the way the public thinks about and responds to the news. So the documentary film clearly has a political importance. Indeed most of the documentary programmes on television have an overt political message, whether they are aiming to influence public attitudes on something quite specific, such as capital punishment, or are aiming at a broader bias towards the left or right of the political spectrum. One school of thought, to which I myself subscribe, argues that it is impossible to film (or in any other way report) the news without expressing a political bias. In other words, every news programme you watch is also expressing a definite attitude towards what is being reported. This bias expresses itself in a variety of ways, including how a story is reported, and also in the decision to report the story or not report it. Consider, for instance, a film report of a conflict between the police and workers on strike, in which the conflict flares into violence. The impact and meaning of the news report will depend on such factors as the differing degree of violence shown by the police and the strikers, and the initial provocation shown by either side. Assuming that the film-maker is able to collect enough film, he or she will then be able to edit the film in order to shift the burden of guilt from one side to the other. The police can be shown to have 'started it' and to have behaved 'violently', or the strikers can be shown as the chief offenders.

Thus, there is no simple truth in what is shown as the news. Perhaps the camera cannot lie – but the film can. Another way of saying this, is to stress the value of film as propaganda. One of the first political leaders to appreciate this was Hitler, who engaged a brilliant director, Leni Riefenstahl, to make documentary films of the Nuremberg Rally (*Triumph of the Will*, 1934) and of the Berlin Olympics (*Olympische*

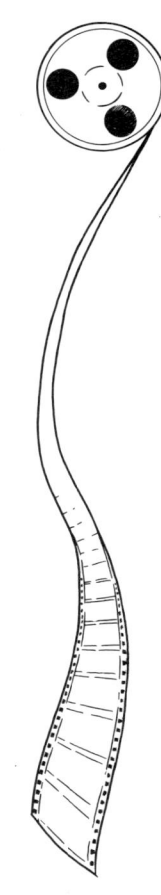

Spiele, 1936). Both were and are superb examples of the art of film-making, and both used real events in such a way as to salute the Nazis' cause.

Fictional films can also be divided into different kinds or genres. Indeed any one who enjoys films is really someone who enjoys particular genres. I doubt if there is anyone who enjoys every genre. Every genre has its own particular conventions. These may relate to a great variety of different aspects of a film, including for example the scenery, the action, the story, the dialogue, the music, and the acting. In particular, every genre has its own sense of an ending. A detective story must end with the detective finding out the murderer's identity. A western must end with the resolution of the conflict between the goodies and the baddies. And so on. Very often, particular actors or actresses become identified with a particular genre, and their mere presence is enough to assure the audience that they are about to watch this genre rather than that.

Any genre can be made the subject of humour. Indeed every genre has its offspring – the 'spoof' genre. The conventions of the spoof are also simple; they slightly exaggerate the conventions that they are laughing at and change one or two of them. Most frequently they change the leading players, perhaps replacing the strong silent hero with a very talkative and nervous character who is in no sense heroic. Or they replace the 'femme fatale' with a homely little chatterbox.

Also, any genre can be made the subject of change and experiment. It is perfectly possible for example to make a western in which the baddies win, not lose, or to make a detective story in which the detective never discovers the murderer's identity. Such experiments, if they are successful, do not mean the end of the genre – there will probably be many more films which follow the old conventions. But they may mean the arrival of a new genre – a kind of western, or a kind of detective story, say, which is distinct from the old type but, eventually, just as predictable.

In other words, genres breed new genres.

For class discussion

1 Talk about any words or phrases of whose meaning you are unsure, such as the terms:
 left or right (second paragraph) in relation to politics;
 conventions of film-making;
 femme fatale;
and any others.

2 Do you agree with this writer that:
 a) all documentary films reveal some kind of political bias? Or can you think of any that do not?
 b) all fictional films belong to one genre or another? Or can you think of any that do not?

The Liberation of L. B. Jones **directed by William Wyler**

For group discussion

1. What is the difference between saying that a documentary film has a political bias and saying that it is propaganda?
2. Briefly outline the contents of any news bulletin you have seen on television, and decide whether or not it had a political bias.
3. What is your favourite genre of fictional film?
   Give two or three examples of films of this genre and work out the conventions they have in common.
4. Can you think of any films that
     a) make fun of a genre? If so, how do they do it?
     b) experiment with a genre? If so, how do they change its conventions?

   Make a note of your discussions, and then report back to the rest of the class.

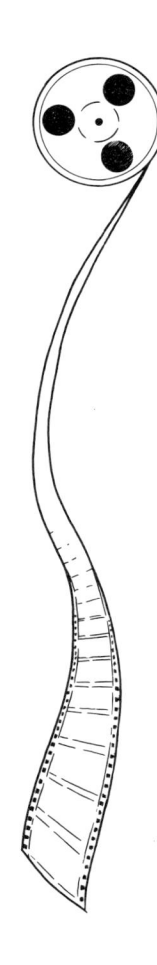

3 Shooting a Film

In the very early days of film-making, shooting a scene was basically a straightforward matter. The camera was placed in front of the action and the players then acted out the scene. In other words, the camera stood still, and the actors moved about as if they were on the stage and the camera was the audience. So it could be said that the early films were much like filmed plays. Indeed many famous stage actors and actresses of the early years of the 20th century repeated some of their most famous performances (in excerpts, at least) for the camera, and there seems to have been little adaptation for the purposes of the film. The camera saw and captured no more than a theatre audience would have captured. So watching a film at that time was in some respects not very different from watching a play, except that there was no sense of contact between the players and the audience.

Needless to say, these early films were, by modern standards, technically limited. Imagine any of your favourite films made in such a way that the camera never moved, that the actors remained on a single stage, and that the distance between the camera and the actors remained more or less the same throughout. Visually, such a film would be very monotonous.

From the beginning, film-makers experimented with the techniques of film-making and it is not fair to attribute particular achievements to specific individuals – many of the experimenters were copied by others who achieved more acclaim. However, one of the great pioneers was the American, D. W. Griffith, who in a series of silent films extended the techniques of the camera and, in particular, established the **close-up** as a basic part of film-making. In other words, the camera no longer remained in one position in front of the actors, but was now being moved to show a player's head and shoulders or any object at close range. The films in which Griffith used this technique included *The Birth of a Nation*, 1915, in which he portrayed the American Civil War, and *Intolerance*, 1916, in which he portrayed four different periods in world history.

Within the next ten to twenty years, the variety of shots available to a film-maker became remarkably sophisticated:

close-up, as already described (CU);

medium close-up, showing the player from the waist upwards (MCU);

extreme close-up, showing only the player's face (ECU);

long shot, showing the complete area in which the action takes place (LS);

medium long shot, showing the complete action or showing the actor full-length, but *not* showing all the setting in which the action occurs (MLS);

extreme long shot, showing an immense area (ELS);

medium shot, showing the player from the knees upwards (MS).

It is also possible to have shots which enable the audience to see the action from a particular character's point of view. For example, the **over the shoulder shot** (OSS) shows the back of the neck of one of the players, and what he or she is looking at – perhaps another player at the other side of the street. These are subjective shots, in which the audience seems to see events through the eyes of a particular player.

Similarly, shots can be taken not only at the same level as the action, but also at a **high angle** (when the camera looks down at the action) or at a **low angle** (when the camera looks up at the action).

There are also *moving* shots, in which the camera moves in the course of the shooting:

boom shot, in which the camera moves up or down;

dolly shot, in which the camera moves towards, or away from, the action;

tilt, in which the camera tilts upward or downward;

pan, in which the camera moves horizontally;

tracking shot, in which the camera moves on tracks to follow the action.

Finally, there are various ways in which a shot may end:

dissolve, in which as one picture fades out another fades in. This is also sometimes called a **mix**;

fade, in which a shot slowly disappears into blackness. This is called a **fade out**. The reverse is a **fade in**;

freeze frame, in which the action seems to be frozen. (This is done by repeatedly printing the same frame or picture);

superimposition, in which two or more pictures are shown at the same time;

wipe, in which a second shot seems to wipe the first shot from the screen.

The Assam Garden **directed by Mary McMurray**

All these various terms will figure in the *shooting script* from which the director will eventually make the film.

An imaginary example might go like this:

Fade in.
Interior headmaster's study. Day.

1. **LS** Head at desk.
   He is writing a letter
   The phone rings on his desk. Cut to

2. **CU** telephone. **Dolly** out to

3. Head picks up phone.
       HEAD   *Headmaster speaking.*
   Mix to

4. *Interior Mrs Calayton's flat.*
   From the door we see Mrs Calayton in **LS** at the other end of the corridor, on the phone.
   She is surrounded by litter and we can also hear a baby crying.
   The camera **dollies** in to Mrs Calayton as she starts talking.
   Fade out Headmaster.
       MRS CALAYTON *It's my Walter. I'm so worried. He*
           didn't come home last night.
   Sound of baby crying becomes more vehement.
   Cut to

5. Baby in **high angle CU** crawling around Mrs Calayton's feet. The baby continues to cry as we hear Mrs Calayton out of view, talking to the headmaster.
       MRS CALAYTON *You're the Headmaster. You must do*
           something.
   Now the baby suddenly stops crying and looks up at Mrs Calayton with great interest.
   Cut to

6. Mrs Calayton and baby in **MLS**.
       MRS CALAYTON (The Headmaster has presumably
           said something by way of reply.)
           I can't do anything. I've got my
           Deborah to look after.
   At this moment the baby starts to howl mightily.
   Mix to

7. Headmaster's study. Head in **CU**.
       HEAD   *But, Madam, you still haven't told*
           me your name . . .

This is a very crude example of the way different techniques may be used in the shooting of a scene or scenes. It does not, though, do justice to the way films (or at least whole parts of them) are often independent of dialogue. In other words, the spoken word is not necessarily the central factor in films.

from *An Introduction to Film-Making* **by Grace Matchett**

The Fall of the Roman Empire **directed by Anthony Mann**

For discussion

1. Can you think of any films in which the dialogue is fairly (or completely) unimportant?
2. Can you think of any films in which it is very important?
3. Discuss anything about this extract (including the vocabulary) that you find difficult.
4. Look at the varous film clips in this Unit. In groups, discuss the various kinds of shots illustrated. Compare your answers with the rest of the class.

Julius Caesar **directed by Joseph Mankiewicz**

Questions on all the extracts

To answer these questions you will need to re-read all the extracts from *An Introduction to Film-Making*. You should work on your own.

1. Explain clearly and briefly the difference between the producer and the director of a film.
2. Explain in your own words what an editor does in the making of a film.
3. How, if at all, does the writer justify her claim that most 'documentary programmes... have an overt political message'?
   (See the second paragraph of *Kinds of Films*.)
4. Give an example of your own (perhaps imaginary) to show how a 'documentary' could be unfair towards its subject.
5. Explain in your own words how, in general, an audience recognises the genre of a film.
6. What is a 'spoof'?
7. According to this writer, how do new genres develop?
8. This writer is doubtful of the importance in films in general of two factors that many people consider crucial. What are the two factors?
9. What seem to be the two or three principal ways in which the technique of film-making has developed since the early days?

Figures of speech

10. In the expressions, 'film star', 'shooting a scene', and 'the camera cannot lie' what figures of speech are used? What do the expressions mean?

Punctuation

11. Rewrite the following with correct punctuation:

    When rené clair came to hollywood he was considered one of the worlds greatest directors if i had a scene at a table and i wanted to cut underneath to show a couple playing footsie he wouldnt allow it why did the camera go under the table he would ask.

For writing

1. Write a story of your own that you think would be especially suitable for filming.
2. Take a small part of the story and rewrite it as a film script.
3. Write a review of three of four films that you have especially enjoyed and discuss what you have enjoyed about them.

15 DILEMMAS

Florence Nightingale at Scutari Hospital, the Crimea

Deciding to Wait . . .

In November 1854, Florence Nightingale arrived with a small team of nurses in Scutari, Turkey, at the height of the Crimean War. Her intention was to create the first professional nursing service ever known. (Until this time, nursing had been either the occasional occupation of amateurs or non-existent.) In wars, the conditions of such hospitals as did exist, were so bad – dirty, overcrowded and carelessly administered – that soldiers who did not die of their injuries, soon died of disease, hunger or neglect.

When Nightingale arrived with her team (which included a group of nuns) she found the attitudes of the army commanders, and of the army doctors, fiercely opposed to her. Her nurses were eager to 'get started'. The authorities were determined to stop her from doing anything.

This is how she handled the problem:

> While the nurses and sisters unpacked, Miss Nightingale went down into the hospital, and managed to procure tin basins of milkless tea. As the party drank it she told them what she had discovered.
> The hospital was totally lacking in equipment. It was hopeless to ask for furniture. There was no furniture. There was not even an operating table. There were no medical supplies. There were not even the ordinary necessities of life. For the present the nurses must use their tin basins for everything, washing, eating and drinking.
> They must be prepared to go short of water. The allowance was limited to a pint a head a day for washing and drinking, including tea, and it was necessary to line up in one of the corridors where there was a fountain to obtain it. Tomorrow the situation would become worse; a battle at Balaclava had been fought on October 25th, and transports loaded with sick and wounded were expected.
> The party had to go to bed in darkness, for the shortage of lamps and candles was acute. Sisters and nurses lying on the hard divans tried to console themselves by thinking how much greater were the sufferings of the wounded in the sick transports. The rooms were alive with fleas, and rats scurried beneath the divans all night long. The spirits of all, wrote Sister Margaret Goodman, one of the Sellonites, sank.
> The doctors ignored Miss Nightingale. She was to be frozen out, and only one doctor would use her nurses and her supplies. Though the patients were in desperate need, and she could supply what was wanted from her purchases in Marseilles, her stores were refused. Her nurses were refused though the patients were being attended by hospital orderlies who were hopelessly unsatisfactory. According to the regulations of the army, orderlies were either convalescents, in which case they were recalled to their regiments as soon as they had learned to be of use, or they were "weak, stupid and clumsy fellows" or

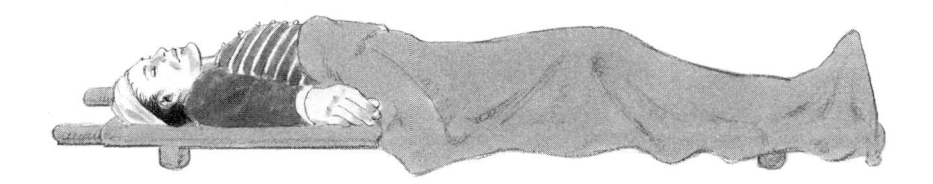

"skulkers" whom the army found useless. The work of attending the sick was forced on them, they almost invariably disliked it, and their numbers were totally inadequate... The medical authorities drew together in a close defensive phalanx. Admit failure! Accept help for the army from civilians, from *The Times* under whose attacks the army authorities were smarting! From a high Society miss who happened to be on dining terms with the Cabinet! Their experience of army methods, of confidential reports, told them that the man who consorted with Miss Nightingale or who supplied his wards through *The Times* fund would be a marked man.

She realised that before she could accomplish anything she must win the confidence of the doctors. She determined not to offer her nurses and her stores again, but to wait until the doctors asked for her help. She would demonstrate that she and her party wished neither to interfere nor attract attention, that they were prepared to be completely subservient to the authority of the doctors.

It was a policy which demanded self-control; the party were to stand by, see troops suffer and do nothing until officially instructed. Though Miss Nightingale could accept the hard facts that a few must be sacrificed in order that the army might be saved, and that the experiment on which she was embarked could never succeed against official opposition, yet she inevitably came into conflict with her nurses.

A day passed and some stores arrived. She made them sort old linen, count packages of provisions. The hardships of life continued. They stood in the corridor to get their pint of water. They ate out of the tin bowls, wiped them with paper, washed their faces and hands in them, wiped them again and drank tea from them. Discomfort would have been ignored if the sufferings of the wounded had been relieved, but they were not relieved. The cries of the men were unanswered while old linen was counted and mended – this was not what they had left England to accomplish. They blamed Miss Nightingale. And she was silent. She did not explain. The capacity to explain had gone out of her nature. The nurses, sentimental and emotionally undisciplined, gained an impression that she was indifferent to the sufferings of the wounded.

On Sunday, November 6th, the ships bringing the wounded from Balaclava began to unload at Scutari. As on other occasions the arrangements were inadequate, and the men suffered frightfully; they were brought up to the hospital on stretchers carried by Turks, who rolled their bleeding burdens about, put the stretchers down with a bump when they needed a rest, and on several occasions threw the patient off. Screams of pain were the accompaniment to the unhappy procession, and Sister Margaret Goodman recorded the case of a soldier who died as a result.

Still Miss Nightingale would not allow her nurses to throw themselves into the work of attending on these unhappy victims. She allocated twenty-eight nurses to the Barrack Hospital and ten to the General Hospital a quarter of a mile away. All were to sleep in the Barrack Hospital and all were to wait. No nurse was to enter a ward except at the invitation of a doctor. However piteous the state of the wounded, the doctor must give the order for attention. She sent her nurses to church to sit through an admirable sermon by the chief Chaplain, Mr. Sabin. If the doctors did not choose to employ the nurses, then the nurses must remain idle.

She was also determined to send no nurse into the wards until she knew that nurse could be relied on. The reliability of the nurse was as important to the success of the experiment as the co-operation of the doctors, and for nearly a week the party were kept shut up in their detestable quarters making shirts, pillows, stump-rests and slings and being observed by her penetrating eye. The time, sighed one of the English Sisters of Mercy, seemed extremely long.

Whatever the regulations laid down, the nurses must submit. Their role was to acquiesce even in what was absurd. By no other means could the doctors be convinced that the nurses were neither critics nor reformers but obedient instruments in their hands.

Miss Nightingale herself rigidly obeyed regulations. On a later occasion she was sitting by the bedside of a man critically ill and found his feet stone cold. She told an orderly to fetch a hot-water bottle. The man refused, saying he had been told to do nothing for a patient without directions from a medical officer. She accepted the correction, found a doctor and obtained a requisition in proper form. For weeks she stood by in silence while the skill of highly efficient nurses was wasted ... Then the situation completely changed. A flood of sick poured into Scutari on such a scale that a crisis of terrible urgency arose and prejudices and resentments were for the moment forgotten.

from *Florence Nightingale* by **Cecil Woodham-Smith**

For discussion

1 Why do you think Nightingale decided to wait rather than insist on using her nurses and medical supplies?

2 Why do you think the authorities were so opposed to her?

3 What two or three different things do you learn from this extract about the kind of person she was?

4 Check the meaning of any of the vocabulary – for example, what does sentimental mean?

5 Check the punctuation – especially the use of semi-colons. When and why are they used?

Deciding to Obey . . .

The celebrated Charge of the Light Brigade occurred in the same war as Florence Nightingale's campaign to care for the sick and wounded.

The charge occurred at the Battle of Balaclava. The commander-in-chief (Lord Raglan), viewing the battlefield from the top of a hill, saw an excellent opportunity for the cavalry to attack the enemy (the Russians) and recover lost ground. So he sent his aide-de-camp (Captain Nolan) with an order to the general in charge of the cavalry (Lord Lucan). The general, unlike the commander, was on low ground and his view was blocked by mounds and ridges. The order to attack did not specify in which direction, and the general chose a direction which led him and his men straight into the enemy's artillery.

Here is a contemporary account by the Poet Laureate of the time.

The Charge of the Light Brigade

Half a league, half a league,
  Half a league onward,
All in the valley of Death
  Rode the six hundred.
'Forward the Light Brigade!
Charge for the guns!' he said:
Into the valley of Death
  Rode the six hundred.

'Forward the Light Brigade!'
Was there a man dismayed?
Not though the soldier knew
  Someone had blundered:
Theirs not to make reply,
Theirs not to reason why,
Theirs but to do and die:
Into the valley of Death
  Rode the six hundred.

Cannon to right of them,
Cannon to left of them,
Cannon in front of them
  Volleyed and thundered;
Stormed at with shot and shell,
Boldly they rode and well,
Into the jaws of Death
Into the mouth of Hell
  Rode the six hundred.

Flashed all their sabres bare,
Flashed as they turned in air,
Sabring the gunners there,
Charging an army, while
  All the world wondered:
Plunged in the battery-smoke
Right through the line they broke;
Cossack and Russian
Reeled from the sabre-stroke
  Shattered and sundered.
Then they rode back, but not,
  Not the six hundred.

Cannon to right of them,
Cannon to left of them,
Cannon behind them
  Volleyed and thundered;
Stormed at with shot and shell,
While horse and hero fell,
They that had fought so well
Came through the jaws of Death,
Back from the mouth of Hell,
All that was left of them,
  Left of six hundred.

When can their glory fade?
O the wild charge they made!
  All the world wondered.
Honour the charge they made!
Honour the Light Brigade,
  Noble six hundred!

Alfred, Lord Tennyson

And here is an account from a twentieth century biography of Lord Raglan.

> The order read: 'Lord Raglan wishes the cavalry to advance rapidly to the front – follow the enemy and try to prevent the enemy carrying away the guns. Troop Horse Artillery may accompany. French cavalry in on your left. Immediate.'
>
> Captain Nolan galloped up to Lord Lucan and handed him the order. Lucan read it slowly, with that infuriating care which drove more patient men than Nolan to scarcely controllable irritation. 'Lord Raglan's orders are that the cavalry should attack immediately,' said Captain Nolan, already mad with anger. 'Attack, Sir! Attack what? What guns, Sir? Where and what to do?' 'There, my Lord!' Nolan flung out his arm in a gesture more of rage than of indignation. 'There is your enemy! There are your guns!'
>
> And leaving Lord Lucan as muddled as before, he trotted away.
>
> The trouble was that Lord Lucan had no idea what he was intended to do. He could not, on the plain, see nearly as far as Lord Raglan could on the hills above him. The only guns in sight were at the far end of the North Valley, where a mass of Russian cavalry was also stationed. These must presumably be the ones Lord Raglan meant. Certainly Nolan's impertinent and flamboyant gesture had seemed to point at them. His mind now made up, Lord Lucan trotted over to Cardigan and passed on the Commander-in-Chief's order. Coldly polite, Lord Cardigan dropped his sword in salute.
>
> 'Certainly, Sir,' he said, in his loud but husky voice. 'But allow me to point out to you that the Russians have a battery in the valley in our front, and batteries and riflemen on each flank.'
>
> 'I know it,' replied Lucan. 'But Lord Raglan will have it. We have no choice but to obey.'
>
> 'The Brigade will advance,' Lord Cardigan said in a strangely quiet voice.
>
> For the first fifty yards the Light Brigade advanced at a steady trot. The guns were silent. Suddenly the beautiful precision and symmetry of the advancing line was broken. Inexcusably galloping in front of the commander came that 'impertinent devil' Nolan. He was waving his sword above his head and shouting for all he was worth. He turned round in his saddle and seemed to be trying to warn the infuriated Lord Cardigan and his first line of his men that they were going the wrong way. But no one heard what words he was shouting, for now the Russians had opened fire, and his voice was drowned by the boom and crash of their guns. A splinter from one of the first shells fired flew into Nolan's heart.

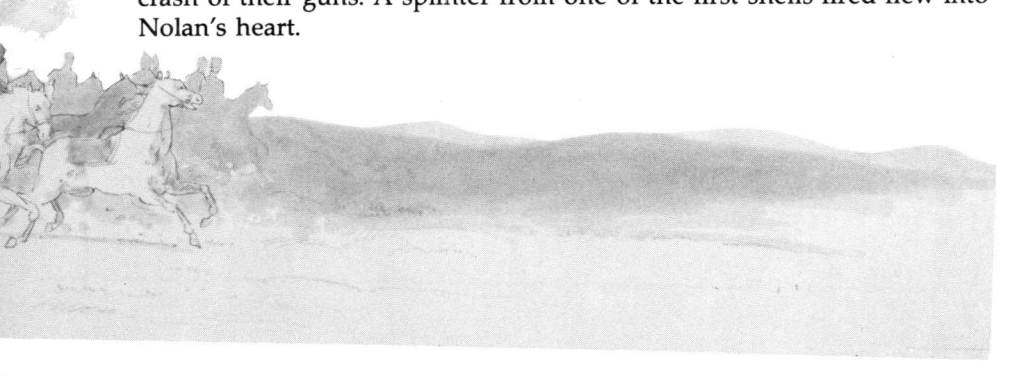

Both Cardigan and Lucan survived the massacre, and then had to meet Raglan – who was furious:

'What did you mean, Sir, by attacking a battery in front, contrary to all the usages of warfare and the customs of the services?'

'My Lord,' Cardigan said, confident of his blamelessness, 'I hope you will not blame me, for I received the order to attack from my superior officer, in front of the troops.'

It was, after all, a soldier's complete indemnification. Lord Cardigan rode back to his yacht with a clear conscience. To Lord Lucan, Lord Raglan said sadly, 'You have lost the Light Brigade.'

Lucan vehemently denied it, and he later wrote, 'I do not intend to bear the smallest particle of responsibility. I gave the order to charge, under what I considered a most imperious necessity, and I will not bear one particle of the blame.'

Of the 673 men who had charged down the valley less than 200 had returned. The Russians, as well as the allies, were deeply moved by such heroism. General Liprandi could not at first believe that the English cavalry had not all been drunk.

adapted from *The Destruction of Lord Raglan* **by Christopher Hibbert**

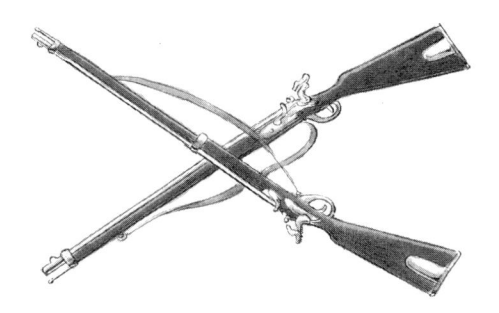

For discussion

1 Is there any difference between the mood created in the poem and that created in the biographical extract?

2 According to a) Lucan b) Cardigan and c) Raglan, who actually made the decision?

3 Suggest two or three different things that you learn from this extract about the characters of the men who led the war. What kind of men were they?

4 Lucan hesitated before carrying out the order. Later he was criticised by Raglan for not checking his position before giving the order. Why do you think he did not?

Los Angeles

Decisions and Restraint

Martin Luther King was one of the leading forces in the struggles of the American Negro to achieve racial equality in the USA. In *Chaos or Community?* he asked the question whether such equality should or could be achieved by violent or by non-violent means. This is part of his answer.

The futility of violence in the struggle for racial justice has been tragically etched in all the recent Negro riots. There is something painfully sad about a riot. One sees screaming youngsters and angry adults fighting hopelessly and aimlessly against impossible odds. Deep down within them you perceive a desire for self-destruction, a suicidal longing. Occasionally Negroes contend that the 1965 Watts riot and the other riots in various cities represented effective civil rights action. But those who express this view always end up with stumbling words when asked what concrete gains have been won as a result. At best the riots have produced a little additional anti-poverty money, allotted by frightened government officials, and a few water sprinklers to cool the children of the ghettos. It is something like improving the food in a prison while the people remain securely incarcerated behind bars. Nowhere have the riots won any concrete improvement such as have the organized protest demonstrations.

It is not overlooking the limitations of non-violence and the distance we have yet to go to point out the remarkable record of achievements that have already come through non-violent action. The 1960 sit-ins desegregated lunch counters in more than 150 cities within a year. The 1961 Freedom Rides put an end to segregation in interstate travel. The 1956 bus boycott in Montgomery, Alabama, ended segregation on the buses not only of that city but in practically every city of the South. The 1963 Birmingham movement and the climactic March on Washington won passage of the most powerful civil rights law in a century. The 1965 Selma movement brought enactment of the Voting Rights Law. Our non-violent marches in Chicago last summer brought about a housing agreement which, if implemented, will be the strongest step toward open housing taken in any city in the nation. Most significant is the fact that this progress occurred with minimum human sacrifice and loss of life. Fewer people have been killed in ten years of non-violent demonstrations across the South than were killed in one night of rioting in Watts.

When one tries to pin down advocates of violence as to what acts would be effective, the answers are blatantly illogical. Sometimes they talk of overthrowing racist state and local governments. They fail to see that no internal revolution has ever succeeded in overthrowing a government by violence unless the government had already lost the allegiance and effective control of its armed forces. Anyone in his right mind knows that this will not happen in the United States. In a violent

Martin Luther King addressing a march, Washington 1963

racial situation, the power structure has the local police, the state troopers, the national guard and finally the army to call on, all of which are predominantly white.

Furthermore, few if any violent revolutions have been successful unless the violent minority had the sympathy and support of the non-resisting majority. Castro may have had only a few Cubans actually fighting with him, but he would never have overthrown the Batista regime unless he had had the sympathy of the vast majority of the Cuban people. It is perfectly clear that a violent revolution on the part of American blacks would find no sympathy and support from the white population and very little from the majority of Negroes themselves.

This is no time for romantic illusions and empty philosophical debates about freedom. This is a time for action. What is needed is a strategy for change, a tactical program that will bring the Negro into the mainstream of American life as quickly as possible. So far, this has only been offered by the non-violent movement. Without recognizing this we will end up with solutions that don't solve, answers that don't answer and explanations that don't explain.

from *Chaos or Community?* **by Martin Luther King**

For discussion

1. What is the main argument that King gives for proposing non-violent change?
2. What do you think would be the main arguments of those who disagreed with King?
3. What does King see as the main difference between a revolutionary movement such as Castro's movement in Cuba, which fought against the Batista regime, and the Black Civil Rights movement in the USA?
4. King was assassinated (by a white gunman) in 1968. Do you think this could be used as a point against his argument here? How do you think King himself would have replied to this?

Review of all the materials in this Unit

To answer these questions, you will need to re-read all the texts in this Unit. You should work on your own. Most but not all of the questions require fairly full answers in which you should refer for evidence to the different texts, but you should always be as economical and as precise as you can. Use your own words as far as possible, but when you quote from a text, always show clearly that it is a quotation.

1. What was Florence Nightingale's method of handling the opposition of the authorities?
2. What do you think is the difference between the *aim* of the writer of the poem and that of the writer of the extract from Raglan's biography?
3. Would you hold anyone responsible for the Charge of the Light Brigade? Explain why.
4. Explain in your own words the main point made by King in:
    (a) his second paragraph, and
    (b) his third paragraph.
5. How (probably) would Martin Luther King have handled Florence Nightingale's problem with the authorities in Scutari?
6. What similarity is there between the way Nightingale handled her problem, and Lucan handled his?
7. What similarity is there between the problem facing Nightingale in the hospital in Scutari, and the problem facing King in the USA?
8. Does the account of Nightingale's problems in Scutari offer any sort of clue as to the possible causes of the blunder of the Charge of the Light Brigade?

For group discussion and writing

Two of the texts in this Unit have been concerned with people who aimed to change the world around them and with the ways they set about doing this. Talk about any *social change* you yourself would like to see happen. It could be a massive change (such as the creating of a ban on nuclear weapons) or a fairly modest and local change, such as creating improved sports facilities for your community.

Compare your views on:
a) the changes you would like to see, and
b) the most effective ways to bring them about.

Then write a pamphlet for distribution to anyone who might be interested, explaining and developing your ideas, and seeking to convert others to your own point of view.

16 FUTURES

In 1400 each person had 354,841 sq yds to himself

In 1971 each person had 49,283 sq yds to himself

In 2000 each person will have 23,656 sq yds to himself

NO ROOM TO BREATHE

Year	Population
2000	7,500
1971	3,670
1950	2,517
1900	1,650
1850	1,240
1800	900
1750	850
1700	800
1650	750
1600	700
1550	650
1500	600
1450	550
1400	500

World population figures in millions

from THE SUNDAY TIMES MAGAZINE 31 March 1

All the texts in this Unit are concerned in various ways with the future – the future of life on earth and of the planet itself. Talk about them, listen to them and read them. Later use them as the basis for your own written report on:

The Future

Listening Comprehension

1 Coping with Change

Technological change is now a basic fact of life. We live in a world that is changing so rapidly that we can hardly keep up with it. In this extract from his book *Rethink,* Gordon Rattray Taylor looks at some of the specific ways in which our society is changing and at the damage that change can inflict upon us.

Before listening to the extract, discuss:
1 In what particular ways is our society now changing?
2 What are the advantages of such change?
3 What are the disadvantages?

Most of our frustrations spring from the intolerably high rate of social change, which results from the expansion of science and technology.

Not everyone appreciates the fantastic scale on which these changes have occurred. Our ability to control disease is perhaps a hundred times what it was a century ago, our energy resources a thousand times as great, our weapons a million times as strong, our speed of communication ten million times as rapid. The growth rate is exponential. The time required for a new invention to spread into general use shrinks exponentially. It took 150 years to diffuse the steam engine, fifty for the car, twenty five for the radio-set, less than fifteen for the transistor. At the same time, change has become more pervasive. Not one, but many fields are changing today. With a lifetime in which to adjust, problems are soluble; when the time comes down to fifteen years, the impact becomes insupportable. The technomaniacs fail to see that the human life-span is the unchanging yardstick in the situation.

The technomaniacs point enthusiastically to the benefits expected to accrue as a result of employing their devices – but even if these benefits are as desirable as they claim, which is doubtful, we still have to consider the costs of making the change. Every competent manager knows that you must get a certain life out of your equipment. There is a point up to which the waste in scrapping machine tools or other equipment is more than the benefit of installing improved equipment. (This is an active issue in telecommunications right now.) The social costs of change which is rapid in relation to the human lifespan are enormous. Sir Geoffrey Vickers has pointed out in his *Value Systems and Social Process*: 'We seem now to be approaching a point at which the changes generated within a single generation may render inept for the future the skills, institutions and the ideas which formed that generation's principal heritage.' To the objection that a man's skills may be obsolete when he is forty the technomaniac replies: 'Then he must be retrained.' He does not see that this is putting production above the man. In all probability the man does not want to go back to square one, giving up his status as a skilled workman and becoming an apprentice again. Why should he? The satisfactions of stability in his life may be more important to him than increased material wealth. I am not asserting that this is always or necessarily the case. I only point out that in a rational analysis the psychological and personal costs, the social cost of re-education, must be made part of the calculation. For it is much more than a question of retraining a workman in an industrial skill. We are talking about changes which render whole life patterns pointless, which disturb value systems, create alienation, make life boring or frustrating or not worth living, raise crime and suicide and alcoholism rates, and much more. We are doing to ourselves what we have already done to many primitive peoples, plunging them into a technological world for which their institutions and values were unfitted. It is well known that this breaks a primitive culture up, leads to loss of motivation, to alcoholism and eventual total anomie. The invisible costs of change are enormous.

It has recently been shown that change – a new job, marriage, divorce, a new home, the death of a parent, even change for the better –

adversely affects health. In a path-breaking piece of research, which must eventually become a standard reference, Dr Thomas H. Holmes, with the aid of a young psychiatrist named Richard Rahe, at Washington School of Medicine, arrived at results 'so spectacular that at first we hesitated to publish them. We didn't release our initial findings until 1967.' Assigning points to major life-changes, they compiled a 'life-changes score' for thousands of individuals and compared them with their medical histories. Al Toffler, in his *Future Shock*, summarises their results like this:

> In every case, the correlation between change and illness has held. It has been established that 'alterations in life-style' that require a great deal of adjustment and coping, correlate with illness – whether or not these changes are under the individual's own direct control, or whether or not he sees them as undesirable. Furthermore, the higher the degree of life-change, the higher the risk that subsequent illness will be severe. So strong is this evidence that it is becoming possible, by studying life-change scores, actually to predict levels of illness in various populations.

Forecasts were made for 3,000 navy men. Afterwards, Commander Ransom J. Arthur, of the U.S. Navy's Medical Neuropsychiatric Research Unit at San Diego, reported: 'It is clear that there is a connection between the body's defences and the demands for change that society imposes.' It follows that no one need be surprised that Western society shows rising sickness rates combined with improved medical services. Toffler's important book recounts many other evidences of the damaging impact, psychological as well as physical, of change – and its wide success shows, I think, that many people already begin to suspect this.

from *Rethink* by Gordon Rattray Taylor

After listening to the text for the first time, discuss:

- **How far do Taylor's answers to the three questions above compare with your own?**
- **What do you think is the main point that he is making?**

While listening to the text a second time, make very brief notes to summarise the main points that Taylor makes and that you think may be helpful to you later when you write your own report on the whole topic of *The Future*. Perhaps write down a very short but relevant quotation.

Now read the various texts below.
Perhaps read them together in small groups, and discuss especially:

- **any questions you may wish to ask about them;**
- **the two or three main points they make;**
- **the ways they relate to the topic of the future.**

Make notes of the points you raise in your discussions so that you can refer to these later in discussion with the whole class.

N.B. Every group should have a dictionary to use when they wish to. Discuss any word that you find difficult *before* checking its meaning in the dictionary. Try to work out what it *probably* means, judging from the way it is used.

2 The demographer's viewpoint
See page 259.

3 Biological Possibilities

Embryology: Cloned mice

By the Staff of *Nature*

Science fiction has moved one step closer to science fact with the announcement by a Swiss biologist at a conference in Basle last week that he has succeeded in cloning a mouse. Until now, the only well-attested clones have been made with frogs, which are technically much easier to clone because they have very large eggs which develop outside the body.

The techniques for cloning frogs were developed by Dr J. Gurdon at Cambridge, and involve the removal of the nucleus containing the genetic material of the fertilized egg and its replacement with the nucleus of a body cell from a tadpole. That technique has now been extended to mice by Professor K. Illmensee at Geneva University.

Cloning a mammal is a much more delicate matter than cloning an amphibian not only because of the size of the egg, but also because the egg must be removed from, and then replaced in a mother, in the right hormonal state to support development of the embryo. Professor Illmensee is an expert in such delicate manipulations, having worked for many years on the creation of what are know as chimaeras.

Chimaeras are animals made by the fusion in the embryo of cells from more than one source. That occasionally happens in nature, when cells of twins are mixed before birth. Artificial chimaeras are used by biologists in the study of embryonic development.

The techniques used to make

chimaeras, however, involve only the removal and replacement of early embryos. To make clones, Professor Illmensee had to perform the extremely delicate trick of removing the nucleus from a fertilized egg and injecting a replacement from a cell taken from a different animal.

Among the questions that cloned mice will enable Professor Illmensee to explore is that of the relationship between the nucleus and the rest of the egg. He has already experimented with nuclear transplants in a strain of mice in which eggs sometimes spontaneously start to develop without being fertilized.

In those strains, the so-called parthenogenetic embryos never survive for more than a few days. Professor Illmensee has, however, transferred a nucleus from such an embryo into a fertilized egg from a different mouse strain and succeeded in producing a fully-grown mouse. That implies that something goes wrong with the relationship of the nucleus and the rest of the egg when parthenogenetic nuclei are left to develop in their natural environoment.

While cloned mice may well help to solve fundamental questions in biology, they are extremely unlikely, if only for technical reasons, to lead to the institution of a brave new world of cloned human beings.

© Nature-Times News Service, 1980.

from THE TIMES 1980

4 Conveyor-belt medicine

Moving Right Along...

In many ways the scene resembles any modern factory. A conveyor glides silently past five work stations, periodically stopping, then starting again. Each station is staffed by an attendant in a sterile mask and smock. The workers have just three minutes to complete their tasks before the conveyor moves on; they turn out 20 finished pieces in an hour.

Nearly everything else about the assembly line, however, is highly unusual: the workers are eye surgeons, and the conveyor carries human beings on stretchers. This is the Moscow Research Institute of Eye Microsurgery, where the production methods of Henry Ford are applied to the practice of medicine. The centre is the brainchild of renowned Soviet Eye Surgeon Svyatoslav Fyodorov, 57, who calls it a "Medical factory for the production of people with good eyesight."

The factory performs a variety of operations, including cataract removal, glaucoma surgery and the implantation of lenses. But the most popular procedure is radial keratotomy, in which a series of fine spokelike incisions are made on the cornea to correct myopia. In a recent two-month period, ...rov, 20 institute surgeons handled ... operations "with only four minor complications." The treatment, which he helped develop, is still controversial in the U.S.

Soviet health officials hope to build more eye-operation factories around the country. The approach not only lowers costs, says Fyodorov, but may actually improve the quality of operations by permitting each surgeon "to perform the part of the operation that he does best." Someday, Fyodorov predicts, appendectomies and even heart surgery will be assembly-line products.

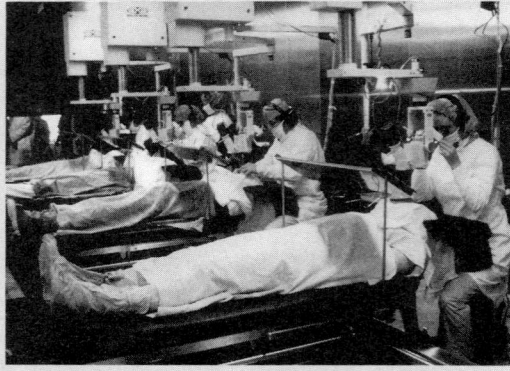

Patients undergo surgery on the assembly line

from TIME MAGAZINE 1 July 1985

5 What we may learn from animals . . .

The bird that never gets a pain in the neck

The animal world offers a number of startling solutions to man's problems in engineering and medicine. We could learn from them – if we allow them to exist long enough. Norman Myers reports

The woodpecker may soon help us to design better crash helmets. High-speed films reveal that when the bird is searching for insects or drilling a nesting place its beak can hammer away at a tree with a speed on impact of 23 feet per second, or 1,300 miles per hour. Yet, in spite of repeated shocks of that order, the woodpecker's brain is never injured. The bird does not even appear to sustain a headache.

One complete peck cycle takes only one thousandth of a second or less, and the deceleration force at each end of a stroke is around 1,000G (one G is the acceleration needed to overcome earth's gravity; an astronaut in a Saturn V rocket experiences only 3.5 to 4G during blast off).

What is the woodpecker's secret? According to Dr Philip May of the Neuropsychiatric Institute at the University of California at Los Angeles, and his colleagues at the Brentwood Veterans Administration Hospital in California, the woodpecker's head moves forwards and backwards in a single plane with no sideways movement at all.

Apparently it is the absence of any whiplash rotation that enables the bird to avoid injury to its skull's contents, and to its neck vertebrae and spinal cord. This suggests that crash helmets could be improved if they were designed in such a way as to restrict sideways movement – meaning that they would have to incorporate some kind of neck brace to limit whiplash movement to the side. In addition, crash helmets could be made of shock-absorbing materials that disperse the shock of crash impact.

A species of wasp may help us with improved design of helicopters. Of more than one million species of flying insects on earth the chalcid wasp is unique in that its wings interact with one another in a manner that allows each to provide a starting vortex for the other. This mechanism provides a model that could enable engineers to fashion a more efficient type of helicopter: if the wasp's mode of aerodynamic lift can be adapted to turbomachinery, it will provide a technological breakthrough for vertical-lift aircraft.

Related examples from the animal world are legion. The cheetah, able to accelerate from a standing start to 40 miles per hour in only three strides, and to sustain a 60 mph chase for 1,000 yards, obviously possesses an efficient heart, and respiratory and circulatory systems; a creature that can sustain a sudden and outsize oxygen debt looks likely to throw light on disorders of the heart, lungs and blood system in humans.

The only animal other than man that is known to contract leprosy is the armadillo, which may thereby

The woodpecker: hitting trees at a rate of 23 feet per second

hold a key to a cure. The Florida manatee, which has poorly clotting blood, may prove useful in research on haemophilia.

The black bear, which possesses hormonal mechanisms that enable it to "sleep" for five months during the winter, supplies information on development of a low-protein diet that helps humans suffering from kidney failure.

Because of their close relatedness to humans, primates are especially valuable for medical research. They have contributed to the development of many drugs and vaccines. Chimpanzees for instance, are the only creatures other than man on which the safety of anti-hepatitis vaccines can be tested. Baboons assist in resolving urinary incontinence in humans. Cotton-topped marmosets, a species of monkey susceptible to cancer of the lymphatic system, help to produce a potent anti-cancer vaccine.

Primates point up a key factor in the situation. While they are, in terms of our daily welfare, among the most valuable creatures on earth, primates rank as some of the most threatened. Exceptionally helpful for research are chimpanzees but there are only 50,000 chimpanzees left in the wild, and their numbers are rapidly declining.

We are now losing, out of earth's 5–10 million species, at least one species per day.

By the year 2000 we could be losing one million. Many of these creatures will take with them a multitude of secrets. By safeguarding the welfare of these endangered species, we are safeguarding our own.

Dr Norman Myers is a Senior Associate of World Wildlife Fund-US and a consultant in environment and development, based in Kenya.

from THE GUARDIAN 9 July 1981

6 After the War...

AN EAST-WEST nuclear exchange – even a war of moderate scale, not an "all buttons pressed" affair – could kill between 750 million and 1.1 billion people in the northern hemisphere during the actual conflict. It could also leave at least half as many people severely injured or suffering from radioactivity during the immediate aftermath – and unlikely to receive any succour.

But there would still be a good few in the northern hemisphere to pick themselves up off the ground and try to remain standing. As for communities in the southern hemisphere, the impact of a northern nuclear war could be quite limited in an immediate sense.

Such, at any rate, has been the conventional wisdom among many political leaders, military planners, civil defence experts and others who seek to determine our destinies in a post-nuclear world. Now it appears, as a result of wide-ranging studies conducted by international teams of scientists, that great numbers of people could die during the course of the first year after the main battle ends. Indeed their eventual total could match those who perish in the immediate aftermath of the war. As for the remainder, they could well find their lifestyles set back to a level akin to the Middle Ages – and many would even find themselves reduced to the status of hunter-gatherers (if indeed they know how to undertake such an activity). In short, the long-term environmental repercussions of nuclear war could prove at least as severe as the immediate damage.

Let us look at a 5,000-megaton scenario, or well under half of the projected 1985 nuclear arsenals of the superpowers. A one-megaton bomb is equivalent to 80 Hiroshima bombs, and can contain more explosive power than that of all explosives used in all wars since gunpowder was invented. Not surprisingly, then, a warhead of just one megaton could "vaporise" 100,000 tons of rock and soil, while the total debris it could loft high into the atmosphere, even into the stratosphere, could amount to around one third of a million tons.

At the same time, bombs directed not only at missile sites and other military targets but at urban centres, industrial installations and oil fields would send out sufficient heat to set fire to forests and croplands on a large scale, thus throwing vast amounts of soot and ash into the troposphere

Hiroshima after the bomb

and beyond. Forest fires could account for some 400,000 square miles on the northern hemisphere, equivalent to the combined territories of Sweden, Norway and Denmark; large as this amount may sound, it is no more than 4 per cent of all forests in the main combatant countries and is only about 20 times larger than what is now accounted for by wildfires each year. These fires could well persist for weeks, releasing as much as 200 million tons of extremely fine and light-absorbing particles. There would also be much similar material hurled upwards from burning oil fields, gas wells and petroleum refineries, as well as from cities with their masses of flammable plastics and other petroleum derived products. Fossil-fuel dumps, often located near cities, contain at least 1,500 million tons of oil.

All this debris is estimated to be capable of reducing sunlight reaching the Earth's surface by as much as 99 per cent during the first six weeks or so, meaning that noontime would appear like a moonlit night. The extended twilight would probably endure for at least another six months, followed by a further eight months or so of only half-normal light. Of course these predictions are no more than informed estimates, and are not so soundly documented as the immediate damages of a nuclear holocaust. They are presented as carefully-analysed assessments of some broad-ranging repercussion.

As the sunlight became blocked out, temperatures would plunge, to as much as minus 43C in the heartlands of continents. This frigid regime would likewise persist for half a year or so, and more than two years could pass before temperatures revert to normal.

As a result of the darkness, photosynthesis would be suspended. In addition, the extreme cold would cause vegetation in much of the northern hemisphere to die. Thus there would be an immediate halt to organised agriculture as we know it.

Moreover, croplands would suffer further from radioactive fallout. A one-megaton explosion leaves a lethal radioactive "footprint" some 15 miles wide and as much as 150 miles long. If we are to envisage thousands of detonations, vast territories could be subject to potent radiation – an estimated 30 per cent of the mid-latitude regions in the northern hemisphere. Generally speaking, plants withstand radiation better than animals. Several crops, however, notably maize, barley, rye, oats, beans and peas, tomatoes, and sugar beets, are more sensitive than others, and their yields would fall by at least one half for a lengthy period. At the same time, small-bodied pests, which are relatively resistant to radiation, would survive and thrive. We might well agree with Jonathan Schell, author of *The Fate of the Earth,* that the outcome would be "a republic of insects and grasses."

from THE GUARDIAN 3 November 1983

rebuilding

7 Happy Days?

Most accounts of the future are depressing. It is almost impossible to find any serious account of what our lives will be like in 20 years' time – let alone in two thousand years – that is not full of gloom and doom. The general picture seems to look something like this: the population is growing at an alarming rate, soon there will be more people than this world can possibly feed or find space for. Additionally, the industrial world's consumption of fossil fuels will continue to cause serious damage to the environment which will in turn cause serious damage to the human race, well before the middle of the 21st century.

Even before this happens, the technological revolution created by the invention and marketing of a great range of computers will have given vast profits to a very small minority and have lumbered the rest of western society with massive unemployment. Most people will simply be poor – unemployed and unemployable. Nor will there be any realistic prospect of the great mass of people eventually finding they are useful to their country in time of war, unlike the generation who lived through the Depression of the 1930s, only to discover that their nation's survival depended on their contribution to the struggles of the Second World War; for when the next World War comes, it seems that the excitement will all be over within an hour or two, and that when the excitement is over, life will be over too. Perhaps the only people to pity when World War III does come (assuming, of course, that it comes) will be the survivors.

So the future looks bleak. But then it has always looked bleak. For as long as people have been looking into the future, they have predicted disaster, calamity, and gloom. There is nothing new about fearing tomorrow. So we can reasonably ask, 'Must it be so awful?' Perhaps the encouraging signs are also the very things that cause us to feel worried. For example, the technological revolution is perfectly capable of creating a society in which very few people need to work and in which the vast majority of people can be supported in a life of comfort and pleasure. In other words, it is now possible to create a new way of life, in which work is unnecessary, because we have available the means to create vast wealth without work. This may be a difficult idea for most of us to imagine, for we have all been brought up to believe that happiness is a reward for hard work. Perhaps we now need to change our educational system so that children are educated to enjoy themselves rather than to "make a living".

It is interesting that nothing is quite as hard as encouraging people to enjoy themselves. I think it is a fair guess that people have always tended to be unhappy, dissatisfied, disappointed with the present and frightened of the future. Similarly, they have always tended to look back at the past with regret, as if it was something wonderful. Perhaps this is no more than a basic desire to stop the future from ever happening: we curse the present and try to turn back the clock in order to make the future go away.

If I am right about human nature, then we can be sure of only one thing when we wonder about the future: people will still be grumbling about the present, looking back with sadness at the passing of the past, and deeply scared of the future!

from *Future Fears* **by Margaret Saple**

8 Life in outer space?

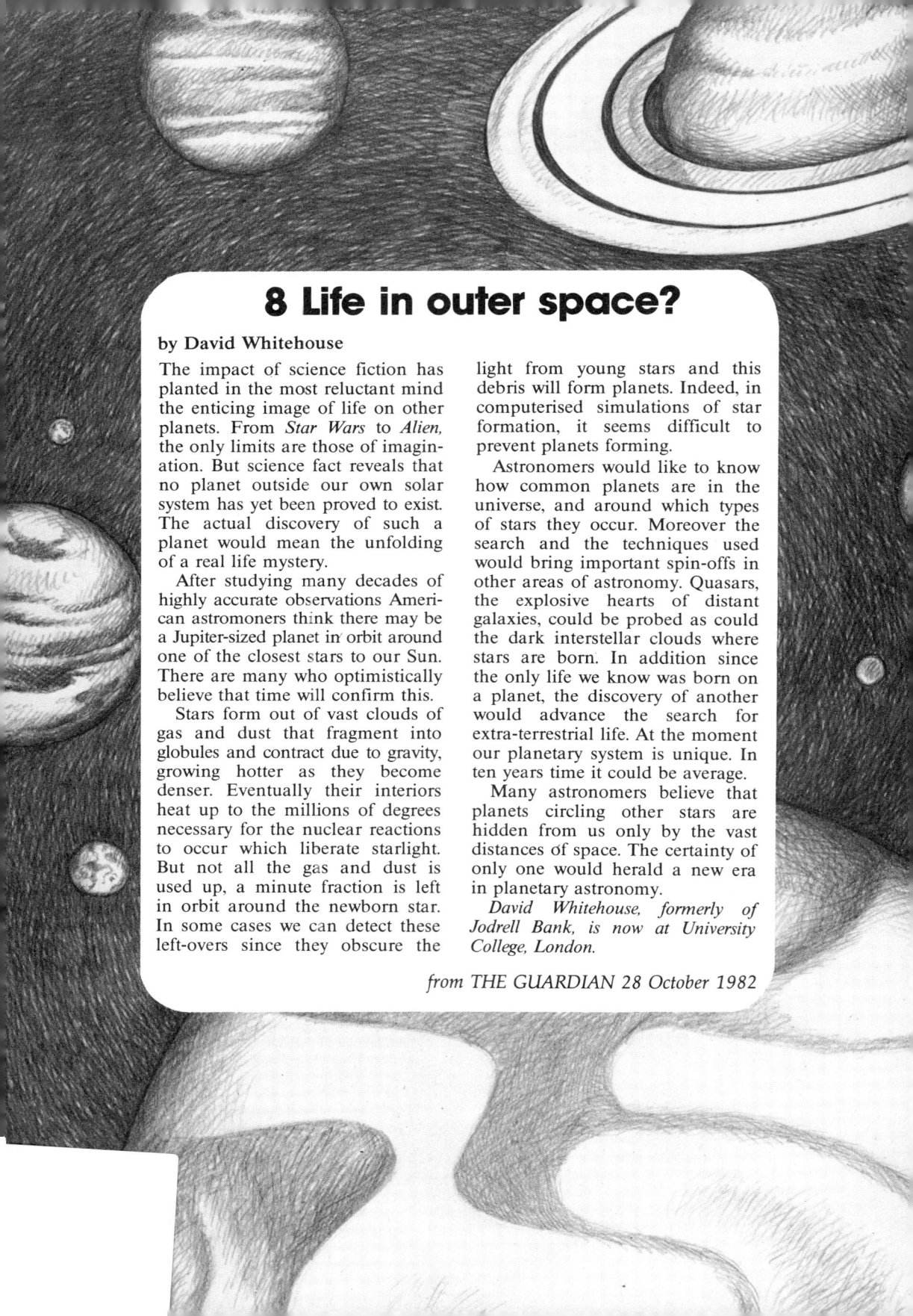

by David Whitehouse

The impact of science fiction has planted in the most reluctant mind the enticing image of life on other planets. From *Star Wars* to *Alien*, the only limits are those of imagination. But science fact reveals that no planet outside our own solar system has yet been proved to exist. The actual discovery of such a planet would mean the unfolding of a real life mystery.

After studying many decades of highly accurate observations American astromoners think there may be a Jupiter-sized planet in orbit around one of the closest stars to our Sun. There are many who optimistically believe that time will confirm this.

Stars form out of vast clouds of gas and dust that fragment into globules and contract due to gravity, growing hotter as they become denser. Eventually their interiors heat up to the millions of degrees necessary for the nuclear reactions to occur which liberate starlight. But not all the gas and dust is used up, a minute fraction is left in orbit around the newborn star. In some cases we can detect these left-overs since they obscure the light from young stars and this debris will form planets. Indeed, in computerised simulations of star formation, it seems difficult to prevent planets forming.

Astronomers would like to know how common planets are in the universe, and around which types of stars they occur. Moreover the search and the techniques used would bring important spin-offs in other areas of astronomy. Quasars, the explosive hearts of distant galaxies, could be probed as could the dark interstellar clouds where stars are born. In addition since the only life we know was born on a planet, the discovery of another would advance the search for extra-terrestrial life. At the moment our planetary system is unique. In ten years time it could be average.

Many astronomers believe that planets circling other stars are hidden from us only by the vast distances of space. The certainty of only one would herald a new era in planetary astronomy.

David Whitehouse, formerly of Jodrell Bank, is now at University College, London.

from THE GUARDIAN *28 October 1982*

9 Is the Earth expanding?

by Peter J. Smith

Several hundred million years ago, the earth's continents were all joined together in the huge land mass now known as Pangea.

It follows that this ancient supercontinental island must have been set in an even larger ocean, equal in area to all the present oceans put together – if, that is, the earth was then the same size as it is now. But it is a curious fact that if Pangea is imagined to be bent round into a spherical shape, it completely covers the surface of the globe with a radius of just over half of the earth's present radius.

So the obvious question arises: Is this remarkable fit merely a coincidence, or has the earth grown, almost doubling its radius? Was there once a much smaller earth completely covered in continental lithosphere?

The first person to carry out the Pangea-bending exercise was the German geologist O. C. Hilgenberg, who in 1933 demonstrated the neatness of the smaller-earth fit using a papier-mache model. Hilgenberg concluded that the earth must indeed have expanded, thus supporting the Russian geologist M. Bogolepow, who had reached the same result (but for different reasons) eleven years before.

Since then quite a number of geologists and geophysicists have toyed with the idea of earth expansion.

from THE GUARDIAN
12 February 1981

10 The end of the future?

by Paul Davies

A sensational discovery made in India last month could shatter traditional ideas about the nature of matter, and provide a once only glimpse of the birth of the universe. Deep within a gold mine a mile underground near Bangalore, Indian and Japanese scientists may have spotted for the first time the most elusive event ever to be predicted by science. The announcement of their discovery nicely coincides with the sixtieth birthday of the man who predicted it, more than a decade ago – the Soviet physicist Andrei Sakharov.

Everyone is familiar with the concept of radioactivity: over-heavy or unbalanced atomic nuclei that disintegrate spontaneously. It was long supposed, however, that nature's simplest, lightest and most ubiquitous substance – hydrogen – is absolutely stable. The nucleus of normal hydrogen consists of just one proton, and protons were supposed to live forever. Now that cosy belief is threatened. Beneath the surface of India, it appears, protons are disappearing.

Protons, along with their cousins the neutrons, are the building blocks of all nuclear matter. Ninety-nine per cent of your body weight is due to them. The Indian vanishing act suddenly makes the world seem rather insubstantial. For what is happening in India must be happening throughout the universe; matter is slowly, but inexorably, decaying. The Earth, the stars, the atoms of this newspaper – all are gradually evaporating away.

Dramatic though it may seem, the effect is not much help for slimmers. At most our bodies will lose only a handful of protons in a life-time. The average proton takes a staggering ten thousand billion billion billion years to go pop. It is only the statistical freaks that the Indian team claim to have spotted, decaying against the odds a mere fifteen billion years after their creation in the fiery furnace of the big bang. At that rate, the Earth will take vastly more centuries to dwindle away than there are grains of sand on every seashore. To have spotted events of such rarity is a tribute to the immense skill of the physicists involved.

The technique used in the experiment was to assemble a huge chunk of matter, in this case 100 tonnes of iron, well away from the polluting effects of cosmic rays. Hence the need for a deep mine. About once a month, a single proton, somewhere in the iron, decays. To catch it in the act, the scientists threw a cordon of no less than 1,650 radioactivity counters around the iron block, forming a 35-layer cake twelve feet tall.

The proton does not, of course, disappear without a trace. Its disintegration is accompanied by a puff of subnuclear debris, and it is this detritus that triggers the counters...

The new discovery conjures up a dismal image for the ultimate fate of the cosmos. As the protons die, one by one, they cough positrons into an electron-infested environment, where they too are soon annihilated. All physical structures are destined to vanish eventually, after an immensity of time, leaving behind just a few gamma rays as testimony to their erstwhile existence. A few electrons and positrons may escape further encounter, and roam the dark chasms of space in solitary confinement, with only black holes to keep them company, but the ten billion galaxies that now blaze so conspicuously across our universe will have disappeared for good.

from THE GUARDIAN 21 May 1981

When you have completed your group and class discussions of the various texts, plan your own report on *The Future*.

1. Work out the particular way in which you wish to explore your own ideas. You might wish to organise your points around some such division as optimistic views of the future, contrasted with pessimistic views. Or you might wish to distinguish the views of different kinds of thinkers, such as geologists, astronomers, psychologists etc., along the lines illustrated in the various texts in this Unit. You might include here the views of novelists and film-makers who have predicted the way the world will progress or decline in the future. In other words, you need a general shape or structure around which to plan your report.

2. Refer to at least some of the texts in this Unit, and to your discussions of them. Make notes before you write, so that you do not have to refer to the texts themselves, but only to your notes. Make your notes brief and clear.

3. Perhaps make a note of further questions you could explore in the Library, and use some of this information also in your report.

4. If one particular aspect of the future especially interests you, then concentrate on that. It could be medicine of the future, or entertainment, or... Here again, though, your report will need a careful structure.

5. When you have finished, add a glossary and a bibliography. Then discuss your reports with each other and perhaps arrange for another class to read them.

   OR

   Write a story in which in one way or another you explore ideas about the future.

from *Back to the Future* **directed by Robert Zeneckis**